A CORSHAM BOYHOOD

GW00684863

Corsham High Street

A CORSHAM BOYHOOD:

THE DIARY

OF

HERBERT SPACKMAN

1877 ~1891

Photoset in 9/11 pt Times Roman
by Chippenham Typesetting, Bath Road, Chippenham, Wiltshire.
Text paper supplied by Howard Smith Papers, Bristol.
Bound by Western Book Company, Maesteg.
Printed in Great Britain by Picton Print
Citadel Works, Bath Road, Chippenham, Wiltshire.

ACKNOWLEDGEMENTS

We would like to express our warmest thanks for the interest, encouragement and co-operation of friends, to Tom Burnard, who has copied all the photographs, to Robin Tanner, Herbert's son-in-law, who has drawn and lettered chapter headings, title page and cover and two illustrations, and to Picton Publishing.

DECEMBER, 1890.

22 Monday

23 Tuesday

24 Wednesday

DECEMBER, 1890.

25 Thursday
Christmas Day

26 Friday
Bank Holiday

27 Saturday.
St. John Evangelist

28 Sunday—*1st Sunday after Christmas. Innocents*—[see page 130]

INTRODUCTION

My father, Herbert Spackman, who wrote these diaries, was born at Corsham, Wiltshire, in October 1864. Spackmans seem to have lived and farmed all over Wiltshire for hundreds of years, particularly in the downland area of Cherhill, Bromham, Calne, Compton Bassett, Calstone and Cliffe Pypard. But the farming tradition was broken with my grandfather Henry, a younger son of William Spackman of Bromham, who told him when he was fourteen that he must not expect 'in these bad times' (1838) to be set up in a farm of his own like his elder brothers, but must go as apprentice to his uncle at the grocery and drapery stores in High Street, Corsham. Later he became a partner, and eventually took over the business.

Herbert was Henry's second surviving son by his second wife, Eliza Hawkins. He learnt Pitman's shorthand at 'Corsham School' – Mr Charles Hulls' school in Pickwick Road (a boarding school which also took day scholars), and started writing his diaries at the age of twelve, purely as a shorthand exercise. Isaac Pitman of Bath, the inventor of the system, was a friend of Henry's, and all the Spackman children learnt his method. But Herbert was the only one who kept up his diaries, every day (with the exception of the year 1878), right through his sojourn in New Zealand in the 1890s and after his return to England and Corsham, until a few months before his death in 1949, when failing sight compelled him to stop.

We three daughters, as children, knew of the existence of the diaries and saw 'Daddy' making his entries, but at that time none of us had learnt shorthand, and in any case it would not have occurred to us, or anybody else, to ask to read them. In 1939 he himself re-read the sixty-two volumes, and thinking we might one day be interested in parts of them he made a much condensed digest of the contents, typed it and gave us a copy each. 'Though the shorthand is still readable', he wrote, 'there are changes in Pitman's system to be met with, and sometimes my outlines are not sufficiently vocalised. As regards the diaries, 60 of them occupy considerable space, and I believe that cremation is advisable!'

The Digest whetted our appetites, and we begged him not to destroy the originals until we could get them translated. But it was not until long after his death, when our old house in Priory Road had to be sold, that we could assemble and check the volumes and assess the task. By that time I was the only one of the family left who could read shorthand, so the diaries came to me. They were a little battered, and varied in size and shape from small pocket-books to large desk diaries; but were all complete, and I could see at a glance that the shorthand, though in parts old-fashioned, was perfectly clear and readable with a good magnifier. Even so, I should not have had courage to tackle them without Herbert's useful Digest. This provided a sort of chart to the hidden treasure, and I picked out a few likely dates and began on them. At once I discovered two things: first, the more I read the easier it became; and second, the more I read the more I wanted to read. There was all the difference in the world between the bare bones of the Digest and the lively details noted on the spot and at the time.

I decided it was well worth making fairly full extracts; not for the general public – there was nothing in the writing to compare, for instance, with the Kilvert Diaries – but just for my sister Heather Tanner and myself, and our immediate families. What chiefly emerges is Herbert's wonderful capacity for enjoyment of both the lesser and the greater pleasures of life, from hopscotch in the home kitchen to conducting an orchestra. He notes the weather almost every day, and describes October 11th, 1879, not just as 'a fine day' but 'a beautiful, splendid, lovely, delicious day, like a summer's day'. The most frequently recurring phrase in the entries is 'Enjoyed myself very much'. One of his personal mottoes was 'Always be doing something you can't do' – and he always was, even in his eighties.

In 1877 the family at High Street, Corsham, consisted of Henry, then aged 53; his second wife Eliza (whose pet name, 'Spring Morning', indicates her personality); grown-up Harry, Henry's son by his first wife Sarah Goold; then the second family with Lewin, Alice (an invalid from infancy), Herbert, Wilfrid, Clara, Ernest and Clare. In spite of shortage of money and other problems, it must have been a happy household for the children to grow up in. They mostly made their own entertainments, and there was no lack of them – concerts, penny readings, evenings with the Good Templars, family outings, choir outings, visits to and from relatives, on foot, by train or with horse and trap; and (according to the weather) cricket in the 'drung', croquet on the lawn, bagatelle or whist at home, learning to swim at Weavern in the summer (usually before breakfast), or to skate on Corsham Lake in the winter (also before breakfast if the shop was busy); making toy fire-balloons, or boats to sail on the river at Lacock. They were keen cricketers (Clare later became famous in several counties), and nearly all, eventually, expert musicians.

The High Street house is still there, though no longer used as a shop; it was Herbert's home until he emigrated to New Zealand in 1891. We don't know what the original house looked like, because it was destroyed, with all deeds and documents, in a disastrous fire in January 1849, when the then proprietor, our great-great-uncle Henry, lost his life (see appendix). But the old gabled kitchen wing, next to the 'drung' (the footpath leading to the Avenue), survived, and was incorporated in the new early-Victorian building. This, if less picturesque, was probably more convenient and comfortable. To us children, when we came to know it more than fifty years later, it was pure enchantment, and it could not have changed much since the 1870s. There was the Grocery with its sanded floor, delicious smells and ranks of neat little wooden drawers all round the walls, labelled with their contents; the dimmer but equally fascinating Drapery; the counters with their tunnels through which one could crawl to the prestigious private side. Then the door through to the back; the big warm kitchen, full of purring cats and shining saucepans, with a long deal dining-table large enough to seat not only the complete family but almost any number of guests as well; the little parlour for afternoon tea; and the long music-room, where a huge wall mirror at one end reflected the low window at the other, giving an impression of space and elegance. Outside the window was an expanse of asphalt (always called 'the gravel', which it probably once was), used for *al fresco* meals in hot weather; then the walled garden led eastwards to the Park, the Avenue, and the Lake (called 'the Pond').

Even in our childhood Corsham was hardly more than a large village, and must have been more rural still in the 1870s, before the second Lord Methuen, with the best of intentions, gave the site for the new Town Hall in the Market Place where the pretty little old Market Hall once stood. Pickwick had been a separate hamlet only a few years earlier; and there is a school certificate of Herbert's (for 'proficiency in French, Class II'), dated July 1877 and showing an engraving of Mr Hulls' school, surrounded by gardens, fields and trees as far as eye can reach. (By the 1900s this school had become The Mansion House, and later was used as a Community Centre.)

One important event in this Wiltshire boyhood is not mentioned in the diaries because it must have happened before they started; probably in the summer of 1871, if Daisy's memory is accurate. (See her poem, 'A Reminiscence' at end of book). It was a visit to Corsham by Herbert's half-cousin Daisy Goold from Nottingham. The Goolds of Corsham were close friends of the Spackmans, and Henry Spackman's first wife Sarah Goold was the sister of Joseph, Daisy's father, who had moved to Nottingham. In 1871 Daisy was five and Herbert six, and they took a great fancy to each other. They did not meet again for more than sixteen years, but kept up a cousinly correspondence, perhaps two or three letters a year, the initiative always coming from Daisy, who never forgot her Corsham idyll. The rather chequered course of their relationship will be evident from the diary extracts; but they did eventually get engaged just before Herbert emigrated. Daisy followed him two years later and they were married in New Zealand in December 1893, but after the birth of their first child and the unexpected death of his beloved mother they decided to return to England, and took up life again in Corsham almost where it had left off, in 1900.

It took me a long time, even after my retirement, to go right through the diaries, and I was held up for some years by poor eyesight. But by the mid-seventies it occurred to me that the extracts, which I had intended only for family reading, might interest others, especially those who remembered the Spackmans of Corsham. At a venture I showed the New Zealand section to the High Commissioner in London, and was much pleased to find that he and his Private Secretary were entranced with the picture it gave of the life of New Zealand settlers in the 1890s, and eagerly accepted from my sister and me the offer of the material on permanent loan to the Turnbull Library in Wellington. This encouraged us to show the Corsham Civic Society some of the earlier extracts, which again were very warmly received. Thus was born the idea of publication. Seventy years of it being out of the question anyway, the years before Corsham temporarily faded out were the obvious choice, especially as many photographs and even the love letters had also survived and would help eke out the story. Eventually, all our material will go to the Wiltshire Record Office at Trowbridge.

Would Herbert have minded his life being exposed? Yes and no: more than once precious documents had to be rescued from the waste paper basket. Yet there is something wistful about his musings as to the ultimate fate of his diary with its meticulously written nightly entries however tired he was: '... I believe cremation is advisable ... perhaps oblivion.' Neither cremation nor oblivion but resurrection.

Explanatory notes, as far as we can supply them, will be found at the end of each year. Some names still await identification, and we shall be delighted to hear from any reader who can throw light on them.

Faith Sharp
with Heather Tanner
1981

The old home kitchen

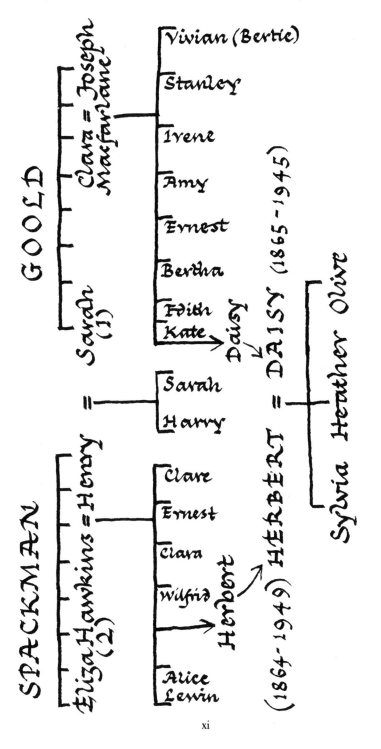

Family Tree

xi

From Herbert's abstract of 1939:

'This was a year of school at Mr Hulls'; attendance at Baptist Sunday School; helping in the shop; going round with Dad in the Calne neighbourhood; a good deal of bagatelle in the evenings; cricket in the Drung, and at school; croquet on the lawn. Poor Alice an invalid in the spare room, where she was often visited by friends; a good deal of visiting by Chippenham musical friends, including Mr Hills (violinist), Mr Brinkworth, Mr Freeth, Miss Poock, Miss Eva Neate, etc.

Discontinued my diary from September, probably owing to holiday at Eastbury.'

JANUARY

1st (Monday) Mr Kenway returned to London. Counted oranges. Ernest Lanham came to tea; went out in the park with our bows and arrows, and had a game of bagatelle in the evening. Dad, Sarah and the two children went to Bath.

4th Went down to Mr Goold's brook and stopped it up. Mr Hills came over in the evening. Blanche Goold came to tea. Mrs Kenway came home from Bath with Maitie and the baby.

5th Went over to Mrs Moore's to tea. Played tag on the gravel all morning. Weighed up some tea.

7th (Sunday) Went to chapel in the morning. Went to Sunday School in the afternoon. Went to chapel in the evening. Lewin played on the harmonium. A very wet day.

8th Hales the lamplighter's son killed in the quarries.

10th Ernest Lanham ... was initiated as a Good Templar in the evening.

11th Went to Mr Hawkins to dinner and tea with Wilfrid, Clara and Clare. Ernest did not go because of his cold. Fourteen sat down to tea. Dad, Ma and Mrs Kenway came up in the evening. Grand ball at Hartham. A starlight and frosty night.

16th Clara, Ernest and Clare went to school ... Went to shorthand class in the evening.

22nd Went to school.

25th Went to Fred Boscombe's to do lessons in the evening. Mr Hills, Mr Brinkworth and Mr Osborne came in the evening and had some music. Lewin done some printing. Alice much better.

27th (Saturday) Went to school in the morning. Had to stand upon the form.

29th Went down to Lacock pond and put my boat on; it went very well but the wind was too rough for it.

30th Did not go to school. Went in the trap with Dad to Melksham and Atworth. Shorthand class in the evening. Fred Boscombe came and done lessons with me in the evening ... A terrible windy day. Ma bad with the headache.

31st Went down Westrop Road after school to the pond with the boat, and tied some string to it. Went to Mr Feaviour's in the afternoon and played bagatelle with Albert for an apple. Albert won it three times, but gave it to me after.

FEBRUARY

3rd (Sat.) Cousin Lizzie here today. Went down to Lacock pond in the afternoon with the boat. Fine till about four in the afternoon, then turned off wet for the rest of the evening. The anniversary of our going to Mr Hulls'. Two years.

6th Went to school. Had jolly fun up there. Went to shorthand class in the evening. A dull day. Fred Boscombe came and done lessons with us in the evening.

7th Fred Boscombe kept in all the afternoon. Lewin, Ma and Sarah Goold went to Wootton Bassett to the concert. Cousin Lizzie and Auntie Lydia came to tea. Cousin Lizzie poured out tea ... Put some sails on my boat. Jessie Goold came and had tea with Alice.

9th Went up to Mrs Thomas's to be measured for a pair of trousers in the evening. Had a bath in the spare room.

2

Charles Hulls' School

4

11th (Sunday) In the afternoon we went (that is Clare, Wilfrid and I) up to Grandma's to tea, and after tea Cousin Lizzie talked to us about Newport. Cousin Albert of Hinton came to Grandma's.

17th Went for a walk with Cousin Lizzie, Minnie Moody, Auntie Emily, Katie Moody, Wilfrid, Clara, Ernest and Clare, out Miss Butler's way in the afternoon.

19th Went to the magic lantern entertainment in the evening.

22nd Myra Twinney and Emily had tea up in the spare room. Members' tea-meeting at the Baptist Chapel. Grandma went.

24th Helped in the shop in the evening. Began putting the turf on for the lawn. Harry went to Eastbury. Slept in Harry's room with Lewin.

28th Went to Mr Boscombe's to tea; Wilfrid, Clara, Frank Wheeler and Joe went also as it was Fred's birthday. Did not come back till eleven o'clock. A beautiful, splendid, lovely, beautiful, fine day.

MARCH

4th Sunday school in the afternoon. Had a library book named 'Tim's Troubles'.

1st Went to the baptising at the Ebenezer Chapel in the evening. Six were baptised: Miss Blandford, Aunt Emily, Lizzie Moody, Cousin Lizzie, Phemie Osborne, Adelaide Aust. Oh, seven though, a young man named Harris.

5th Clara's birthday. I gave her a drawing slate.

6th Went to the popular entertainment in the evening. Liked it very much.

7th Corsham Fair. I was down at the fair nearly all day. Spent twopence. I was electrified at the fair. A cold windy day.

12th Gave sixpence to the subscription for Sir Rowland Hill.

14th Went to the practice for the Temperance Service of Song at the British Schoolroom. Put sixpence in Alice's missionary box.

15th Missionary meeting at the Baptist Chapel ... A missionary from China came; he sang a song in the Chinese language.

16th In the afternoon an old gentleman came to Mr Hulls' and Mr Hulls told us that he was going to give us some recitations and we were not going to have any school. So we all sat round to hear him. Amongst his recitations were 'The Bashful Man' and 'The Charge of the Light Brigade'. We went home at half past three.

18th (Sunday) Chapel in the morning. They all broke down in the first hymn. Sunday School in the afternoon. Miss Haslem read us a story about Robert Malcolm. Had a library book named 'A Spanish Cavalier'.

19th School from nine to eleven and the rest of the day was a holiday because it was Mrs Hulls' birthday. Went in the park with our bows and arrows ... Had romps up in the hayloft with Fred Boscombe, Clara, Ernest and Clare. Dad a little better; Alice about the same. Mr Brinkworth and Miss Tanner came over from Chippenham in the evening and had music and singing.

20th Went to the entertainment in the evening, threepenny seats. Mr Glock sung a song and made a muddle in the middle.

21st A lovely cloudless day. Went with Cousin Lizzie, Auntie Emily, Clara, Ernest

Harry Goold Spackman

Sarah Goold Spackman (Mrs Kenway)

and Clare out in the park to pick some primroses; we could not find many primroses but found some beautiful white violets and we sent them to the folks in London.

23rd Joe and Fred Boscombe had a game of hopscotch in the kitchen in the evening. Ma, Sarah, Harry, Lewin and Eva Neate went in the fly to the Chippenham concert. Had a bath in the evening; Grandma washed me.

26th A great storm of hail came on and I got nearly wet through coming home from school. Lewin helped me with my Latin in the evening.

28th Helped Ma clean the windows in the parlour in the afternoon. Cousin Lizzie cried about walking with Alice in the garden. Clara, Ernest and Clare broke up for a week's holiday.

30th (Good Friday) Had a game of darts in the morning in the nursery. Had some hot cross buns for breakfast. Went to church in the morning and sat with Dad, Cousin Lizzie and Sarah. Went up to Grandma's ... Grandfather's birthday. Played skipping and 'sedan carrying' out in the garden after tea with Wilfrid, Clara, Ernest and Clare. A magnificent day.

31st Went down to Pound Pill in the morning. Mr and Mrs Kenway came from London with Maitie and the baby. Had a game of cricket out in the drung with Wilfrid, Ernest and Clare, for the first time this year. The Chippenham Rifle Volunteers' Band came to Corsham in the evening. They went up to the top of the town and played a few pieces and then went into the Methuen Arms and after that they had half an hour's stroll and then they went down the town home playing. I followed them to Lord Methuen's gates. Mr Brinkworth and Sergeant Bass were there.

APRIL

1st (Easter Sunday) April Fools' Day. Only made one once, and then by Wilfrid. Made Ann, Clare, Joe, Fred Boscombe, Ernest, Cousin Lizzie, one. Went to chapel in the morning. Maitie went. Went for a walk after tea in the park ... Had a library book, (from Sunday School), the title of it 'Harry's Perplexities'. Went to chapel in the evening. Stopped to Sacrament. Went for a walk up Westrop road and round the park after chapel with Fred Boscombe and Joe. A beautiful day.

2nd Did not go to school because it was Bank Holiday. Went out in the park with our skipping ropes before breakfast. After breakfast we asked Dad if he would let us have the carriage out and he said he would, and so we took Maitie and baby out in it in the garden. Went for a walk with Lewin and Wilfrid and Cousin Lizzie to Hartham Park and we got a basket of primroses.

4th Did not go to school. Helped Lewin in the shop. An awful tremendous rainy day; it was like a river in the street. Played bagatelle in the evening with Mr Martin. Mr Humphries came to tea.

6th Harry came home from Eastbury. Cousin Lizzie and Lewin went to the Grand Popular Entertainment at Pickwick in the evening.

7th An April-shower day. Wilfred, Ernest, Clare and I had our hair cut up at Mr Little's.

9th A sultry day. Mr Uriah Goold's sale.

17th Got up at six o'clock and mowed the lawn and afterwards rolled it with Mr Martin. A fine cold windy day.

19th Helped Lewin get up the orders. Went to the tea meeting at Box; Lewin drove. Ma, Wilfrid and Sarah went. We had a beautiful drive home. A nice, fine, beautiful, splendid, lovely day.

24th Got up at seven and went for a long walk with Wilfrid, Ernest and Clare ... Miss Poock and Miss Neate came to tea. Mr Brinkworth came later in the evening. Went to practice for the Whitsuntide hymns up at the chapel.

26th Ernest and Clare had a holiday. Us five went out in the park and got some cowslips.

29th (Sunday) Us five got up at six and went for a long walk. Chapel morning and evening. Sunday School in the afternoon. Had a library book, title 'Vivian and his Friends'.

MAY

1st (Tuesday) Grandma's birthday. I gave her a packet of writing paper. Lewin bought five doves, two old ones and three young ones. He gave Wilfrid and me one young one each.

2nd Holidays over. Went to Lodge in the evening. Joe chose me as his right-hand supporter. Dad came back from London. He brought us some Banbury cakes.

4th Went to school. Three new boys came. Saw Mr Christie the new French master.

6th (Sunday) Us five and Dad went to Box in the train and walked back. Dad went up to the top of Mr Pictor's house. A beautiful day.

17th Chippenham concert. Ma, Sarah, Lewin and Harry went and brought back Cousin Joe and Miss Poock. They both slept here. Seventeen slept in the house.

21st (Whit Monday) Dad, Lewin, Cousin Joe and us five got up early and went to Pickwick to see the bicycle race. We saw 30 ... Went to tea meeting in the evening at the chapel. 170 sat down to tea. A fine day.

22nd Band came through the street in the morning. Sunday School treat in the afternoon. Had tea in the school room then went out into Mr Burchell's field. Had a game of cricket out there and several other games. A fine day.

31st Went to Calstone in the trap with Dad and Wilfrid – Mrs Spackman's birthday.

JUNE

5th Cousin Louie Butler and her young man came.

6th Shocking catastrophe at Widcombe Bridge (Bath). Dad went to see it. A lot of the boys (from school) went to Bath. Harry went.

7th Miss Dinah Spackman died about five in the morning.

10th (Sunday) Father, Mother and Clare went in the trap to Bromham. Went to church in the morning. Went to church in the evening. Went for a walk after church. An African day.

12th Got up at six and started at seven with the bier to go to Calne with Eli to bury Miss Dinah Spackman and got there at eleven and came back by train at 2.30. Walked to Chippenham in the evening to help Grandfather with bier. A fine close day.

19th Went to Wootton Bassett in the trap with Dad, Wilfrid, Ernest and Clare. We went up on the White Horse and the Monument. Lewin and Aunt Jane came from London. Cousin Bessie came from Wootton Bassett. (to stay).

JULY

10th (Tuesday) Had tea out on the lawn. All in the house went out there. 24. Played croquet. Enjoyed myself. A fine day.

15th (Sunday) Went down to the Weavern in the afternoon with Fred Boscombe and Wilfrid and took off our shoes and stockings and waded into the water. A fine day.

24th (Tuesday) Ernest's birthday. Wilfrid and I went to Wootton in the trap with Dad. I took an algebra and done some sums. A stormy day. Mr Brinkworth and Mrs Cole came to tea.

30th (Monday) Went to school. Mr Hulls gave out prizes. I had one. Broke up for the holidays. A very fine day.

AUGUST

1st Went to Weavern in the morning with Robert (Wild), Ernest Lanham, Wilfrid, Ernest and Clare. The water was very cold. Clare's birthday. He had six little boys to tea.

2nd Went to Lodge in the evening. Election of officers. I was elected Vice Templar, Wilfrid Left-hand Supporter, Clare Chaplain, Ernest Deputy Marshal.

6th (Monday) Bank Holiday. Went to the Good Templars' Fête. Marched in procession down the town and through Pickwick. Fireworks were set off in the evening. Went up to Mr Hulls' and got my certificate. A stormy day.

9

8th Made a silk winder.

14th Ernest Lanham ground coffee, 2500 turns without stopping.

22nd (Wednesday) [Account of the visit to Eastbury.] We watched the cricket match till half past three and then Dad took us down to the station and saw us off. We went to Shrivenham in the train and then Cousin Joe came to fetch us and drove us to Eastbury. We got there about half past seven. A beautiful day.

23rd In the morning went for a walk with Cousin James. Played croquet and rings. We watched the eclipse of the moon. A beautiful day.

24th Went for a walk with Cousin James and Cousin Clara to the Downs in the morning. Went for a walk with Cousin Mary, Cousin Clara and Cousin James to Lambourn in the evening and afterwards went to church.

25th A very wet day. Played bagatelle and cricket in the garret.

26th (Sunday) Went to church in the morning. Went for a walk with Cousin Joe to East Garston in the afternoon. Went to church in the evening. A dull day.

27th A wet day. Played bagatelle, draughts, etc. Aunt, Mary and Clara busy in the school room.

28th A wet day. Went to the bazaar in the afternoon. Went out in Mr Mills' meadow in the evening.

29th (Wednesday) Went for a walk with Cousin James to the Holly Bush in the morning. Went to the bazaar in the afternoon. Mr Footman came to supper. Harry came in the evening.

30th Had a game of croquet in the morning with Harry. Harry, Aunt, Mary and Joe went to Newbury in the wagonette. Went to the bazaar in the evening.

31st Had a game of croquet in the morning. Went to Woodlands with Joe's dinner. Went to Woodlands with Joe's tea and took ours too. Played hide and seek with Alice in the evening.

SEPTEMBER

1st Played croquet in the morning. Went to Bockhampton in the wagons. Went to Bockhampton with Joe's dinner. Played cricket and croquet in the afternoon. Had tea out in the fields with Joe at Bockhampton. Played hide and seek and tag with Alice in the evening.

3rd A very wet day. Played bagatelle, draughts, and cards. Cousin James went to plantation in the morning.

4th Played cricket and croquet in the morning. Went to Bockhampton in the afternoon with Mary and Clara: had tea there, and played Old Man and asked riddles in the evening. A fine day. Cousin Joe fell off his horse.

5th Played cricket and croquet in the morning, and in afternoon. Played hide and seek with Ann in the evening. A fine day.

NOTES FOR 1877

January 1st Mr Kenway had married Herbert's half-sister Sarah. They had three girls, Maitie, Katie and Ethel. At this time they lived in Bath, but Sarah seems to have spent much of her time in Corsham.

4th Blanche Goold: Sarah Kenway's cousin. Mr Goold's brook: at Pound Pill, where Sarah's grandfather had his tannery.

5th 'The gravel': the space, later asphalted, at the back of the house, before the garden beds.

11th Mr Hawkins: Herbert's mother's father. Hartham House: home of Lord Islington, then Sir John Dickson-Poynder.

16th, 22nd Back to school after holiday: Clara to Claremont, a private school for girls, beyond Prospect; Ernest and Clare to the 'British' (elementary free) school, at the end of the cricket field (now Corsham Primary School). 'British' was of course short for 'British and Foreign Bible Society'. Herbert and Wilfrid went to Mr Hulls' school, Pickwick Road, which they had attended for two years from 1875. Mr Hulls also appointed the head mistress of Claremont.

25th 'Done' (for 'did'): this occasional archaism is almost his only grammatical slip. Or is it an obsolete shorthand outline?

February 3rd Cousin Lizzie: Herbert's mother's niece.

7th Sarah Goold: Herbert's father's niece by first marriage. At home she was exploited to mother the young children of her father's second marriage, and at last left Bath to help in the Corsham shop as one of the family. Lydia Hawkins: Herbert's mother's sister.

8th Jessie Goold: another cousin on the Goold side.

17th Mr Moody was gardener at the Mayos' (bottom of Priory Street, then called Stumps Lane: the Stumps family used to live at The Priory). Katie, Minnie and Lizzie Moody were his daughters. Auntie Emily: a Goold relative, *née* Emily Freeth, later Emily Hayes when she lived at Prospect.

22nd Emily Hawkins was Herbert's real aunt, his mother's youngest sister, living with the family as help and, after their mother's death, as second mother. Myra Twinney was a cousin of Emily's: Grandma Hawkins was a Twinney, from Steeple Ashton.

24th Harry: Herbert's half-brother and Sarah Kenway's brother. Eastbury: home of Herbert's late Uncle Clare Flower Spackman, of Pigeon House Farm (now a listed building).

March 19th Mr Brinkworth, first of many entries. See Note for March 12th, 1887.

31st 'Drung': the passage leading from Corsham High Street to the Avenue (etym. 'through-ing'). Cricket in the drung follows almost daily for the rest of the summer.

April 4th Albert Martin: see January 1879. Mr Humphries: he married a Berkshire Spackman, Cousin Bessie.

9th Uriah Goold: Herbert's father's brother-in-law. His tanning business at Pound Pill had failed, and Herbert's father became liable.

May 2nd 'Lodge': the Good Templars.

June 5th Louie Butler: daughter of Herbert's father's sister, Ann of Bromham.

7th, 12th Dinah: daughter of Henry Dunsdon Spackman (Herbert's father's cousin and former partner) whose father died in the fire of 1849. Grandfather Hawkins helped in the garden and, apparently, with undertaking!

10th First mention of church, where his half-brother Harry was now organist. Herbert gradually transferred to the church choir.

15th Weavern: a beautiful wooded valley a few miles from Corsham, part of Hartham Park estate.

July 24th Mr and Mrs Wolper: Herbert's half-cousin Mary (Polly) Goold had married a Dr Wolper of Germany. Mrs Emily Cole, wife of Alfred Cole of Church Street, is to figure a good deal in the diaries; she was related to the mother of Harry and Sarah, Herbert's half-brother and sister.

30th The prize was 'for proficiency in French'.

August 1st Robert: a cousin on the Spackman side.

8th Silk winder: there is mention of 'mulberry leaves from Mr Saddler's'. The winder survived for his children's silkworms!

26th East Garston: the Manor Farm there, an early seventeenth century building near the church, was later the home of Cousin Joe Spackman.

Alice Spackman

From the 1939 abstract:

'I kept no diary for the year 1878. I must have left school at
the end of 1877, and am established in the grocery
department now' (the consequence of 'Mr Goold's sale'; see
April 9th, 1877.) 'I do not appear to have been studying
music, but choir singing gave me a good start. Apparently I
must have heard a lecture addressed to the young, for I find a
note, "Determined to study music and read sensible books"!
My friends at this period were Ernest Lanham, Frank
Wheeler, Joe Ward and Fred Boscombe.'
Ernest Lanham was the station-master's son, and the
friendship lasted throughout their lives.

Lo and behold I dreamed a dream and I saw in my dream a large fish, and it opened its mouth and spake and it said, 'Oh Tarpy, thou king of gardeners, thou hast offended the king of fishes by neglecting thy duty'. And lo and behold at these words the fish vanished. And Tarpy fell on his face and wept, and he was a changed man from that day.

JANUARY

1st (Wednesday) With Wilfrid as my partner and Clare and Dad as my antagonists we whisted the old year out and the new year in, Clare and Dad winning the game. Went to Grandma's to tea with Wilfrid, Clara, Ernest and Clare. Mr Goold's sale; Cousin James Butler came down to go to it. Wesleyans' tea meeting; Lewin went as reporter. A nasty wet drizzly day, snow in the evening. Ernest Lanham came up and stayed to tea.

3rd We heard of Lieut. Coker's death by the bursting of a cannon. Mr Linton had to tell the news ... Church practice in the evening. We tried sitting in the Tower to see how it would do; the sound was much better. Lord Methuen is going to sit in the chancel till his chapel is built.

4th Pretty busy today. Got the orders off at the eleventh hour. Bought a money box to put my money in. A clear moonlight night.

5th Went down to the pond to see if it was frozen over. The ice was about three quarters of an inch thick. A beautiful moonlight night. Went for a walk with Fred Boscombe and Ernest Lanham after church. Put down some water in the garden for the slide.

6th Got up early and brushed out the shop, dusted the tins, etc., then had a good slide. Ernest Lanham came up after breakfast and had some slides. Mr Mayo and the boys went on the pond; the boys skated but Mr Mayo contented himself with walking on it. Ernest went down to the pond and while in the act of jumping across the brook he slipped and fell in. He came home and went to bed. Harry and Sarah went to Mrs Amoore's to an evening party.

7th Woke up and looking out of window beheld snow on the ground ... Lewin went down to the pond after breakfast and stayed till dinner time. Tarpy and I went down in the afternoon, but besides the ice being rotten it was snowing all the time so we soon came off.

9th Went down to the pond ... it was pretty good ice, mostly covered with frozen snow – frozen so hard in some parts that it was quite smooth to skate on.

10th A very hard frost. Went down to the pond about eleven and stayed till dinner time. I enjoyed myself very much. There was a good skater down there from Melksham; she could go backwards as swift as anything. Mr James Humphries came to Corsham and went down to the pond to learn to skate; he got on capitally. Minnie and Katie Moody came to tea.

14th Went to practice in the evening. We had 'Dame Trot', 'The Lass of Richmond Hill', 'How Gentle the Moonlight', 'Night Winds', 'Stay Prithee Stay' and a few others; we had a pretty good attendance. Raining nearly all day and very bad walking too.

15th Got up most of the parish orders in the course of the day. Tarpy was out nearly all day attending to the chapel tea meeting. Went to Lodge in the evening to be initiated. There were only 14 there but they managed it somehow. Ernest Lanham was there. We had a comfortable little tea party, nearly all of them being up at the chapel. I did not go because it began so early and I wanted to be initiated rather badly. A beautiful clear starlight night, freezing sharp. Broke the bank window.

17th Anniversary of the fire, Jan. 17th 1849. Practice at church in the evening; had no voice at all. All us boys had our ten shillings given us by Mr Linton.

18th We put our money in the bank. Wilfrid put 12s, Clare put 33s, Ernest put 17s, and I put £1. 16s. 0d.

20th (Monday) Went down to the pond after dinner ... and stayed till five o'clock. It was pretty good ice, about the same as Friday. Ernest Lanham went back to school by the ten o'clock train ... All the little chicks got their books ready for school.

21st We were all up very late in the morning, about 7.30 or later. The children went off to school like good little dears. Went to the entertainment in the evening. There were nine Spackmans there. I enjoyed myself very well, especially Mr Stantial's reading. A very cold wind today. Mr Brown had a slight accident in the street in the morning. He was going down the lane when the horse shied, and on Mr Brown's pulling him back the horse slipped and fell on him, but beyond a strained thumb he sustained no injuries.

22nd Went down to the pond ... but it was not really safe. Mr Willie Yockney fell in close to the island and had to scrabble a good bit before he got out. I went in over my feet.

23rd A Dr Seaton came here and performed some tricks down at the British School Room and ran away without paying, the dirty spalpeen.

24th Went down to the pond after breakfast and stayed till about 12.15. It was the most splendid ice I ever skated on ... Dad and Mr West went down to Box after Mr Seaton to make him pay for the school room.

27th Cousin Joe came from Eastbury on his bicycle and went down to the pond with Lewin and Harry.

28th Had a game of hockey on the pond with Joe. Practice in the evening at the Methuen Arms; Dad and Joe came to listen.

FEBRUARY

1st (Saturday) A light fall of snow covered the face of Mother Earth when I woke up this morning and continued to fall till after dinner and it soon got into a deep snow. This however did not stop the skaters from having a turn on the pond, which after being brushed was not so very bad. Reckoned up the cash account for the month. Not a very busy day owing to the weather.

3rd Went down to the station for the cake from London which Aunt Jane had sent

Emily Hawkins

for Dad's birthday. Lewin went up to the Pickwick Readings in the evening to play for Miss Amoore.

4th Dad's birthday, 63 years old. We had his Christmas pudding for dinner and his cake for tea. The little boys stayed at home as it was Dad's birthday.

5th Went to Lodge in the evening. It was installation and I took my office as assistant secretary.

8th (Saturday) Uncle William came in the evening. It rained most of the day but that did not stop customers coming as we were pretty full. Went up to Lord Methuen's in the morning with Albert with a cask of soda and explored the vaults.

9th In the afternoon counted my stamps and found I had 3000 all but 18.

10th Uncle William went home. Albert drove over to Melksham with him. He left us a sovereign. Had a game of whist with Dad after supper. My side won. Did not go to bed till 12.15.

11th Superintendent Baldwin came to examine our weights. Our horse got into the weigh-house and ate some sugar.

12th Mr Freeth came over from Chippenham in the morning to tell us that Mr Brinkworth could not come to the concert as his brother-in-law was killed on the railway. Mrs Widburn offered her services to sing two songs instead of Mr Brinkworth. Cousin Mary and Bessie came from Eastbury to the concert and I mistook Cousin Bessie for Emily. Went to the concert in the evening and there was a pretty full room. Harry had to make a speech about Mr Brinkworth and had to make a good many alterations in the programme. 'Betsy Baker' went off well. Mr Reynolds was there, much to Sarah's delight.

13th Sent a comic Valentine and a few scraps to Maitie.

14th Wilfrid stayed at home because he did not know his lessons. He went to Allington in the afternoon with Dad in the trap. Did not have one Valentine. Lewin had one ugly Valentine but quite inappropriate. Went up to the Institution and had a game of billiards. Tarpy was beaten for the first time by me, by two hundred, and the next game left me the victor. Cousin Bessie and Mary had a game of whist in the evening with Dad and Ma.

15th (Saturday) A very busy day. Ernest Lanham came up in the afternoon and showed us an illustration of electric light. It was very pretty. He had a little piece of wire which the chemical master gave him, and he stuck this little piece of wire between the hinge of his knife and then lighted the wire. We put down the gas by the fire so as to have it dark, and when he lighted it, it was almost like day.

17th Sarah was very bad with the toothache, so Clara stayed at home and helped in the shop ... Cousin Bessie and Mary went back to Eastbury. Harry drove them to Chippenham.

22nd It was a sharp frost in the night and not very much snow, but it soon began to come down again. Ernest made a rather hard snowball and flung it at Clare, and Clare said it was nearly a stone ... Albert made a snow man down the garden and frightened me; then we brought the others down and made them believe it was a ghost. Had games of snowballs at intervals during the day. We were pretty busy today considering the weather.

25th (Shrove Tuesday) Had pancakes for dinner. Went down to the schoolroom rather early to put the people in their seats, but I did not like the job much. Miss Butler's girls came in, and Ernest Lanham and I sat just behind them and had a jolly bit of fun. Mr Hulls' boys acted Shakespeare's play, 'The Merchant of Venice'. Crisp did his part the best. Emma Aust came in in the evening and Minnie Moody also. A beautiful day. Peace was hung.

MARCH

3rd (Monday) Uncle William came in the afternoon and had a game of whist in the evening with Lewin as his partner and Dad and Ma as his antagonists. Went out for a walk in the evening and smoked a cigar and then went to the Institution and had a game of draughts with Fred Day and beat him. A beautiful moonlight night. I wrote the first order in the order book.

4th Dad and Uncle William went to see the hounds at Rudloe Firs and all the youngsters went too. I received the 'Boys' Sunday Reader' from Ernest Lanham by post and am very well satisfied with it. Dad and Uncle William went to the Pickwick Readings in the evening. It was the last of the entertainments and Harry said that he should think it was quite 400 there.

5th Clara's birthday. I put a button-hook in her shoe in the morning, so as when she went to put it on she would find something hurting her foot and then take it out. Uncle went to Reading in the morning and from thence to Newbury. Clara had about half a dozen little girls to tea and Mr Humphries had a cup also.

6th A beautiful day, clear blue sky and quite warm. Some of the shows for the Fair came in the day. One of the showmen's dogs went mad and they had to kill it.

7th Fair day. It was a pretty good fair for cattle but there were no sheep and very few pigs. I went down in the evening with Ernest Lanham, Wiles and Fred Boscombe and bought some swishers and swished at the girls but the policeman stopped it soon after. Mr Barrett had hold of me and took it away. I had two or three shots down the shooting galleries and hit the bull's-eye once or twice. I did not go to choir practice so I had my name put down. It was a beautiful moonlight night. I went in the show to see some performing fleas. Did not get home till nearly 11.30. Ernest Lanham did not spend a halfpenny all the time he was down there.

10th Stayed at home in the evening and read the 'Boys' Own Reader'. I had nearly a dozen customers after shop was shut and Martin was gone.

13th Mary Newman came from Atworth and stayed to dinner. Mr Pitman came in the evening.

14th Murfwa had three kittens.

21st A man from London sold watches by auction in the market place.

22nd Aunt Sarah came from London. All the youngsters had tea up in the nursery.

24th A dreadfully cold day. Albert Martin was not very well so we had to do without him for the day. Emily wanted me and Frank Weller to go to the Neston Lodge with Miss Hodges, Miss Aust, Miss Emma Aust and herself, so I went up for Frank Weller and we started about seven. It was a pretty good meeting and it was cold coming back. Went up to the Court and Mrs Pike gave me some cake for tea.

APRIL

4th Had a lecture on book reading and music, and I determined to learn music and read sensible books.

5th A very changeable day and a beautiful moonlight night. I looked at the Queen of the Night through the telescope.

7th (Monday) Fred Boscombe wanted to walk over to Melksham to get his bicycle and he wanted me to go, so as there was something to go to Mrs Butler's I went. We started about 7.30, got to Melksham about 8.30, then we had a few refreshments and then started for home as Fred could not get his bicycle as the man was out, and we got home about ten. It came on to rain when we had got up top of the hill.

10th A dismal day and very cold for April. Sarah's birthday. She went to Bristol to stay till Monday night.

14th (Easter Monday) (At Bristol) Got up at 8 o'clock and had a bath in Mr James's bath. We all went gardening to help to build the fernery which Mrs James wanted made. In the afternoon Gilbert and I went down to the Colston Hall ... We intended to go to Dr Linn's, but went in the wrong door, and so instead of seeing Dr Linns we saw H——'s Mysteries, but we enjoyed ourselves very well indeed. In the evening all the people went out and left Gilbert and I on our own, so we had a game of draughts, lotto, etc., and then had a look at some books and then went to bed.

27th (Sunday) Went for a walk with Harry in the afternoon and then went into Hartham Church and saw the organ and Mr Noble played on it. Thundered and lightened in the afternoon, rain all the evening.

MAY

1st A nasty wet cold day and snow even ... Went into Baines's and engaged to take in the Boys' Own Paper instead of the Sunday Reader. Frank Baines promised to lend me some books to read. On the telegram (*sic*) at the Institution we heard that there had been some great losses on the English side.

6th A wet morning. I collected all my treasures into the cupboard in the bookcase which was to be my future place for all my things. I fitted a lock on to my clothes drawer in the nursery.

15th A nice morning. Tarpy went round for orders. Bought a Boys' Own Paper and Boys' World and also a knife from Mrs Bromley. Albert went down to Mr Jennings for the tea things but the horse ran away and then stopped short and sent the basket flying over the horse's head, and nearly everything was smashed.

21st Went to the newly made Corsham Mechanics' Institution in the evening with Ernest Lanham. I enjoyed myself there.

27th A fine morning but soon turned off to wet unfortunately. We started for Christian Malford about 12.30 in the Chippenham brake; it was rather a squeeze. My hat was knocked off just before we got to Cross Keys. The Festival went off very well considering. We had a very good tea, then the concert. We started about seven and got back soon after eight.

29th A fine morning. Clare's anniversary. We kept it up by going down to Mr Mayo's to tea; we had it in the summer house. We had a game of tennis and a game of cricket. While Martin was driving round the parish for orders the shaft broke off. It seems as if May 29th is a rather unlucky day for the horse and trap. I got some oak leaves early in the morning, so I was free from attack all the day.

JUNE

2nd (Whit Monday) A fine morning. Went up to Rudloe Firs to see the bicycle race but we had to wait a long time, but at last they came. They went down Pickwick Road. Had a game of cricket in the drung in the morning. They did not have the cricket match as it was too wet; it rained pouring all the afternoon. Went up to the chapel tea-meeting with Wiles and Fred Boscombe.

3rd Mrs Methuen died.

9th We shut up about 10.30 ... I went down the avenue about 12.15 and there were a lot of people there already. Some policemen were down there keeping the people out of the square. Went into church rather early as we had to practise the hymn. Everything went off nicely. The choir were to follow behind the procession, but the people got in the way and we couldn't get up the aisle, so we had to see the best way we could. Went down to the grave and looked in afterwards. There were a lot of flowers on the coffin.

10th A fine day. Tried ginger-beer making but had a lot of difficulties to surmount, but succeeded pretty well as far as I went. Lewin was making up a report of the funeral to go to the Wiltshire Times nearly all day.

16th A pouring wet morning. Made some more ginger-beer. Did some painting in the evening. Mr Cole and his men papered the parlour.

19th The painters and plasterers were working about the house most of the day. An entertainment was announced to take place in the British Schoolroom, but owing to the managers being short of money the entertainment did not take place.

20th Did some more of my picture in the evening. We received news of Prince Louis Napoleon's death in Africa by assegais of the natives.

22nd (Sunday) Put on our new clothes in the morning. Went to church. Went to see Grandma in the afternoon and stayed to tea.

27th Went to Bath (in wagonette) to see 'H.M.S. Pinafore'. I enjoyed it very much; it was a splendid play. We sang going home and got home about one o'clock.

JULY

9th (Wed.) A fine morning. Went down to Clifton with the junior schools. We started at 12 o'clock. There were four extra carriages put on. About 180 children had to wait a long time at Bristol station. While we were waiting we distributed a bun each to all the children. Went straight to the Zoological Gardens. We had one or two storms there. Had a very good tea and then home again; a very short stay there. Got home soon after seven. Went along to Mrs Lanham's and had a few strawberries and then went to the Institution and had a game of billiards.

16th A fine day. Got up early and done some pasting in my scrap-book. Went out in the parish with Martin. Went in Mrs Charles Jones's and saw her idiot son. Went in Mr Fuller's garden with Martin. In the evening went over in the shubbery and got some catapult sticks.

17th Got up the orders today. Had a game of croquet with Ernest in the afternoon, the first this year and the first time with the new croquet set. I won ... A fine day, not much sun though. Expected Edwin Lee to come to tea and have a game of croquet but he has not come, much to Emily's disappointment.

21st Ordered another painting book at Mr Baines's.

24th A beautiful day. Overslept myself and was not in the shop till nearly eight o'clock. Ernest's birthday. I gave him a little box with soap in it.

25th A fine day. Got up at half past four and went out with Jack, though I meant to paint but forgot to bring the paints. Ernest came with me as he slept with me; we went round Easton.

26th A dull day, inclined to rain ... A wild beast show came here and performed up in Batley's field in the evening. We had a very busy day as we were rather backward with the orders.

28th Got up at half past five and went down street to wake Wiles and Fred Boscombe to have a game of cricket. I shot up at the windows to wake them, but shot at the wrong ones, but I got them up at last. We played till seven o'clock. Fred Boscombe went off to London by the 12.30 train and Aunt Lena and Lewin went too ... Went down in the shrubbery to cut some more catapult sticks and made a catapult. Had a game of croquet after shop but it got dark and we had to leave off. Edwin Lee came to tea and played croquet all the evening.

29th A splendid day. In the sun it was pouring hot. Lewin, Harry and Wilfrid went down to Box to play a cricket match and got beaten in one innings. After the match they went in to Bath and had a bathe. We had the whitewashers in the kitchen and outhouses ... Kate Webster was hung in the morning.

30th A fine day. Had a sponge bath in the morning for the first time. Hulls' school broke up. Last day of Wilfrid's schooling.

31st First practice for H.M.S. Pinafore, but I am not going to sing in this concert as I know I shall not be good.

AUGUST

1st (Friday) Clare's birthday. He had Frank Ryall and Freddie Cole to tea.

4th (Bank Holiday Monday) Got up at six o'clock and had some breakfast and then we started. We were seven in number: Dad, Lewin, Wilfrid and I, Mr Henry Barnes, Mr James Barnes and Edwin Lee. Ernest Lanham came with us as far as Chippenham as he was going to Bath, and we potted some windows going along. I lost my catapult at the last minute so I had to have Harry's and it broke very soon. When we got to Calne we walked up to Cherhill and had a look at Cherhill church, and went up on the White Horse and Monument, and went from there right across to Castle Hill and rested while we had a view of the splendid scenery around. From there we went to Roundway and then to Mr John Butler's and had some lunch, and then went into Devizes and looked at St John's Church. We then walked to Rowde and had some milk at Annie Franks's and then on to Bromham. We went in Bromham church and Lewin played on the organ and then we went up in the belfry. We then went to Bromham House and had some tea. After tea we had a row on the pond in the farmyard in the flat boat; it was jolly fun. About eight o'clock we had some supper and then had some singing. We had some of the 'Pinafore' songs and one or two of another sort; we did kick up a row too. Albert came round with the horse about half past ten and then we took our farewell of Bromham House and got home just at twelve o'clock after spending a most agreeable day. We walked about 20 miles. It was a splendid day for a wander on a Bank Holiday.

6th Mr James came in the morning and told us that he had brought an action against Mr Jolly of Bath for sending away Alice, his daughter, from their shop without a moment's notice. The jury gave an immediate verdict for Mr James, damages £87.

7th A fine day. Mr Humphries and Cousin Bessie his wife came to tea. Wilfrid, Clara, Mr Humphries and I had a game of croquet before tea ... A woman came in the shop and offered to cure any of our corns. She had a lot of testimonials; one was from Mr Macfarlane. Her charge was too much for me.

8th A fine day. Mr George Humphries and a Mr and Mrs Taphouse came to tea, and while we were at tea Mr Isaac Humphries came in, so we've had a pretty good show of Humphrieses the last two days.

11th Got up early and cut the lawn with Martin ... Went up to Frank Wheeler's house after shop and looked at his papers, paintings, essays and puzzles. The lamps were lighted in the streets for the first time. A fine day, very sultry and oppressive.

12th A splendid day, very hot. Edwin Lee came in the shop as apprentice. Had tea on the lawn with Minnie and Katie Moody, Aunt Sarah, Aunt Jane, Wilfrid, Ernest, Clare, Clara, Alice, Lewin, Dad, Ma, Emily and Martin, a pretty good party.

15th A fine day. Uncle William came to see us and tipped us half a crown for the Weymouth trip. Went for a walk with Edwin Lee, Frank Wheeler and Ernest Lanham; walked all about the town and had some jolly larks. Eva Neate came to supper and sang afterwards. She has a splendid voice.

18th (Monday) When I woke in the morning it was pouring wet; not a very nice prospect before us. Had some breakfast and then started. There were a good many over 30 went from here. We got there (Weymouth) about 10.30 and then we went and had a bathe directly; we 8 in our bathing machine included Mr Arthur Little. Had some tea after the bathe and then went over to Portland in the steamer and had another tea. Sarah was seasick going across the water so she came back by train. Frank Bromley took her. After tea we had donkey riding. Clara and I nearly fell off. Did not see Harry all day. We had no light going home. Got home about 11 and recounted our adventures.

20th Got ready for my journey (to Bristol) in the morning. I got to Bristol all right but it was a wonder I got any farther as I didn't know where to go for the place where the Clifton train starts from. I found it at last though and got to Mrs James's all right about dinner time. Took the train to Clifton Down in the afternoon and went down the Avon, but it came on to rain and spoilt it all. Went down town in the evening with Gilbert and ran after the girls. I enjoyed it very much.

24th (Sunday) Got up early and had a bath which was all the more pleasant as there was a lot of water in it. May James came in the morning, and went back in the evening.

25th A beautiful day ... Got to the Clifton cricket field about 11 o'clock ... Lancashire went in first and made 53 and then Gloucester went in and made 123 and 6 men out; W. G. Grace making 75 not out. I brought a card and scored on it. We took some sandwiches for dinner and tea. After the match we went on to the Downs and came home by the last train.

26th A dreadful wet day. Went down to Budgett's with Gilbert and he cried because he was wet. After we came home we had to change our clothes. Went to the Orphan House (Number 2) in the afternoon with Gilbert. We saw all the little beds all in a row, and the children singing and going through their exercises. (Back to Corsham the next day.)

28th Tried to paint a new picture in the 'Boys' World' in the evening but made a mess with the sky and determined to give it up.

29th Went up to Mr Little's to be measured for a pair of shoes.

30th A splendid morning and it kept fine till the evening when we had just about a storm of rain. We had some empty sugar casks in the yard and the bees came in them in swarms, so we rolled the casks bang up against the wall and made them all fly out. It was a splendid moonlight night and Lewin, Sarah, Emily and myself went for a walk ... Harry played out in the street on his violin about eleven o'clock.

SEPTEMBER

2nd (Tuesday) A beautiful day. In the evening went to Chippenham to visit the Lodge. Lewin, Polly and Addie Aust, Miss Hodges, Miss Ward, Frank Wheeler and Ernest Lanham formed the company. Frank Wheeler and I managed to get into a second class carriage. We walked about the town a bit before the meeting. After it was over we had a coffee, and wretched stuff it was too. We had a nice walk home, but it would have been better if Frank Wheeler hadn't been there. Didn't get into bed till 12.30.

4th Two men came in the shop in the morning and asked Edwin what was the name of the young lady in the drapery shop. He told them, and then they went over to Mrs Bromley's and told Miss Hart that Miss Goold had looked at the books they were selling and told them to tell her that it was a very nice book and recommend her to take it in. She was completely deceived and ordered the book, but when she found it out she wrote and countermanded the order.

13th In the evening at supper Dad related some of the adventures at the fire.

15th Lewin came of age; a pity he was not at home … Practice in the evening; we practised the anthem for the opening of Lord Methuen's chapel. Clara played the organ while Harry led the boys.

16th Patty Baines died suddenly at her home.

17th Went to Lodge in the evening and took the office of secretary in the place of Rosie Churchill as she was going away from Corsham.

20th Had a talk about love and marriage and also about Heaven in the shop.

21st (Sunday) A rather dull day. Went for a walk down Collett's Bottom and got some nuts and afterwards went in Hartham Church and heard Mr Noble play two or three pieces of music.

25th A splendid day. Miss Fowler's wedding. We put up our banner (the same that we used when Colonel Methuen and his wife came into Corsham) across from the top of our house into Mrs Southey's window. There were not many decorations besides ours. The ceremony went off very well.

26th Gertie Baines came into the shop in the afternoon and asked to see a bottle of almond. I saw on the label outside the words 'Free from Prussic acid' which aroused my suspicions as to whether Patty had taken impure essence of almonds that had some Prussic acid in it.

27th (Sat.) A fine day. Found my catapult and shot at intervals in the day. We had just about a row here in the evening. Two men began fighting and Barrett went up to them to stop them and one of them hit him. He got up, handcuffed them and dragged them up to the police station. Jobbins took one of them, but when they nearly got up there, he got loose and ran home. Jack Barrett ran after him and brought him back, and they telegraphed to Chippenham for some policemen. Baldwin and another came and soon took them over. There was just about a crowd of people all about the town.

29th (Monday) A fine day. Cleaned the counter, weights and scales in the shop in the morning. Uncle and Aunt Laurie went up to Grandma's to dinner and tea. They and Dad and Ma had a game of whist in the evening. Some of the gentry in this town were busy today decorating the church.

30th Harvest Festival and opening of Lord Methuen's chantry. Shut up shop at ten o'clock. Went to church in the morning. The service went off very well. A very dull day.

OCTOBER

2nd Uncle William came in the afternoon and went to the concert in the evening. I had to sell the programmes. It went off very well. We had a very full room taking into consideration the wet night. We shut up shop at seven o'clock so as to be in plenty of time. The Chippenham people had supper here.

5th (Sunday) Went for a walk with Jack to the Batters in the afternoon and when I came home found Cousin and Mrs Butler of Bromham House in the parlour. They stayed to tea and church and went home in the evening.

7th A fine day. Dad and Uncle (William) went for a walk in the morning and in the afternoon they went up to the Court and went all over it. Went up to fetch Alice

Back view of the old home

Skating on 'the pond'

from Mr Burchell's in the evening. I got in the chair and Ann pushed while I guided. After I came back played whist with Uncle as my partner and Dad and Wilfrid, afterwards Ma, as my antagonists.

8th A fine day. The painters were varnishing the front of our shop today. Uncle William went away in the morning after tipping us four bob each. Harry went with him. Albert cheeked Mrs Hill in the morning in the shop and Lewin boxed his ears for him and we didn't see any more of him that day.

9th A fine day but rather dull. Batty's Circus was here today. We had the Grand Procession at one o'clock. I went to the circus in the evening; it was very good, same as usual. We had a good many circus men in in the course of the day.

11th (Saturday) A beautiful, splendid, lovely, delicious day, like a summer's day. It was very foggy in the morning but the sun soon came out. Ann went home in the afternoon. We slept in the nursery as it would be less trouble to Emily to make the beds. In the afternoon the football club had their first practice in the cricket field. Albert Feaviour had his neck hurt very badly and Alfred Kinneir had his wrist put out, a very nice beginning.

13th A foggy day as usual. Cleaned out the shop windows and cleaned the panes too in the morning. Ernest Lanham had a holiday as it was the birthday of the founder of the school, Edward VI. Found two robin redbreasts in the greenhouse and shot at them with my catapult for some time with no result.

14th Mrs Woodburn and Miss Luchford came to tea.

16th A boy named Lodge fell down the well in the quarries at Hudswell and was smashed to pieces.

20th Dad had a very bad attack of bronchitis and we had to telegraph for Harry to come home and attend to a funeral.

22nd Dad was a good bit better.

24th My birthday. (15th) Received most of my presents in the morning. I invited Penny and Hudson (Hulls) to tea, also Ernest Lanham. We had games in the kitchen in the evening and Edwin Lee, Sarah, Minnie and Katie Moody came in and joined us. It was rather a wet day.

25th A very fine day. Used my bloater paste in the morning for breakfast and enjoyed it very much. Cousin Fred from Newport came in the afternoon and slept here. We shut up rather early in the evening, but after we had shut up Mr Feaviour came down and gave us an order and I had to get it up and take it. It was a splendid night.

NOVEMBER

2nd (Sunday) Went for a walk to Rudloe Firs and through Mr Poynder's park to the church, and after it was out went in and heard Mr Noble and his son play and one of his daughters sing.

5th A beautiful day. Made six crackers in the morning. Bought Alice a book for her birthday. Set off fireworks in the evening. We had a good many to see them: all the Elvises and Neates, Miss Hart, Frank Wheeler, Edwin Lee. The balloon caught fire and one of the Roman candles hurt Wiles's hand; that was all the accidents. It took from 8 to 10.

7th A fine day. Frank Baines lent me a book called 'The Phantom Ship'. In the afternoon Jack came back. Edwin went up Pickwick with some biscuits for Mr Smith and saw him come out of the hedge and run up to a wagon and then follow it, so he went up to the wagoner and asked him how long the dog had followed him, and he said only from Pickwick, so we couldn't make out where he could have been all the time. Edwin brought him home and we had great rejoicings on his account.

15th A beautiful day. There were three funerals: Mr Fido's, Mr Mark Taylor's (Mr Chichester's coachman) and a little boy. Sarah Goold said 'damn' twice. We had a nice slide in the morning. Ernest and Clare went down to the pond and found it frozen nearly all over and about a quarter of an inch thick.

18th Went to Mr Hale's the shoemaker and was measured for a pair of boots. Went to the first Penny Reading in the evening and enjoyed myself very much, except for one thing, and that was that I had to put people in their seats. There was no-one to bring the piano away afterwards and it had to stop there all night. Ma could not go as she had a bad cold, so they had to leave out the trio.

20th (Thursday) A piercing cold day; it snowed in the morning a bit. In the evening we saw in the 'Wiltshire Times' an account of Charlie Brinkworth's death by drowning. He was on the mizzen-mast in a violent storm and slipped somehow and fell in the sea, it being too rough to try and save him ... Had a game of Pope Joan till supper time.

24th A fine day. Lewin went round collecting subscriptions for the missionary meeting ... he went in the trap and Minnie Moody and Clara went too. Minnie Moody was here to tea. Went to the missionary meeting in the evening. It was very well attended. I was tucked up at the top along with the choir boys.

25th Went to the Pickwick Reading in the evening; it was awful rot, nearly all comic songs and vulgarly sung too. We put down our new carpet in the parlour.

26th A cold day; we had a good bit of snow ... Got some steel wire down at Child's and made it into a cheese cutter.

27th Went to Mr Moody's in the evening; Edwin and Wilfrid and Ernest Lanham too. We solved puzzles most of the evening. We had a game of Consequences. It was the meteor night but it was too cloudy for any to be seen.

DECEMBER

2nd (Tuesday) A hard frost again. Went down to the pond before breakfast and had some very good skating. After dinner I went down again with Edwin and hadn't been on about ten minutes when I thought I would go round the island, as I understood Lewin went round; but I hadn't gone far when I went in. I partly kept myself up by kneeling on the mud under me and holding on to the ice till they had the rope, and after one unsuccessful attempt they flung it to within my reach, but they could not get me on to the ice until they had pulled me some way as the ice was not strong enough. I ran all the way home, Edwin with me, and got into bed. Had some hot tea and a hot water bottle and had soon recovered from the effects of my bath. I got up about seven o'clock. Nearly everyone in Corsham soon knew of it.

3rd A dreadful hard frost. Lewin, Sarah, Clara, Ernest, Clare and Edwin went down to the pond before breakfast. There were a lot of people there in the course of the day, a great many from Bath and some from Chippenham. I had lots of inquiries as to my health after my baptism yesterday. I was awfully stiff, especially on the left-hand shoulder.

4th An awfully cold day. Went down to the pond before breakfast with Lewin, Clara, Sarah, Ernest and Clare and I enjoyed it very much. Worked hard at the orders after breakfast and went down to the pond again after dinner for about an hour. There were a great many people down there mostly from Bath and Bristol. I saw the place where I fell in Tuesday. Martha Bromley died in the evening. Went to the Institution to practise carols.

6th (Saturday) A beautiful day. Went down to the pond about half past eleven and stayed till dinner time. It was very good skating where they had brushed paths (in the snow) the day before, but the rest of the ice was awfully rough. After shop wrote for a shorthand paper and also applied for membership of the 'Evercirculator'. Put some water down the path. Went over to see M. Bromley in her coffin in the afternoon. It was the first dead person I had ever seen. She was awfully thin.

9th Ma's birthday, 45 ... Practised reporting in the evening; Edwin read to me. [After a temporary thaw the pond froze again and stayed frozen right over the New Year.]

16th We arranged the Christmas window ... Went to Pickwick in the evening to the readings and enjoyed myself ever so much more than last time. Lewin, Harry and Clara played the Pinafore waltz. Did some more of my Dictionary after supper.

18th Went up to Frank Wheeler's and had a look at his model of a Chinese house. It was a splendid piece of workmanship.

24th We were very busy today in the shop ... Went up to Mr Baines's and ordered 'Round the World in 80 Days' by Jules Verne.

25th (Christmas Day) Went to church ... all the singing went very well except the anthem.

29th We heard of the fearful accident that happened to a train going over the River Tay bridge. Lewin and Harry went to the Court to attend the Servants' Ball, and didn't get home till 6.10 in the morning. A very changeable day; wind, snow, hail, rain, snow alternately. (30th)

NOTES FOR 1879

The dream of 'Tarpy'! This was the nickname for Albert Martin, general handyman, shop assistant and gardener. As an old man he had a magnificent long white beard.

January 1st Mr Goold's sale: see April 9th, 1877.

10th Minnie and Katie Moody: see February 17th, 1877.

17th The fire: January 1849, when the shop was burnt and Herbert's great-uncle died. See Introduction and Appendix.

February 3rd Aunt Jane: his mother's sister. She married Samuel Laurie.

8th Uncle William: his father's elder brother, farming at Kingsclere.

12th Sarah Goold: see Note for February 7th, 1877.

25th Miss Butler: head mistress of Claremont School for girls. 'Peace': presumably the murderer Charles Peace.

March 13th Mr Pitman: Isaac Pitman, the inventor of Pitman's Shorthand.

14th Murfwa, the cat, may have been christened by Wilfrid, who specialised in names!

May 1st Losses: in the Zulu war?

29th Anniversary of Clare's accident: he was thrown from the trap on the grocery rounds, and had a compound fracture of the leg. Oak leaves: this was Oak Apple Day.

June 9th Herbert's father had been undertaker from the age of 15, when he assisted his uncle. Hence the diary's frequent notes of deaths and funerals.

16th Mr Cole: the Coles were builders, painters, etc. See Note for July 24th, 1877.

22nd Grandma Hawkins, his mother's mother.

July 25th Jack, the dog.

28th Aunt Lena Hawkins, his mother's sister.

30th Sponge bath: a practice kept up for most of his life. Last day of Wilfrid's schooling: a regrettable but necessary retrenchment after the failure of the Goold tannery. See April 9th, 1877.

August 12th Sarah (Rowell): another of his mother's sisters.

September 13th The fire: see January 17th.

October 5th Batters: then a walk among hillocks thrown up when the railway was excavated. Now preserved as an 'open space' for Corsham.

13th 'With no result'; catapult and cat unfortunately got them in the end.

November 2nd Mr Poynder: later Lord Islington (Hartham Park).

7th Jack had got lost the day before.

24th Minnie Moody to tea. And almost daily!

December 2nd, 3rd, 4th 'The pond'. From the files of the 'Wiltshire Times' for 13th December, 1879:

'CORSHAM. Fast Trains Stop for Skaters.

During the past week the lake in Corsham Park has been well frozen over and the Rt. Hon. Lord Methuen, with the kindness of former years, has allowed all comers to enjoy the pleasure of skating. Consequently, the inhabitants and a great many ladies and gentlemen in the neighbourhood and adjoining parishes have availed themselves of the opportunity so kindly offered.

The ordinary train service by the Great Western Railway is by no means inconvenient for Bathonians and Bristolians, but in addition to these, the company have kindly stopped some of their fast trains to give additional accommodation and relieve the regular passenger traffic. We learn that several hundred persons arrive daily. The lake, therefore, wears a very animated appearance. No accident has been recorded.'

The summer must have been exceptionally fine and warm,
both before and after St Swithin's day, which was also fine.
Nearly every entry records cricket in the Drung, croquet on
the lawn, long walks over the Batters, round the Dry Arch,
etc., bathing at Weavern, sometimes several times a day, or in
the river at Lacock. The fine weather lasted well into
September. The year was also noteworthy for measles in the
family, and for Herbert's change from treble singing to 'bass'
and from piano practice to violin.

JANUARY

6th (Tuesday) A dull damp day. Put paper room tidy in the morning. Had a game of nap after shop with Ernest and Clare and afterwards went up to the Institution and had a game of billiards with Tarpy and Frank Wheeler, Tarpy taking us both on and he beat us. Had three games of draughts with Frank Wheeler and beat him all three. Sarah in bed today with her cold.

9th Went to practice in the evening and had our money given to us, 12s 6d, and Mr Linton remarked that I must not have any next year as I was a man now.

12th My Evercirculator came by the mid-day by post and glad I was to see it too ... Went down to Mrs Alfred Cole's in the evening and fetched Clare up ... I measured myself and weighed myself also and found that I was 5ft 3in in height and 110lbs in weight.

13th A very heavy snowstorm in the morning; the snow was six inches thick and a capital sort for snowballing, and Martin, Edwin and Harry got up top of the house in the afternoon and cleared the snow and snowballed each other.

19th A very hard frost. Tried the slide but it was not very good. Had two rubbers of whist in the evening; Martin played. I won one and lost one. Mr Mayo and his children went on the Park pond and Mr Mayo fell in up to his knees.

20th A fine day and very hard frost; the thermometer went down to 18 degrees ... Went down to the pond directly after dinner and stayed till after 3; it was splendid ice. Pickwick Readings in the evening; Lewin went. I went down to the pond after shop with Edwin and Ernest Lanham but the keeper came along and ordered us off ... A clear moonlight evening.

22nd There was a wedding at the church and the couple gave Mr B—— the grand sum of 6d for his fee. A great many down at the pond in the afternoon, about 400. I went down with Edwin in the evening and had a jolly time of it.

23rd Went down to the pond dinner time and stayed till 3.30. I enjoyed myself very much. There were a great many down there. I got into the 'outside edge'.

MARCH

1st (Monday) Ann came in the morning to resume her duties as servant. Played a new game called Demon in the evening.

3rd Went down to Ann's house after shop for Ernest, Clare and Clara to come up and play Demon with Wiles, and stayed there a short time and heard the musical box.

8th (Monday) Corsham Fair. There was quite a lot of cattle down there. I didn't go down till the evening and then there was not much to see; I went in to see some marionettes, and had a swing, and had one or two shots;

13th A splendid magnificent day. Mrs Kenway went out in the donkey cart in the afternoon with Clara and the three children. I held a horse for a lady in the afternoon and she gave me threepence.

14th (Sunday) Went to church in the morning and evening. Went for a walk with Lewin, Wilfrid and the three dogs before breakfast. Went out for a walk in the afternoon with Ernest Lanham and Jack, and met Miss Goold, Miss Jessie Goold and Miss Alice Kinneir, and then walked with them. Went for a walk

Henry Spackman ('Dad')

Eliza Spackman ('Ma')

after church with Frank Wheeler and Ernest Lanham. Had tea at Mr Lanham's.

20th (Saturday) After shop went down to the British Schoolroom to hear the speakers (Mr Fuller's candidature) but the chief speakers had finished before I got down there. When Mr Fuller was going off in his carriage we gave 3 cheers.

24th A black man came in the shop in the evening and a lot of boys collected at the shop door to look at him.

25th The Conservatives had their meeting down at the Royal Oak, Dad went to the annual Vestry Meeting. Missionary meeting at the chapel.

26th (Good Friday) Had two games of croquet before church; Wilfrid won the first and I the second. Had some more games before dinner and in the afternoon as well. Mr and Mrs Brinkworth and the baby came in the afternoon and Mr Brinkworth played croquet. We went at it again after tea and then went to church.

30th Went to the entertainment at the British Schoolroom in the evening; the room was crammed. The play went very well and I enjoyed myself immensely.

31st Lewin went to Chippenham by the 4.30 train for the declaration of the poll; Mr Goldney got in by 23. Aunt Sarah and Louie went away and gave me 6d. Took my best coat down to Mr Churchill's to have a pocket made in it.

APRIL

6th (Tuesday) A showery day. In the evening went up Stumps Lane and watched the roundabouts and swings.

9th Polling day. Tarpy, Lewin, Wilfrid and Clare were employed down there. It went off very quietly till afternoon … in the evening a mob collected about the town hooting and yelling, etc. till a very late hour. A lot of Mr White's windows were smashed.

10th Heard news of Mr Fuller's defeat. He only lost by 50. A lot of policemen paraded the town in the evening but they did not succeed in keeping order.

27th (Tuesday) A fine day but cold. Miss Awdry's wedding. I went down and blowed. Made some ginger beer in the afternoon; went up to Mr Feaviour's for the barm. Practice for the concert in the evening and Mr Brinkworth came over; I stayed at home and listened to it.

30th Mr Goldney came home and was drawn through Pickwick in honour of his being created a baronet. Bottled my ginger beer. Finished 'Frank Mildmay' and began 'Jane Eyre'.

MAY

12th The anniversary of Jack's appearance in our yard.

17th (Whit Monday) Stayed in bed all day; my measles broke out. Bicycle race from Bath to London. A regiment of artillery passed through Pickwick. Baptist Chapel tea-meeting.

18th Dr Kemm came to see me in the morning. Wilts Friendly Society Fête. I got out of bed to see the band pass by. Children's treat at the chapel. We shut up the shop at six o'clock.

19th (Wed.) Shop closed for the first time at four o'clock. Measles much better.

20th Joe Ward came to wish me goodbye in the morning and Miss Blandford also. Grandpa came to see me too. Mrs Beavan came to see me in the afternoon; Aunt Lydia came in the evening; Willie Moody for a short time in the morning. The measles are much diminished on me. It was a beautiful warm day. Ma again sat with me all night.

21st A beautiful day. Had a good night's rest. Had some ham and chicken paste on my bread and butter for breakfast. Had some mackerel for dinner. Murfwa was brought up to see me but she seemed frightened and soon ran away ... Had some turtle soup for supper. Read a good bit of Byron in the evening.

22nd Solved a Chinese puzzle that Ma brought up. Finished 'Handy Andy'.

23rd Earache better in the morning. I was dozing all the morning as I had no sleep all night. Read some Boys' Worlds in the afternoon. Sarah came up for a short time after tea and Aunt Anna afterwards. Emily sat with me at night.

24th Had an egg for breakfast. Dr Kemm said I could get up tomorrow. Ma had her tea with me and sat with me for a few hours. Cricket match with Box; Corsham made 119 and Box 21 and 26. Harry made 43.

25th A beautiful day. Festival Day. I got up after dinner and came down in the parlour. Had tea in the parlour with Emily, Clara and Alice. After tea Miss Sainsbury came in and talked to me for a short time and brought me some buns, and Tarpy came in afterwards with a large piece of cake from the tea-meeting. The bells rang at intervals during the day. Some band went by in the morning.

26th A delicious day. Took some medicine before breakfast and it made me very sick. Ernest went up to Mr D....'s and brought down a large volume of the 'Graphic' for me to look at ... Wrote to the 'Boys' World' office for the title page and index of Boys' World, first volume. The Boys' Newspaper came and Lewin brought it in to me. Minnie Moody came to tea.

28th Dr Kemm came and said Wilfrid had measles and Clare would soon have them. Did painting morning and afternoon. Tea in the parlour with Clara as the kitchen had just been washed. [Ernest also developed measles soon afterwards.]

JUNE

5th (Saturday) Did some painting in the morning, afternoon and evening. Finished 'Husbands and Wives' at tea time. Cricket match between Corsham school and Bloomfield cricket club. Lewin played for the school, made 118 and then gave up his bat. Willie Moody came up and helped in the shop. Bought a Reynolds Newspaper.

6th Clare came down in the afternoon and we played with the telephone for a short time.

7th A windy day. Bessie Hulbert came to see Alice in the evening. Dad brought me from the Institution two volumes of 'Monte Cristo' and 'Verdant Green'.

8th Wilfrid, Ernest and Clare got up after dinner. Dr Kemm came and I got under the table. I was reading 'Monte Cristo' nearly all day.

36

13th (Sunday) A fine day. Went for a walk with Mr Wiles and Ernest Lanham down to Collett's Bottom and met a lot of others down there ... Took Alice up to Chapel in the morning.

14th A beautiful day. Some good practice in the cricket field till nearly 9 o'clock. Hung up in our bedroom the pictures I had painted during my state of convalescence.

20th A stormy day. Went for a walk in the afternoon with Willie Moody and Wiles down to the Chequers and around by Stowell Farm.

21st Clara got up (after measles). Grandpa, Willie Moody and Lewin were gardening a great part of the day and made the borders and path look very pretty. Finished 'Monte Cristo'.

23rd A fine day. The 'Patriots' fête. They engaged Bradford brass band ... Went in the club field and watched a young man climb the greasy pole. Had one or two turns at the coconuts and hit down two.

24th A beautiful day. Wilfrid, Ernest, Clare and myself were christened at church in the morning and Mr Linton gave us a prayer book each.

27th (Sunday) A beautiful day. Went down to the Weavern in the afternoon with Wiles, Ernest Lanham and Wilfrid, but only Wiles and I got in; the water was not very cold.

29th A beautiful day. Got up at five o'clock and went down to the Weavern with Wiles and Edwin and had a good bathe. Back by 7.15.

JULY

2nd A stormy day. Uncle William went home about dinner time and left a sovereign between us.

4th (Sunday) A beautiful day. After dinner went down to Mr Uriah Goold's house to have some strawberries.

11th A beautiful day. Got up at 7.30 and went for a walk with Jack, Ruff and Wilfrid by the coach road and down Westrop road, Went for a walk with Wiles, Ernest Lanham etc. in the afternoon.

22nd Amy Coxall came here in the evening.

27th We heard of the elopement of Mr Noble, organist at Hartham church.

28th Emily, Sarah and Miss Coxall went to Velly to the tea-meeting; Edwin drove them out.

29th Went up to Mr Hulls' in the morning to see the distribution of prizes with Clara. Mr Mayo promised to give a history prize to the boys next year.

30th Harry and Miss Coxall, Ernest and Clare went to the Court to see the picture gallery.

31st Went down to the fair (Bartlett's Steam Circus) after shop and had two rides on the horses.

AUGUST

5th Practised piano.

8th Went down to Mr Uriah Goold's in the evening for some gooseberries.

16th Mrs Wolper wished us goodbye.

17th A beautiful day. Sunday School Treat. Went down to the Weavern in the morning with Mr Lucas, Ernest Lanham and Edwin. Went down to Mr Mayo's field about half past two and played a game of cricket and had some tea and afterwards walked about the field a bit and then came home. I ran in one race and got a shilling.

19th Alice went up to Grandma's to stay for a few days. British School broke up.

22nd Ruff died.

23rd (Monday) We buried Ruff after breakfast. Willie and Mrs Wild came to dinner and tea ... After shop went up to Mr Batley's field to see the show there (Ghost Illusions).

25th Chippenham Flower Show. Edwin and Wiles and I went by the 4.30 train and went to Mr Edwin Brinkworth's to tea and then went to the field. The band played a nice selection from 'Pinafore' which I enjoyed very much. At seven o'clock we went to meet Ernest Lanham, then walked about the town till the fireworks began. Walked home afterwards.

26th A beautiful day. Choir treat. We started at 11 o'clock. When we got to Cherhill we had our lunch and then went on to the monument and White Horse and then to Silbury Hill and saw Willie Wild as we were coming back. Had some tea ... then on to Avebury Church and Harry and Lewin played the organ ... Got home about ten o'clock. It was lightning all the way.

SEPTEMBER

6th Mr Spackman of Calne died.

8th A beautiful day. Had a game of cricket in the drung after breakfast. Cricket match between Harry's eleven and Mr Mayo's. They won the toss and put us in and we made 60, Wilfrid making 27 and me 10. They made 43. Then we went in and made 121, Wilfrid making 19 and me 36. They followed on and were all out for 50 when time was called. We won by 17 runs on the first innings.

10th Dad and Uncle William went to Mr Spackman's funeral at Calne.

11th Pouring rain a good deal of the day. Cricket abandoned ... Edwin locked in the shop all night.

12th Rain nearly all day. Cousin James Butler came from Bromham in the afternoon and stayed to tea.

14th A drunken man made a row in the street in the evening and Mr Barrett took him up to the station house.

16th Uncle John and Aunt Margaret and Vaughan came. Ernest and Clare went to school.

20th Lewin done some printing; he had some new type come.

28th Went up to Mr Hulls' to confirmation class. Gertie Baines had lost her poll parrot for two or three days and today it got up in Hulls' trees.

OCTOBER

4th Aunt Jane came from London.

7th Wilfrid and I were confirmed at the church. Took a football out into the park and had some kicks.

10th Went to church and sat in the bass seat. Interesting discussion on Heaven in the evening.

11th Went up in the belfry in the evening with John Burston, Frank Wheeler and Fred Bryant and helped ring the bells.

17th Went to Hartham church in the afternoon with Minnie Moody, Mrs Cole, Sarah, Emily, Aunt Jane and Aunt Lydia. Emily and I entered the seat together and got turned out. Had tea at Grandma's.

19th Counted stamps in the evening; 7,785. Practised on the violin.

20th Snow in the morning. Miss Fry practised her song for the concert with Harry in the drawing room in the evening.

24th My birthday. Had presents from Aunt Jane, Edwin Lee, Clara, Alice, Ernest and Clare.

26th First of the penny readings in the evening. I went and enjoyed myself very well.

27th Stayed up till 1 o'clock and finished 'The Heir of Redcliffe'. Ernest Lanham gave me a pair of solitaires.

NOVEMBER

1st Made a fire balloon. In the evening tried to set it off but it was a failure.

5th Harry Neate got some fireworks for Edwin at Bath, Lewin made some and I made a few crackers, so we had a pretty good display in the evening. My balloon didn't go up.

18th Very cold; snow in the evening. Shut (shop) rather early as it was such a bad evening. Did some shorthand and then we sang some glees in the drawing-room. After supper had a rubber of whist with Aunt Jane, and I and Dad lost.

20th Put down some water for the slide. Porchester Waxwork Exhibition came here.

22nd A very hard frost. Went down to the pond after breakfast with Wilfrid but after throwing a stone the keeper came along and ordered us off. He ran after us and told us he would take us up but it was only to frighten us.

23rd On waking up found it snowing hard and all thoughts of skating quickly disappeared. Went to the entertainment in the evening. Enjoyed Mr Brinkworth's reading, 'Horatio Sparks', very much. Miss Lena Moore's song and Miss Young's pianoforte solo were the only two pieces that I didn't care about. It was not a very full room owing to the dirty roads and fog.

29th Went to violin practice. Frank Wheeler played the harmonium. Fred Hulls broke his violin by hitting Win Merrett with it.

DECEMBER

3rd Mr H. D. Spackman from Chippenham came here in the evening.

9th Ma's birthday. 46.

12th In the afternoon went to Biddestone with Dad and Wilfrid and met Ernest Lanham and Wiles with Dick Balch's dog 'Noble', and we had some fun with him by sending him for sticks. Went up to the Baptist Chapel in the evening and heard the choir practise the 'Nativity'. Practice for Melksham concert at 5 o'clock.

13th Had some practice on the violin with Ernest Lanham in the drawing-room. We had some Christmas carols; Ernest played 1st and I played 2nd, Clara played the piano.

16th Went to Melksham concert in the evening in the Chippenham brake. I sat along with the coachman going. Sat with Minnie at the concert; I enjoyed it very much. Went to Mr Barker's to supper and then came home. I sat inside coming home.

27th Joe Ward came to tea and we had cards afterwards. Went to the carol practice at the Methuen Arms in the evening.

28th Went to the carol entertainment in the evening. It went off very well except Mr Hulls' and Mr Budden's duet and Charlie Hulls' violin solo.

30th Joe Ward went back to Street and took Ernest and Clare with him. Went to the cantata, 'Nativity', at the Baptist Chapel in the evening. Sat at the bottom of the chapel so had a good view of the singers. Enjoyed it very much. Eva Neate took the solo parts; she has a splendid voice.

31st We sat the Old Year out and New Year in. Lewin went to Biddestone for the watch night service there.

NOTES FOR 1880

January 9th Mr Linton: the popular Vicar.

12th Evercirculator: a kind of Round Robin letter, to which each recipient added a contribution before passing it on.

13th Edwin (Lee): apprentice in the grocery shop.

March 20th Mr Fuller (of Neston): Liberal candidate. The Conservative candidate was Mr Goldney.

April 30th Jane Eyre: he is also reading 'Peter Simple' and 'All the Year Round'.

June 13th 'Took Alice to Chapel': a regular practice on Sundays; Alice continued to prefer the chapel to the church. Collett's Bottom, in Hartham Park, on the way to Weavern.

July 4th Mr Uriah Goold's house, Ash Villa at Pound Pill. Herbert's father was responsible for the empty Goold home and adjoining field after the failure of the tanyard business.

11th 'The coach road' – for the Methuen coach? from the Avenue to the Chequers, via the Dry Arch.

22nd Amy Coxall: later engaged to brother Harry, who had met the Coxalls in London. Henceforth the Spackmans often stayed there when visiting London.

August 22nd Ruff: one of three dogs. This date is heavily ringed in black.

26th Willie Wild: cousin on Spackman side.

September 16th Uncle John: John Hawkins, his wife and son.

November 22nd 'The keeper ordered us off': Lord Methuen's permission for skating, when the ice was safe, always had to be obtained first. See December 1879.

23rd See March 12th, 1887.

A full year, almost un-cut, with work in the grocery department, and much music, outings, firework-making (usually with Ernest Lanham!), and the beginning of love affairs. It ends with Grandpa Hawkins's death, involving the appearance of relations not mentioned earlier or afterwards.

JANUARY

4th (Tuesday) A fine day but dull. Eva Neate and Mrs Cole came to tea. Mr Cole and Florrie Neate came after tea. Wilfrid and I went down to Mr Moody's after shop and had cards etc. Lewin brought up his fiddle and played it in the street; it was pitch dark.

8th The organ came and was deposited in the church.

11th A dull cold day. Came on to snow rather fast in the afternoon. Pickwick Readings; Ma and Lewin went. Went down to church in the afternoon and had a good look at the organ. Practised my violin part for the Melksham concert all the evening. Evercirculator came.

13th A fine day though very cold. Ernest Lanham and I went to Melksham in Mr Alway's wagonette in the evening. While the singing was going on I had my hair cut and we had some refreshments . . . afterwards came back to the Town Hall and had our violin practice. Coming home took up Mrs Osborne. There was some skating down on the pond but it was not safe; Mr Mayo, Hansard Yockney and Mr Johns fell in.

14th A fine day and a very hard frost. Went down to the pond about ten o'clock and stayed till dinner time.

17th (Monday) A fine day. Went down to the pond in the afternoon and stayed till tea-time, and enjoyed it very much. Learned the Outside-Edge backwards. In the evening practised 'Macbeth' with Ernest Lanham, Miss Wall and Harry in the drawing-room and afterwards went to the Institution and got 'Ernest Maltravers'.

18th A most wretched day, the worst I can remember having, and even Dad and Martin said they had never experienced such weather. It was very windy and snowing, so that the snow drifted into heaps so as to prevent all traffic. Practised on the violin. Shut up (shop) at six o'clock as there was no chance of any customers coming in. At 7.30 I had my shorthand class, but as there was only Frank Wheeler and Edwin we had it by the fire in Harry's den. Practised my pieces for the Readings and Melksham concert after supper.

19th A wretched day; it came on to snow very thick about breakfast and kept on all day. Martin couldn't go out for orders in the parish. No practice in the evening owing to the weather. Edwin didn't go home but stayed here in the evening and slept with Wilfrid and I in the spare room. We had no daily papers except the 'Bristol Post' and we had no letters delivered.

20th A fine day and a hard frost. Martin went for orders on horseback. Went up to Mr Feaviour's in the evening to practise our pieces for the Readings. Miss Wall played the piano and Harry the violoncello and Ernest and I the violins.

23rd (Sunday) A dull day, thawing most of the day though rather slow. Went to church morning and evening; in the morning the water came dropping down close by me and in a great many other places. Went down to the church in the afternoon with Sarah to hear Harry play the organ. Went to Ernest Lanham's after church and practised our pieces for the Readings.

FEBRUARY

4th (Friday) A wet day. Dad's birthday. Harry played some pieces on the organ after practice. A telegram in the 'Daily Telegraph' to the effect that Colonel Methuen had saved a man from drowning at Berlin, and the church bells were set ringing.

5th (Sunday) A beautiful day. Went down to church after breakfast and Harry tuned the trumpet stop. Went to church in the morning. Went down to the church in the afternoon; Mr and Mrs Lanham, Ernest and Miss Wall were down there. Harry brought home one of the trumpet pipes as the water had got into it. Went to church in the evening; Harry played the Hallelujah Chorus after church. Practised our pieces for the Readings in the drawing-room and then had 'Judas Maccabeus'. Mr and Mrs Cole to tea.

8th A very windy day. Went down to the church after breakfast and blew for Harry, and afterwards Mr Bell came and played for a long time and gave me a shilling for blowing. Went to the entertainment in the evening. Harry, Ernest Lanham, Miss Wall and I played one of Simpson's Minuets and the March in 'Judas Maccabeus' and it went off pretty well. Harry put a disorderly fellow out of the room towards the end.

13th Mr Rowell and Aunt Sarah were here to breakfast and dinner.

15th Our concert in the evening; I had to take the tickets. It went off very well, but the tenors made a little mess of it in 'Alan-a-dale'. Mr Freeth and Mr Brinkworth rode back in our cart with the harmonium.

17th A dull day. Went to Melksham in the evening. I called at Mr Bell's on business for. Dad. Went in Burgess's and regaled ourselves with gooseberry tarts.

28th A hard frost and a nice fine day. Went to Chippenham by the seven train with Ernest Lanham and Wilfrid to the concert. Us three sat in the front seats for two tickets; Harry gave them to us. The concert went off very well. I liked the 'May Queen' best. We walked home and got home about 11.30. Ma, Sarah, Clara and Harry and Lewin helped the singers.

MARCH

1st (Tuesday) A fine day. I, Lewin, Ernest Lanham, and Clara went over to Melksham in the afternoon to the concert. We started at about 5 o'clock; it was a very nice drive. We had a rehearsal at 6 o'clock and afterwards went down to Burgess's to get some coffee, after which we again made our way to the Town Hall. The concert didn't go off very well; there was a muddle in 'Disdainful of Danger', that was the worst, and then there were a good many similar muddles. Ernest Lanham, Clara and I came back in Griffin's brake along with the rest.

3rd A cold windy day. Went down to the church in the morning with Harry and a commercial traveller and he played some pieces on the organ for him to hear. Had a new black apron.

9th A very windy day ... Evercirculator came. I sent off a postcard to the next member. Wrote an essay in it on 'On the Importance of a Good Character'.

10th A dull day. Went to Bath in Griffin's wagonette to see 'The Pirates of Penzance' at the theatre with Wilfrid, Bill Burraston, Bill Elvis, David Merrett and Ernest Woodman. We went down to Griffin's about 5 o'clock and expected to see a lot

43

down there, but beside the six mentioned none turned up. Played whist going down, but it got so dark that we couldn't see. Went to the theatre directly we got there; we took young Griffin with us and he and Wilfrid sat in the middle and I went to the back along with Ernest Lanham. Enjoyed it immensely. It wasn't over till eleven o'clock; Ernest Lanham rode back with us and they sang a lot of rotten songs going back. Got home soon after one o'clock.

11th A glorious day. Wasn't up till 8.30. Lewin got up a large party to go to 'The Pirates of Penzance' and they had Griffin's brake; we wished we had waited and had went with them.

12th Went down to the church in the afternoon with Harry and tuned some stops. Alice came in in her chair and Harry played some pieces for her to hear, and I wheeled her home. Mr Rowell came in the evening and had supper.

20th A fine day. Went up with Alice to chapel after breakfast. Went to church in the morning and evening. Went down to Ernest Lanham's after dinner and had a look at his new music stand. Afterwards went into the church and listened to Harry playing the organ. Dad and Ma went to Bromham in the pony trap and afterwards went on to Calne and brought Lewin back. Ernest Lanham came to tea and also Minnie Moody. [Lewin's fiancée. Minnie was almost as ever-present as Ernest Lanham.]

24th Went to Melksham in the evening. It was fine going but stormy coming back. Had a long walk before we went to the Town Hall. Went to Mr Burgess's and took home one of Huntley's and Palmer's lists and also a few macaroon biscuits.

25th A fine day. Went to Chippenham in the evening to see Poole & Young's 'Biorama'. Ernest Lanham came with me; we went by train and walked back. It was an awful crush going in, but it was a splendid entertainment ... Got home at a quarter to twelve.

27th (Sunday) ... Went for a walk with Ernest Lanham in the afternoon down to the Weavern. In the evening Mr and Mrs Alfred Cole came up and there was a long discussion on religion.

APRIL

1st (Friday) A beautiful day and a little warmer; the dust flew about in clouds. Someone sent me a letter with the Corsham postmark on it to try and make me an April fool, but I guessed what was up and didn't open it.

4th ... Lewin and Wilfrid went round to collect Census papers.

5th A beautiful day. Went to Bradford in the afternoon with Clara and Wilfrid in the pony trap; it was a nice drive. When we got there we went out for a walk with Lily and Nellie (Beavan) and then had tea; afterwards went in to see Mrs Weobley and then came home, leaving Clara to enjoy a week of Bradford.

8th Wilfrid drove Ma to see Mrs Gane in the Chippenham Workhouse.

14th A fine day. Went to Melksham in the evening. Went in to Mr Burgess's and had some tarts; Miss Burgess served us. Went and had a look at the churchyard and went into the church. Afterwards went in Mr Burgess's bakehouse and saw him making hot cross buns. After the practice was over we went to Mr Badham's to supper and I went and got the horse ready and brought it up.

15th (Good Friday) A fine day. Had some of Mr Burgess's hot cross buns for breakfast. Went down to the church and blew for Harry till church-time ... Dad, Ma and Sarah went to Marshfield in the pony trap. Heard that one of the Miss Notts had gone mad.

16th A beautiful day. Great excitement here owing to Miss Nott's madness.

18th (Easter Monday) A fine day but very dusty and the wind blew the dust about very much. Played croquet in the morning ... Went over to Melksham in the trap in the afternoon with Harry and Ernest Lanham. I drove. We took the instruments to Mr Ainsworth's and then went to Mr Burgess's and had a long talk with Miss Burgess. Afterwards went up to Miss Fowler's hall where the speeches relating to the opening of the Coffee Tavern were going on, and waited till the procession went down to the Coffee Tavern and saw old Tuddy playing his instrument and also our cornet player. Went to Mr Ainsworth's and had tea and afterwards played croquet with Mrs and Miss Ainsworth and afterwards with young Ainsworth. Harry came in and we had some music. Miss Smith sang her song and Mr Wall also. Ernest Lanham and I, Miss Smith, Mr and Mrs Ainsworth and the two children played Nap and afterwards we came home. Forgot my coat, also Harry's music, and forgot to bring home the oranges ordered at Mr Burgess's.

19th Lord Beaconsfield died about five o'clock in the morning.

MAY

2nd (Monday) A fine day. Uncle William came in the morning. Harry went over to Melksham by train. He telegraphed Lewin in the afternoon for he and I to go over, so we started at 5.30; went to Mr Walls' and Lewin played on his organ for an hour; I blew. Mr Wall showed us over the garden afterwards, and after some time Harry came in and we had supper. About a quarter to twelve I went down for the horse and gave the fellow a shilling, but he said that would not do and so I had to go and fetch another sixpence. Harry lost his umbrella going home.

3rd A beautiful day. Harry took Uncle William down to the church and played on the organ for him; I blew. Uncle William went away by the 4.30 train ... A boy at the British School stabbed another boy with a knife; nothing very serious though. Edwin had his 4 o'clock holiday.

4th A fine day. While I was practising on the fiddle in the drawing-room in the afternoon Dad ushered in Miss Burgess and Mrs Stratton; they had come over to hear our organ. Called Harry and then we all went down to the church; I blew ... Uncle William came again in the evening.

5th A beautiful day. Had a gooseberry tart by post from Miss Burgess; ate half of it and sent the other half out to Ernest Lanham ... Edwin's birthday. Had our first game of cricket in the drung before tea.

8th (Sunday) A splendid day ... Ernest Lanham and I walked to Melksham in the afternoon; I took some flowers for Miss Burgess. We started about 1.30; we went Witley way. After taking the flowers to Miss Burgess we went into Mr

Ainsworth's and rested ourselves ... we had a little violin and after tea went to church. Didn't care for the service much. After tea went for a short walk with Ernest and Harry Ainsworth. When we went in again we sang some hymns, and presently Miss Burgess was announced; she came to thank me for the flowers. We sat down and had a little talk; Ernest also came in. After supper we started; it was nearly eleven o'clock. It was beautiful moonlight and we got home about 12 o'clock having spent a most enjoyable Sunday. Had my first cold bath in the morning.

11th A fine day. Had a periodical sent by post in the morning from Mr Bucknell of London, advocating his system of shorthand; after reading it through I came to the conclusion that it was not very good. Mr Bodman and his two daughters came in the afternoon; after tea Harry took them down to the church (first having a look at the lake and the Court); I blew for a little time and then Lewin came down and told me Monty Comber was waiting for his shorthand lesson and so I went up, but he was gone; I had forgotten all about him. Went to the class in the evening at the Methuen Arms; the two Miss Bodmans went, and after supper we had some music in the drawing-room. The eldest Miss Bodman sang two songs and Harry and Sarah sang a duet ... Had my hair cut by the new barber who goes to Mr Marks's every Wednesday. Dad cut down a good deal of the bay tree.

18th A wet day, raining nearly all day. Brought down my alarum and after repeated failures succeeded in making it go for five or six hours ... Martin borrowed Mr Balch's trap and went out for orders, our trap being unserviceable as Mr Cole hadn't finished painting it.

21st A beautiful day. Framed Harry's pictures of Shakespeare and Gladstone and put them up in his room ... Harry went to Melksham to play in the cricket match. ['The boys' seem to have devoted most of their time this summer to cricket matches. Harry was in much demand over several counties.]

26th A beautiful day. Had a bath in the morning. Stained a picture frame and varnished it. Mr Cole and one of his men stained the drawing-room floor and varnished it.

28th A fine day, but a heavy thunderstorm in the afternoon. While Fred was out with some orders in the parish a shaft of the cart broke, so he took the horse out of the cart and rode back on it and told us; then Edwin went back with him and they managed to get it up to Mr Duck's and had it mended. Three new fiddles that Harry bought in London came in the evening and we tried them in the drawing-room.

30th A beautiful day. Fred went over to Chippenham to fetch the harmonium. Went down to the church in the afternoon to blow for Lewin while he played on the organ to Mr and Mrs Harris of Calne. Coming back, between the two stiles a girl pointed me out a little snake, a species of viper I should think. I took it up in my hat and brought it home, and after showing it to all of them at home, Edwin killed it with an iron bar. Edwin, Wilfrid, Ernest and Clare and I went down to the Weavern in the afternoon and we had a capital bathe. After that played cricket and after that Ernest Lanham and I and Harry practised our piece for the concert.

JUNE

1st (Wednesday) A beautiful day. Played in the cricket match between Corsham second eleven and Bath Association second eleven. I made 1 and 5 and Wilfrid 6 and 17. Corsham lost by 12 runs on the first innings. Afterwards went and dressed for the concert. Miss Burgess came in the afternoon ... Mr Freeth came over ... and stayed a little after supper and had some music in the drawing-room. Ernest Lanham and I were very glad that our piece was over. The concert went off very well. Had a little of Mr and Mrs Frank Baines's wedding cake.

6th A fine morning. Played in the cricket match with Rockley's. Wilfrid and Harry played also. Rockley's went in first and made 300; one fellow made 105, a left-hand man; another made 70 and another 58. Poor Corsham went in and a heavy storm of hail came on, and it was six o'clock before we went to the wickets. We were 5 men out for 10 runs when Callingham went in and he and Arthur Kinneir brought the score up to 40, and when Callingham was bowled time was called. The score: Corsham 8 wickets for 45 runs. So we saved the defeat nicely. Harry made a duck, Wilfrid one, and I didn't go in. Harry, William, Lily and Nellie Beavan came over in the evening ... and Harry, Ernest Lanham and I played our 'Andante Cantabile' on the violins. Miss Olding came in and sang 'Come back to Erin' and Sarah sang 'The Lady of the Lea'. After some refreshments they went back; they had a nice covered vehicle. After supper I went down to Ernest Lanham's and went out for a walk with him. Lewin went to Bradford in Mr Mayo's carriage.

7th A stormy day. Ernest Lanham came up in the afternoon and stayed in the shop till four o'clock and then I went to Chippenham with him by the 4.30 train. The Fete was held in the Market Hall owing to the rain. We went in there about six o'clock and listened to the band; it was very good. There was a theatrical performance afterwards by the same company as we heard the other night, but they had such a job to get the people out of the Market Hall. We started to come away about 9.15 and then they hadn't got all the people out, so if we had stopped to that I don't know what time we should have got back. When we had just got out of Chippenham Jim Balch overtook us on horseback and walked with us as far as the tunnel. It was a beautiful moonlight night. We got home about 10.30.

8th A fine day. Had a bath in the morning. Corsham branch of the Wilts Friendly Society's Fete. They engaged the Melksham brass band for the day. They came through the town twice in the morning and then went to church; Dad went to the dinner. We shut shop after tea and then Dad, Wilfrid, Edwin, Martin and I had two games of croquet, though I was interrupted by Monty Comber coming for his shorthand lesson ...

13th A fine day ... Harry went down the park with his fiddle serenading in the evening.

16th A very wet day. Choir went to Christian Malford to the Festival. We had a brake from Chippenham and Miss Sainsbury had Griffin's brake. We started at 12 o'clock. The service went as well as could be expected, the anthem very fair. I didn't enjoy the tea much. We didn't stay for the concert but started for home soon after tea, and stopped at Mr Garlick's for some refreshments. We came home through Pickwick and got here about 8 o'clock.

17th A beautiful day ... Finished 'The Channings' at tea-time; I enjoyed it very much. Wrote in Clara's confession album and also in Nellie Beavan's text-book.

20th Wrote in Minnie Moody's confession album.

22nd A very stormy day. Lewin and Minnie Moody went to Claverton as there was an excursion train going from here. Edwin went to Chippenham to have some teeth out, but the man wasn't in.

24th A fine day ... Went for a walk with Ernest Lanham after practice and saw the comet. Saw the new curate at practice.

27th A very wet day. Had cricket in the shop with a soft ball at intervals in the day.

28th A fine day. Cricket match between Wootton Bassett and Corsham. Corsham won on the first innings. Lewin made 55 not out ... Had some music in the evening. Ernest Lanham, Harry and I took our fiddles out on the gravel and played some pieces out there, and afterwards Ernest Lanham and I played in the drawing-room with Sarah at the piano.

JULY

8th (Friday) A fine day. Went up to the cricket field in the afternoon to watch the athletic sports by Mr Hulls' boys. Ernest won a cup ... Mrs Fowler gave the prizes. Came home and had some tea and then started for the station to go to 'Pinafore' at Chippenham. Ernest Lanham, Clara and Wilfrid came with us. Enjoyed it very much ... Had a very nice walk home, beautiful moonlight.

18th A beautiful day. In the afternoon at four o'clock Edwin, Wilfrid and I went down to the Weavern to bathe; I enjoyed myself very much ... Went up to the cricket field afterwards and had a very good game. Afterwards went in the Institute, then had some music in the drawing-room with Harry and Sarah.

19th A beautiful day. Joe Ward came in the shop in the morning. Cricket match between Corsham and Prior Park. Corsham made 101 and 102 and Prior Park 163, leaving them about 40 runs to get, time not allowing them to go in a second time ... After tea Edwin and I filled a bladder that we had bought in the morning with gas and let it go; we went down the park and watched it out of sight ...

20th A beautiful day but much colder owing to the rain the night before ... Gave Monty Comber his shorthand lesson after tea up in my bedroom and watched the Claremont girls go by. Had a game of croquet after shop with Martin, Edwin, Frank Wheeler and Ernest Lanham; Martin gave up before we had finished as he was in a temper. I won the game ... Jack bit Mr Abbott on the leg.

24th A fine day though with a few slight showers ... Ernest's birthday; gave him a book. Went up to Grandma's to tea with Wilfrid and Clara and took my violin and played to her. After church went for a walk with Ernest Lanham and Wilfrid out to Linley's. Dad was very bad with asthma.

AUGUST

1st (Monday) Bank Holiday ... Lewin, Minnie Moody, Aunt Lydia, Emily, Sarah, Wilfrid, Ernest Lanham and myself went to Farleigh Castle in Mr Alway's wagonette. We started about eleven o'clock. Willie Moody, Clara and Katie Moody drove behind us in Mr Ryall's trap (or Riley's) as far as the 'Horse and Jockey' and then turned off to Neston. We stopped at Mr Beavan's at Bradford and then Lily and Nellie got in the trap and Ernest Lanham and I walked on with Harry and Willie Beavan. When we got there it came on to rain, so when we had had some dinner outside the 'pub-house' we started for Bradford; we then had tea and then we had some music, 'Pinafore' etc, and then went for a walk up 'Tor Hill'. I took Harry's opera glass with me and we had a nice view from there. After supper we started for home. I had toothache all day which greatly marred my enjoyment.

2nd Put some gutta-percha stuff in my tooth.

4th A splendid day. Went over to Melksham in the trap in the afternoon with Harry and Lewin to witness the opening of the new organ. Fred came with us and took back the trap ... The service went off pretty well, though once, Sir Herbert Oakley began to play the 'Amen' to one of the hymns before all the verses were finished; and the minister who preached the sermon, towards the end of it, said 'And now ...' and the people thought it was 'And now to God the Father' etc. and rose, but they soon found out their mistake and resumed their seats. After the service we listened to Sir Herbert Oakley till he had finished, and then went to Mr Wall's to tea. Afterwards went to the church and had a closer inspection of the organ and I took down the stops; a man was tuning them. Lewin spoke to Mr ... about the Calne organ ... After (evening) service listened to Sir Herbert Oakley till about 9 o'clock and then went to Mr Ainsworth's and had supper, and then walked home. Got home about 12.30.

5th A beautiful day and very hot ... Clara had a letter from Blanche Pelham with two small photographs, one of which I possessed myself of.

11th (Thursday) I took Clara, Ernest and Clare to Portskewitt. [Sarah Kenway's home.] We started by the 8.45 train; Dad came down to the station with us. We got to Portskewitt about one o'clock. The wind was very rough going across in the steamer. After dinner Clara, Ernest, Clare and myself went to 'Caldecott Castle'; we explored every nook and cranny of the place though rain was drizzling all the time. After tea played cricket with Clare up in the nursery and then we had some music in the drawing-room.

12th Mr Kenway started early for his holiday. Sarah sang some songs in the drawing-room after breakfast. It was raining all day. I passed away the time somehow or other. After dinner Sarah and Clara got ready to go to the station with me; it was a very dirty walk ... A young man named David Little was in the carriage. He used to live at Corsham but hadn't been there for six years. He knew Sarah and then asked me if I was her brother. I rode with him all the way to Corsham. He treated me to a bottle of lemonade at Bath ...

29th (Monday) A very wet day. Choir outing. We went to Roundway Park. Harry, Ernest Lanham and I took our violins. Had dinner directly we got there; afterwards went up to Castle Hill and then back to tea. Had some fiddle and Mr Burraston sang a song and Mr Duck gave a recitation ... Home about 8.30.

31st A fine day but cold. Chippenham Flower Show. Cricket match between Corsham and Mr Herbert Awdry's eleven. Corsham won on the first innings. After the match went to Chippenham with Harry. The fireworks were pretty good ... Ernest (Lanham) and I had got as far as the milk factory (walking home) when Griffin came up with the brake and so we got up and had a jolly ride home; it was about 12.30

SEPTEMBER

4th (Sunday) A fine day ... Went down on the lawn in the afternoon and read 'The Two Destinies' by Wilkie Collins.

5th A fine day ... Went to the Institute and got 'The New Magdalene' by Wilkie Collins from the library.

12th A dull day. The grand piano was taken out to Claremont. Cousin James and his wife went to Devizes and from thence to Bromham. Cousin James Butler drove them to the top of Bowden Hill and I and Fred went to meet them at the bottom in the trap. Harry, Arthur and Lily Beavan came from Bradford in the pony carriage to bring the bazaar things, and stayed to tea and supper ...

14th A beautiful day. The first day of the bazaar. We shut shop at four o'clock and having dressed and had tea went up in Griffin's brake. Watched the first violin of Millington's band all the evening. The room was crowded. Walked home with Ernest Lanham.

15th A beautiful day ... In the afternoon went down to Mr Chapman's to see if Ernest Lanham could come up to the bazaar and play the violin, and he could, so went home and dressed, then went down for him and went up in Griffin's brake. Went in and saw the museum and then 'Punch and Judy', then played at intervals all the evening. The Chippenham fife and drum band was there.

18th (Sunday) A fine day. I was up at eight o'clock ready for our drive to Bradford, and after we had breakfast we started, Sarah and Martin in front and Wilfrid and I behind; it was a beautiful drive. Got there about 10 o'clock and after putting the horse in went to chapel. It was a pretty chapel but very poorly attended. Started about 3.45 for home; Sarah and Nellie walked to the top of the hill with us and then we wished them goodbye. Came home Atworth way. Church in the evening. It was raining very hard when church was out and the people were very slow going out.

21st A wet morning but turned off fine after breakfast and continued so all day. Miss Awdry was married. I went down to blow. Uncle William was in the shop at times and we had some fun with him ... Uncle, Dad, Ma and Ernest had whist in the kitchen in the evening.

27th A beautiful day. Made a fire balloon in the evening and with Edwin and Ernest Lanham tried to set it up, but it burnt; so came in and had some 'Pirates'.

Mervyn Comber came in and we had a jolly spree. Sarah (Mrs Kenway) came in the afternoon with her three children.

28th A fine day. Made another fire balloon in the morning. Uncle John came to tea. Harry and Lily Beavan drove over with Sarah Goold in the evening and after shop we again had 'Pirates' with a larger orchestra than ever. We also had other music. Ernest Lanham was here with his violin. While they were at supper, I and Ernest went out in the yard and set off the balloon; it went about as high as the park trees and then burnt; I had made the hole a little too small. It frightened Wilfrid and Mervyn Comber who saw it out in the street. Had my hair cut.

29th A fine day. Made another fire balloon before breakfast. Went down to church to blow for Harry as Mr Linton and Mr Webb wanted to practise their intoning. Afterwards Mrs Kenway and Uncle John came down. Before Uncle John went he gave me sixpence for blowing. In the afternoon we heard that the balloon we set up last night had come down on Mrs Bromley's house and the policeman seeing it gave the alarm of fire and frightened Mrs Bromley very much; she sent for Mr William Bromley and he removed some tiles to see if there was any fire, but only discovered my wire that was at the bottom of the balloon. After supper went down to Ernest Lanham's and set off another; this one went capitally and went out before it reached the ground; afterwards had some music with Mrs Kenway, Sarah, Clara and Ernest Lanham. Went as far as the Methuen Arms with Ernest.

30th A fine day. Made another fire balloon … The bobby was busy trying to find out who set the balloon up last night, and asked Wilfrid about it …

OCTOBER

1st (Saturday) A beautiful day. Made another fire balloon … Wrote in Blanche Pelham's confession album in the shop in the afternoon.

7th A fine day but dull. Made a warm-water apparatus to put in our bedroom, after much trouble and perseverance. Had my violin practice in the drawing-room and after a bit Lewin came and we practised together, then Clara, then Ernest Lanham and Harry, then we all had the Overture to 'Pirates of Penzance', afterwards played some duets with Ernest, then Sarah came in and we had another dose, then Clara came down from her studio and played one or two things.

10th A fine day. All the choir went down to the church at one o'clock to have their photographs taken. Of course us six were taken. I am rather afraid how I shall turn out as I moved my eyes while we were being taken …

11th A beautiful day. Finished three more balloons … The first public entertainment in the evening. Mr Gane and Mr Freeth came over from Chippenham and helped us. We had the 'Overture to the Pirates of Penzance' first. Harry played the American organ, Lewin our piano, Clara the Institute piano and Mr Blouet, Ernest Lanham and myself violins. It went off very well. The programme was very good and altogether it was a success. The room was well filled, it being a splendid moonlight night.

12th A fine day. Finished another balloon, making six in all ... First practice of the 'Choral Society' at the Methuen Arms; Miss Stone came with Miss Pelham and Miss Gilbert. There was a very good attendance. I enjoyed it very much ... The painters were varnishing the front of the shop all day.

13th (Thursday) A wet day ... First practice of the Melksham Choral Society. Harry, Lewin, Ernest Lanham and I went over in the trap; it was a wet drive. We put violins etc. in Mr Ainsworth's and stayed there a bit and then went to the schoolroom; it was not a very nice place but much better than the Town Hall both for playing and singing. Mr Ainsworth's children had the measles. We played a little with the singers but not much as we didn't know it, and then went to Burgess's and had some grub. We came back and after the singers were gone we played 'Pirates' with the rest of the band. It was a wet drive back too. We got home about 11.30.

14th A very windy day. Three trees were blown across the avenue and a great many besides in other places. I went down there in the afternoon. There were a lot of poor people there all day sawing and chopping off the branches. His Lordship came up the avenue in the afternoon and told the people that they must not saw the boughs off but they could pick up what were already broken off. The drying shed down at the tanyard was blown right down; I went down to see it. The telegraph wires were broken up by Mr Cruse's.

15th A fine day but cold. Washed and oiled the croquet set in the morning ... In the evening went up to Mr Lee's and set off a fire balloon with Edwin and Ernest Lanham; when it was a little above the house the wind took it and it caught fire. Ernest and I went home Bence's Lane way.

16th A beautiful day ... Dr Kemm didn't feel well in church this morning, so walked out and fainted outside the door; Mr Burraston and some church wardens went out to him ...

17th (Monday) A beautiful day ... The photographs of the choir came in the morning and they were pretty good though rather too dark; I came out better than I expected. Set off a fire balloon in the evening down at Ernest Lanham's; Edwin came down. While we were lighting it Ernest caught it on fire, but blew it out before it had made a very big hole, and then it went up beautifully. Edwin then went home and I went in with Ernest and had a nice quiet talk up in his sanctum.

19th A beautiful day. The stoker of the train due here at 11.55 was killed by his head coming into contact with the pillar of the aqueduct opposite Mr King's; he was taken to Mr Allway's and Dr Kemm was sent for and pronounced death to be instantaneous; Lewin went down and saw him and sent an account to the 'Bath Herald' ... Went down to the British School as there was a man named Tom Horrocks, a converted —— [?], giving a temperance lecture; Ernest Lanham came with me, but we soon came out again; he hollered so it was enough to give you a headache.

20th A fine day ... Lewin went to the coroner's inquest on the body of that man that was killed yesterday ... Started for Melksham at 7 o'clock. Ernest Lanham and I went in the Coffee Tavern and had some refreshments and then went to

Burgess's and relieved them of a dozen gooseberry tarts. We then proceeded to the schoolroom and had a very good practice, although the band was rather diminished; Harry Ainsworth had the measles, Badham wasn't there, and the viola man and the young second fiddle didn't intend to come at all simply because they would have to pay for the music. Lost our black rug over there; it dropped out between the Coffee Tavern and the 'Bear'; we spoke to the ostler and a policeman and they promised to make inquiries about it.

24th My 17th birthday. Wilfrid, Ernest, Clare, Clara and Alice put together and gave me an album; Emily a pair of warm socks; Sarah a purse; Alice a pair of carpet slippers; Ernest Lanham a scarf pin; Edwin Lee a pot of bloater paste; Aunt Lydia sixpence and Grandma sixpence and Aunt Lena a birthday card. Ernest Lanham came up to tea and Edwin came in after shop. We had the second part of 'Messiah' through and afterwards our class music and then 'Norma' and ... Gounod's Serenade. After supper we set off some crackers that I made in the afternoon and also put some benzoline down the path ... Afterwards we played 'Pope Joan' till eleven and then the party broke up.

25th A beautiful day. Harry's cold still very bad. He could hardly speak at the choral class in the evening, which was held this day owing to the 'Court Leet' on Wednesday. Made a few crackers in the afternoon.

26th A fine day. Made a few crackers in the morning. An old schoolfellow of Harry's came in the shop in the afternoon and after shaking hands with Harry commenced a sort of entertainment consisting of ventriloquism, imitation of a brass band and various animals. He was half drunk, said he was coming into a legacy of £1500 and then asked Harry for some money ...

27th (Thursday) A beautiful day ... Clara brought home my text-book which she had taken up to school to have the girls' names written in it; they all conceded to my wishes and inserted their names. Went to Melksham in the evening; it was cold riding. Went into Burgess's and had their cheese-cakes and then went on to the schoolroom. Ernest Lanham and I went up and played with Harry along with the singers, and afterwards with the band. Got home soon after eleven.

28th A fine day. Mr Cole's men were in the two shops today whitewashing, and then Miss Simmonds washed the floors of both shops ... Made some crackers ... Pasted some articles from the 'Grocers' Journal' in the book which I bought for the purpose. Went to church practice in the evening and afterwards went down to Ernest Lanham's and meant to set off the fire balloon but we hadn't enough spirits, so went up in his den.

29th A fine day. Miss Simmonds finished the shop in the morning and it looked very nice. Finished cracker making in the afternoon. Ernest Lanham came up in the paper room and with what powder there was left we laid a train under the shed and set it off ...

NOVEMBER

1st A fine day ... The second public entertainment in the evening. Mr Blouet, Ernest Lanham, Harry, Lewin and I played 'Cloches de Corneville' ... Mervyn

CORSHAM MECHANICS' INSTITUTION.

PROGRAMME OF
ENTERTAINMENT

IN THE

BRITISH SCHOOL-ROOM,

TUESDAY, DECEMBER 13th, 1881.

INSTRUMENTAL. "Gavotte, 'Louis Quinze'" ......*Maurice Lee*.
Miss CLARA SPACKMAN, Messrs BLOUET, LANHAM, H. G.,
  L., & H. SPACKMAN.

SONG................ "The Village Blacksmith" ....*Weiss*.
               Mr. W. FREETH.

SONG................"We'd better bide a wee'" ....*Claribel*.
               Miss BURGESS.

READING...
               Mr. STANTIAL.

QUARTETTE........ "Night, Lovely Night !" ....*F. Berger*.

SONG............. "I am a Friar of Orders Grey" ....*Reeve*.
               Mr. C. H. HULLS.

(muted)
VIOLIN QUARTETTE......."Gavotte" ....*Scotson Clark*.
   Messrs BLOUET, LANHAM, H. G., & H. SPACKMAN.

SONG......................"Visions of Home" ....*Hartog*.
               Miss OLDING.

SONG................... "'Tis jolly to Hunt"......*Sterndale Bennett*.
               Mr TUCKER.

READING...
               Mr. C. H. HULLS.

SONG......................... "Love Not" ....*Blockley*.
               Miss BURGESS.

OVERTURE.......... "Pirates of Penzance"......*Arthur Sullivan*.
Miss C. SPACKMAN, Messrs BLOUET, LANHAM, H. G.,L., &
  H. SPACKMAN.

Doors open at 7 o'clock ; to commence at 7.30.
ADMISSION—SIXPENCE, THREEPENCE & ONE PENNY.
A few Reserved and Numbered Seats—ONE SHILLING.

CORSHAM MECHANICS' INSTITUTION.

PROGRAMME OF
ENTERTAINMENT,

IN THE

BRITISH SCHOOL-ROOM,

TUESDAY, NOVEMBER 22nd, 1881.

MARCH. ...."Inauguration" ....*Scotson Clark.*
Miss C. SPACKMAN, Messrs GOULD, PRICE, A. E. HULLS,
BLOUET, LANHAM, H. G., L., & H. SPACKMAN.

READING. ...."Her First Appearance" ....*Temple Bar.*
Mr. C. F. OSBORNE.

SONG. ...."In the Cloisters".........*Odoardo Barri.*
Miss JENNIE AMOORE.

SONG.........................."Punchinello" ....*Molloy.*
Master T. J. GOULD.

READING.......... "A Dull Day on Exmoor" ....
Rev. E. A. WEBB.

OVERTURE. ...."Der Freischutz"....................*Weber.*
The Misses GILBERT, PELHAM, C. SPACKMAN, & Mr. L.
SPACKMAN.

SONG. ...."Cleansing Fires" ....*V. Gabriel.*
Mrs DUNN.

READING...
Mr. E. HATHERELL.

SONG...................."The Frenchman" ....*Lloyd.*
Mr. HARRIS.

READING...

INSTRUMENTAL......."Lucrezia Borgia"................*Donizetti.*
Messrs BLOUET, A. E. HULLS, H. G., & L. SPACKMAN.

Doors open at 7 o'clock; to commence at 7.30.
ADMISSION—SIXPENCE, THREEPENCE & ONE PENNY.
A few Reserved and Numbered Seats—ONE SHILLING.

LACOCK.

A GRAND EVENING CONCERT

OF VOCAL AND INSTRUMENTAL MUSIC,

Will be given under the Patronage of the Clergy and Gentry of Lacock and the Neighbourhood,

IN THE NATIONAL SCHOOL-ROOM,

On TUESDAY, November the 8th, 1881,

by Ladies and Gentlemen of Chippenham, Corsham, Melksham, and Lacock, who have kindly consented to give the Entertainment for the Benefit of the Lacock Coffee Tavern.

PROGRAMME.

PART I.

OVERTURE.....	"Pirates of Penzance."	Sullivan
Miss C. Spackman, Messrs. Lanham, H. G., L. & H. Spackman.		
Song.....	"The Lover and the Bird."	Guglielmo
	Miss Porter.	
Duet.....	"The Flight of the Swallow."	Kucken
Miss Burgess and Miss C. Spackman.		
Song.....	"In the Clousters."	Barri
	Mr. Zebedee.	
Glee.....	"Hark! the Lark."	Dr. Cooke
Miss Porter, Messrs. Smith, Freeth, and Tucker.		
Song.....	"The Lost Chord."	Sullivan
	Mr. A. Knee.	
Song.....	"Thy Face."	C. H. R. Merriott
	Miss Fry.	
American Organ & Piano.. "Adelaide."		Beethoven
Messrs. H. G. & L. Spackman.		
Song.....	"Tis Jolly to Hunt."	S. Bennett
	Mr. Tucker.	
Song.....	"The Better Land."	Cowen
	Miss Burgess.	
Song.....	"The Village Blacksmith."	W. H. Weiss
	Mr. Freeth.	
Quartett.....	"Night, Lovely Night."	Berger
Miss Burgess, Miss C. Spackman, Mr. A. Knee, Mr. Zebedee.		

AN INTERVAL OF TEN MINUTES.

PART II.

March.....	"Coraline."	Mendelssohn
Miss C. Spackman, Messrs. Lanham, H. G., L. & H. Spackman.		
Song.....	"Thady O'Flinn."	Molloy
	Miss Porter.	
Duet.....	"The Larboard Watch."	
Mr. Zebedee and Mr. A. Knee.		
Song.....	"Do they think of me at Home?"	Harry Clifton
	Miss Simco.	
American Organ & Piano.. "Marche Militaire."		Scotson Clark
Messrs. H. G. & L. Spackman.		
Song.....	"What'll Mith Wobbiegidoon Thay?"	
	Mr. Zebedee.	
Song.....	"Like Englishmen they Died."	Ernest J. Symonds
	Mr. Tanner.	
Instrumental Trio.....		
Miss C. Spackman, Messrs. H. G., & L. Spackman.		
Song.....	"The Children's Home."	Cowen
	Miss Burgess.	
Song.....	"The Vagabond."	Molloy
	Mr. Knee.	
Quartett.....	"Good Night, Beloved."	Glee Pinsuti
Miss Porter, Messrs. Smith, Freeth, and Tucker.		
Finale.....	"God Save the Queen."	

Comber sang 'Mrs Brown's Luggage' and for his encore sang 'The Bashful Young Man', to which he added some local verses ...

2nd A fine day but dull. Had a bath in the morning. Had my hair cut up at Marks's ... Had a bath before class in the evening. Enjoyed the class very much. Ma was in bed today with a headache, and Clara took the solo in 'A Wealthy Lord'. Mr Newnham went out just before we sang 'Blow Gentle Gales' simply because Harry didn't carry out his suggestion with regard to the word 'gentle'.

3rd A foggy damp day, very mild ... Mr Hulls' birthday; the boys gave him a silver salver and the girls a cut glass water jug; they all had a holiday. Clara went out to tea, and Ernest and Clare went up to supper as a sort of commemoration. Went to Melksham in the evening; but for the fog it was a very pleasant drive there and back.

5th (Saturday) A beautiful moonlight night but rather damp all day. Alice's birthday; gave her a pair of mittens ... In the evening there were high festivities; Osmond's in Pickwick Road sold fireworks and gangs of kids went up and down town setting them off; there was some benzoline lit too. After shop we went out in the front garden and set off a balloon and then some of my crackers and some of Ernest Lanham's fireworks; afterwards we set off two more balloons; they all three went very well but they took such a long time to inflate. Ernest Lanham and I took Aunt Lydia up home. Miss Burgess, Martin, Edwin, Fred and all our people watched the fireworks and we flung crackers amongst them.

7th (Monday) A dull foggy day. Had a cold bath in the morning ... After shop set off my last balloon. It went up very well and we followed it up Stumps Lane where it came down in the middle of the road. Edwin who had run on was just in time to catch it and brought it back to us, followed by a troop of kids. After taking off the burnt wadding I put it under my coat and brought it home ready for another journey.

8th A dull day and damp ... After tea I dressed for Lacock; Harry went in the cart with the piano; Ernest Lanham and I went with the harmonium afterwards, and Lewin, Clara, Minnie Moody. Jane Amoore came with Mr Coates. The programme went off very well and afterwards we had supper in the room adjoining the concert room. Harry came home with Ernest Lanham and I in the cart with the harmonium; the piano was left till the morning.

9th A fine day but dull ... Tried to set off the last balloon again after tea but it burnt soon after I lit the spirits ... Went to practice in the evening at the Methuen Arms. Mr Newnham again went out when we commenced 'Blow Gentle Gales'.

10th A beautiful day though rather dull. Made two more ballons ... Practice at Melksham. I took a few flowers to Miss Burgess. Had some gooseberry tarts at Burgess's and then went to the schoolroom where we had a very nice practice. Went into Burgess's again afterwards and Miss Burgess gave me a box of gooseberry tarts to take home to Ma.

12th Still went on with fire balloons at intervals till I had finished seven. Finished 'The Vicar of Wakefield'.

15th A fine day. Wrote in Lily James's confession album and in three more of Mr Hulls' boys' confession books. Received a note from Miss Burgess inside Sarah's letter and answered it. In the afternoon played the violin with Clara; we played hymns, I the treble and Clara alto. Afterwards Jenny Amoore came in and sang 'In the Cloisters'. Ma made me a hood for my coat. Attempted to set up a balloon in the evening, but it burnt when it got as high as the house.

16th A wet day ... Miss Burgess drove Mrs Ainsworth and her daughter Edie over in their conveyance in the afternoon; Mrs Ainsworth and Edie went to Mr Baines's and Miss Burgess came here and she and I had some dance music etc. in the drawing-room; she stayed to tea and Mrs Ainsworth called for her soon afterwards. Went to class at the Methuen Arms in the evening. Mr Newnham again went out directly we began 'Blow Gentle Gales'.

17th A beautiful day ... Went to Melksham in the evening. Went to Burgess's when we got there and had some gooseberry tarts and then went to the schoolroom; had a very good practice; went in Burgess's again afterwards. Harry bought four pounds of toffee.

19th A beautiful day ... Finished 'The World of Kant' in the evening; in my opinion the best book I have read.

22nd (Tuesday) Went up to Mr Feaviour's and helped Harry tune two pianos and the harmonium in the morning. A beautiful day. Went to the entertainment in the evening ... sat up in the front and had a very good view of the girls ...

23rd A stormy day ... Tarpy went to Chippenham to hear Mr Spurgeon's son. Went to practice at the Methuen Arms in the evening; Mr and Mrs William Farnoll were there and also Harry Neate. Mr Newnham went out before 'Blow Gentle Gales'.

28th A fine day ... Sent a postcard to the next member of the Evercirculator to advise him of the approach of the Evercirculator. Set off two balloons in the evening; one went right out of sight, the other caught when it was over the vicinity of Lord Methuen's.

29th A beautiful day ... Wrote to Withers & Co. for a violin mute and some rosin. Went to the missionary meeting at the British School in the evening with Ernest Lanham; it was a most enjoyable lecture by the Rev. Mr Hutchinson, a missionary of China; there was a good room and a very orderly audience too ... Lefroy was hung at nine o'clock in the morning.

30th A fine day. Received a letter from Miss Burgess and answered it ... Lewin attended an inquest at Gastard on the body of Sally Barnett who hung herself the other day.

DECEMBER

1st A beautiful day and a splendid moonlight night ... I sent down to Ernest Lanham to know if he could go with me to Chippenham to the concert, but he sent back to say he couldn't; so Dad and I went in Mr Allway's fly with Lewin, Jenny Amoore and Sarah. Enjoyed the concert very much, especially Mr Dyer from Bristol. We got home about 11.30; Jennie Amoore came in and had some supper and then I took her home.

3rd Lewin took up his duties as secretary of the 'Wilts County Club'; people were in and out all day and the room was crammed in the evening. A beautiful day. Cold bath in the morning and a warm-water bath in the evening.

5th A fine day ... Watched the eclipse of the moon in the evening; got Harry's opera glass and looked at it; I could see it very well. Went to the British School to hear a lecture on India by Sir Charles Hobhouse; enjoyed it very much.

7th Practice at the Methuen Arms. Mr Newnham was not there ...

8th A fine day ... Bought a new diary for 1882. Went to Melksham in the evening; went in to Burgess's and had something to eat and then went to the school-room; when we had played 'Blow Gentle Gales' and 'Jack Frost' the band came and we had the 'Messiah'; I enjoyed it very much, also the band practice afterwards. I played 'first' in some of the things. Went in Burgess's again afterwards. It was a splendid night and we got home about 11.30. Found Mr Rowell playing whist when we got home.

13th (Tuesday) A fine day but cold and foggy. Very busy in the shop in the morning. Miss Burgess came in the afternoon. Ma was in bed today with a headache. In the evening went to the entertainment at the British School; Harry, Lewin, Clara, Mr Blouet, Ernest Lanham and I played the Gavotte Louis Quinze, and Mr Blouet, Harry, Ernest Lanham and I played Scotson Clark's 'Gavotte' for four violins, muted. And at the end of the programme all of us played the Overture to the Pirates of Penzance. Miss Burgess sang two songs and was encored both times but did not respond. There were some 'Christmas Boys' outside the schoolroom when we came out and they frightened Miss Stone and the girls.

14th A wet day. Practice at the Methuen Arms in the evening. Played our violins to the 13th Psalm, 'A Wealthy Lord', 'Acis and Galatea' ... Ma was a little better.

15th A dismal wet day. Miss Burgess went back to Melksham by the 12 train. Busy all day getting up orders. In the evening went to Melksham in Mr Coates' trap as ours had been hard at work all day. Had a very good practice and afterwards went to Mr Burgess's and had supper and played ... didn't get home till after twelve.

17th A dull day and some rain ... In the evening the choir boys came in Harry's music room and practised some carols, and Ernest Lanham, Harry and I played violins. Mr Linton came in. Grandpa was very ill. Ma was there all night and stayed till supper time; when she came away he was quieter but weaker.

18th A very windy day. Went up to Grandma's with some oranges for Grandpa after breakfast. I went up and saw him and he looked very ill; I kissed him and said goodbye as I was afraid I should not see him again ...

20th A very rough day ... Our choral concert in the evening at the British School; it was an invitation concert, invitations being given by the members and the committee. The room was crammed; a temporary stand was erected for Mr Blouet, Ernest Lanham and I and it looked quite like an orchestra. The programme went off very well except Mr Hulls' solo which was a dead failure; he had to stop and commence again. Charlie Hulls accompanied him. After it was over Mr Hulls went out and didn't come in again. Clara's solo in 'A Wealthy Lord' was encored, the only encore of the evening. Blanche Pelham and Lizzie Gilbert played in the 'March of the Priests'.

21st A beautiful day. Grandpa was much worse, but Ma was up there all day. Lewin put three Chinese lanterns in the shop window in the evening and lit them and they looked very pretty.

22nd A fine day. Grandpa died about 1.30 in the night. In the afternoon I went up and saw him; he looked very nice. Coming down I went in Mr Hulbert's and was measured for a pair of trousers and Wilfrid was too. In the evening went to the Institute with Ernest Lanham and afterwards went down in his den and talked and he brought me up some cocoa.

24th (Saturday) A fine day and a frost. Clara had some Christmas cards sent her from Blanche Pelham and amongst them was one for me; she gave it to me at breakfast time and so they all knew it; it was a very pretty card and on the back of it 'With Blanche's best wishes to Herbert'; she sent Clare one as well. I had toothache bad all the morning, and in the afternoon went over to Dr Kemm's and had it taken out by Mr Wood; he hurt very much at the time but was not long about it. It bled a good deal and kept on all day as he didn't put anything in to stop the bleeding; I didn't go in the shop afterwards but stayed in the parlour. After tea Ernest Lanham came and talked to me. Uncle and Aunt Laurie and Aunt Polly came by the 5.45 train ... Finished reading the 'Life of Swedenborg' and commenced 'The Evening and the Morning'.

25th (Christmas Day) Got up and went to Holy Communion; Ernest Lanham was there and he collected. When I came home practised on the violin till breakfast time which was not till ten o'clock. Uncle and Aunt Rowell slept here and had breakfast in bed ... In the afternoon I wrote a letter to Blanche Pelham and also sent her a New Year's card.

26th A wet dismal day ... Cousin Fred from Newport came by the 11.55 train and brought Cousin Willie, his son, with him. We had some music before dinner ... After dinner I dressed for the funeral and went up to Grandma's with Ernest and Clare; we went up and saw Grandpa in his coffin ... The funeral went off very well; Mr Hurlstone gave the funeral address in the schoolroom. After it was over Wilfrid, Ernest and Clare and I came home and had tea by ourselves in the parlour; after tea we played games and sang carols. Uncle and Aunt Rowell, Uncle John and Uncle Laurie went back to London after tea, and Cousin Fred and Willie to Newport.

27th A dull day but not much rain ... Lizzie, Minnie and Katie Moody were here to tea. Uncle William and Cousin Edward came in the evening and went to the entertainment and stayed here for the night. The carol entertainment went off very well and there was a pretty good attendance. Mr Mayo lent his magic lantern for exhibition and that represented the second part of the programme; Mr Alfred Cole managed it.

28th A dull day. Opened shop in the morning again. Went down to the church and blew for Harry while he played to Cousin Edward. Uncle William and Cousin Edward went back by the 11.55 train ... In the evening played some dance music in the drawing-room for Sarah, Clara and Aunt Polly to dance to.

29th A fine day and very mild. Received a letter from Ernest Lanham in the morning and wrote back to him by return of post ... Ma made Wilfrid and I presents of two nice silk handkerchiefs.

31st A fine day though rather dull ... Blanche Pelham wrote to Clara and sent her some photographs of herself when she was a little girl and enclosed one for me. Ernest Lanham came back from Bristol and came up in the afternoon and evening; I packed up the books he had lent me and gave them back to him ... Finished 'The Evening and the Morning' while the old year was passing away. The bells were ringing.

NOTES FOR 1881

February 4th Colonel Methuen: Frederick Henry Paul, 2nd Baron, who succeeded in 1849. His son, Paul Sanford Methuen, 3rd Baron and later Field Marshal, succeeded in 1891.

17th Burgess's: baker's and tea shop. Miss Burgess was a good singer; she and the gooseberry tarts play a large part in the diary!

March 12th Mr Rowell: second husband of his mother's sister Sarah.

April 5th Lily and Nellie Beavan of Bradford-on-Avon: relatives by marriage. Lily lived in the Round House. Nellie married Mr Dotesio.

18th 'Forgot': a lifelong characteristic!

July 20th 'The Claremont girls': first mention.

August 1st Horse and Jockey: no longer an inn. It stood at the junction of the Corsham – Bradford and Bath – Atworth roads.

4th The Calne organ: Lewin was organist at Calne.

5th Blanche Pelham: Clara's schoolfellow at Claremont – first mention! See programme for Nov. 22nd, and note in diary!

12th David Little: he later wrote a novel about the Corsham neighbourhood, 'by D. le Litt'.

September 12th Cousin James: eldest son of the Spackman family at Eastbury.

October 11th Mr Blouet: master at Hulls' school. Teacher of French?

12th Miss Stone, headmistress at Claremont.

28th 'Pasted some articles': these scrapbooks were kept throughout his life.

November 8th See programme.

23rd Spurgeon's sermons were published separately in booklet form.

December 13th Christmas boys: mummers?

This year was remarkable for the various sightings of a comet, for daily violin practice, much cricket, especially in August, brother Harry's emigration to New Zealand in October, and Herbert's clandestine correspondence with pretty Blanche Pelham at Claremont school – a romance which ended abruptly with the year.

JANUARY

2nd (Monday) A wet dismal day. Put five shillings in the bank in the morning. Went up to Mr Little's to be measured for a pair of boots. Dad went to Bath. Harry, Lewin, Clara, Minnie, Jenny Amoore, Sarah and Mr Barnes went over to Chippenham to the practice for the concert – they went in one of Mr Allway's conveyances. After tea wrote a short note to Blanche Pelham to thank her for the handkerchiefs she sent me.

3rd A fine day. Had a bath in the morning. Practised on the violin ... Chippenham concert; besides some glees and songs they performed 'The Ancient Mariner' ... Dad went over by train to hear it and Fred drove over to fetch him back. There was a servants' ball at the Court in the evening and Harry, Lewin and Clara went after the concert was over.

4th A fine day ... After dinner dressed for Mr Neate's party. We spent a very pleasant evening; it was the first party I had been to for a very long time. We had 'Proverbs', 'Blind Man's Buff', 'Spoons' and music, also 'table-turning' (or trying at it). The two Miss Amoores [were there] and Miss Wiles, Miss Luchford, Ada Ayliff and Mr and Mrs Alfred Cole, which with the Neates and Fred Bryant made up the party to over sixteen. We came home about 12.30.

6th A very stormy day. After church practice ... had some dance music with Sarah in the drawing-room and Clara, Emily, Minnie Moody and Sarah danced.

9th We heard that the Market Place was given to the town for the Town Hall, chiefly through the Colonel.

10th ... Went to the 'Pickwick Reading' in the evening. Harry and I played 'Norma' and then 'Pirates of Penzance' (Ernest Lanham played in that) and then Dancla's 'Andante Cantabile' and 'Valse'. Jennie Amoore and Sarah sang a duet (Rose in Heaven). The room was pretty full but it was a very dark night.

11th A fine day. Grand hunt at Hartham. Went to class at the 'Methuen Arms' in the evening; I enjoyed it very much, the pieces were so pretty. Afterwards went down to Ernest Lanham's and had some supper and then Mrs Lanham and Miss Wall came in, and Miss Wall and Ernest played 'Voices' and 'Lucrezia Borgia' ...

12th A fine day. There was a cricket concert at the British Schoolroom in the evening. Mr Lane came from Calne, Mr Freeth and Mr Tucker from Chippenham, Mr Kelly from Reading and a Miss Edith Cokey from London ... Mr Bell and Charlie Hulls gave songs too ... Mr Kenway came on the 4.30 train and went to the concert ... I turned over the leaves in two pieces for Mr Lane, and took the tickets. After the concert Mr Kelly came in and sang us a lot of comic songs, and then Mr Clarke drove him over to Chippenham to take the train for Reading. Eva Neate contributed a good deal to the programme; her 'Softly Shines' with harmonium and piano accompaniment was the best thing of the evening.

15th (Sunday) A fine day but dull ... Nellie Beavan walked over from Bradford ... Emily and Sarah walked to meet her and they got back just in time for chapel ... In the afternoon Jennie Amoore, Nellie Beavan, Sarah, Clara, Wilfrid and I went for a walk up the coach road and down Lacock Road. After tea we all sang parts of 'Messiah' and after church I had some music with Sarah in the drawing-room.

17th A fine day but foggy and much colder ... Went to Mrs Alfred Cole's in the afternoon to her party; amongst the guests were the Amoores, Miss Luchford, Miss Goodyer, Minnie and Katy Moody, us six boys and Alice and Clara and Sarah and a great many smaller fry. Mr Cole exhibited Mr Mayo's magic lantern after supper, which was very good. We didn't come away till after twelve.

19th A foggy day. Ma was in bed all day with the headache. Clara, Ernest and Clare went back to school. Harry, Lewin, Ernest Lanham and I went to Melksham in the evening to the practice; we put up at the 'King's Arms'. We had a splendid practice and afterwards went to Burgess's for some refreshments. We got back about 11.30.

22nd (Sunday) ... In the afternoon we practised a new madrigal for the class ... then we had 'The Shepherd's Farewell' and 'Gather Ye Rosebuds'. Afterwards I took my violin up to Grandma's and played to her and had tea there. After tea I drew Alice down to the chapel in her chair, and then went home but couldn't get in as everybody was out, so I had to climb over the garden wall and leave my violin outside the drawing-room window and then went to church ...

25th ... After practice (at the Methuen Arms) Ernest Lanham and I went for a short walk, but Ernest was in a cynical (silly) mood and we quarrelled about girls.

29th A wet day ... After dinner we had 'Messiah' in the drawing-room; I played violin and Harry the violoncello. Afterwards Ernest Lanham and I went down to the church to help Harry tune. Miss Olding was down there. At a quarter past four I left them to go and fetch Jessie Light to tea, and after tea we had 'Messiah' again ... Before Jessie Light went I got her to write in my text book.

31st A beautiful day ... Mr Freeth's Benefit Concert. We started from here at 4.15 in a sort of cab of Griffin's; Ernest Lanham and I rode outside with Everard Griffin. There was a rehearsal at five o'clock and then we went to Mr Freeth's and had a little refreshment and prepared for the concert. It went off very well; the orchestra was composed of Mr Lane, Mr Thomson, Harry (violoncello) Mr Rudman (cornet) and Ernest and I, with the harmonium and piano. Ma, Sarah, Clara, Mrs Cole, Minnie Moody and Miss Burgess helped the singers ...

FEBRUARY

2nd (Thursday) A fine day. Had some music with Miss Burgess after breakfast; she went back by the 10 train. Harry went down with her. He went to Melksham by the 4.30 train. Ernest and I and Lewin started for Melksham soon after 6.30 and went in Burgess's and were introduced to Miss Jones and another young lady and had some gooseberry tarts, then went to the school-room. Had a very good practice ... Gertie Baines was there and I spoke to her ... Called in at Burgess's and brought three gooseberry tarts home. Uncle and Aunt Rowell and their little girl Katie came in the evening.

5th (Sunday) A beautiful day. Got up at 7.30 and drove Lizzie Moody and Wilfrid to meet Willie Moody at Bathampton in Ryle's trap. Down Box Hill it was very slippery and I had to walk the pony ... Had two letters from two young ladies in the morning (Miss Pelham and Miss Burgess).

6th A fine day. Wrote a love letter to Blanche Pelham and inserted it in Clara's letter. 'Penny Readings' at the British School in the evening; if it hadn't been for Mr Hulls' boys and girls the room would have been very empty.

7th A beautiful day. Harry, Lewin and Clara went to Calne for a concert; Harry and Clara sang a duet, 'When the wind blows in from the sea' ... After shop Ernest Lanham came up and we had some music with Sarah; Uncle and Aunt Rowell were there and Uncle Rowell sang a comic Irish song and Aunt Rowell sang two or three songs.

8th Clara had a letter from Blanche Pelham and inside was enclosed a letter for me; such a nice long one it was.

10th A fine day ... Mr and Miss Burgess came over from Melksham in their four-wheeler in the afternoon and stayed to tea; Mrs Burgess came down to the church and Harry played the organ to her. Miss Burgess took a pocket-book out of my pocket and I didn't notice it at the time, but after she was gone I missed it and sent a postcard for her to send it back, as there was something particular in it.

11th A fine day. Had a letter and a Trowbridge paper from Miss Burgess ... Ernest Lanham went to Melksham in the afternoon and brought back my pocket-book ... Ernest and Clare went to Chippenham to buy marbles. After shop had a discussion with Wilfrid, Sarah and Emily on different subjects, health and religion chiefly. (Very deep it was.) Wrote a letter to Miss Burgess explaining about the pocket-book.

12th Wrote a long letter to Blanche Pelham and enclosed it in Clara's.

13th A fine day ... Went up to the Mechanics' Institute with Ernest Lanham in the evening and read a tale out of 'Cornhill Magazine'. Afterwards walked about the town and watched the people buying and posting Valentines. Bought one and sent it to Blanche Pelham.

14th A fine and beautiful day. Had a Valentine from Daisy Goold; she drew it herself. I wrote to her and thanked her for it in the evening. Harry had one Valentine describing all his occupations on the envelope.

15th A wet stormy cold day. Had another Valentine in the morning, but from whom I couldn't tell. Practice at the 'Methuen Arms' in the evening; very good attendance. Afterwards went down with Ernest Lanham and then he came up with me.

16th Very good practice (at Melksham). Miss Burgess was corky about the 'pocket-book'.

19th (Shrove Sunday) A beautiful day. Got up at 8 o'clock and had some violin practice and also had a letter from Blanche Pelham and read it ... In the afternoon Dad, Ernest Lanham, Wilfrid, Clare and myself went to Box in the train and walked back, and Miss Goold, Emily, Clara and Minnie Moody came to meet us; afterwards we met Mr and Mrs Alfred Cole, and we saw the drunken clergyman talking to them and he talked to Dad. We stayed and listened to him; he was a regular canting fellow, making out that it was only

Valentine

Corsham
Feb 14/82 (Herbert was 17, Daisy 16.)

Dear Daisy

I write to thank you for the pretty Valentine you sent me this morning.
I don't believe I ever had a more unexpected one, and I could not make
out who it came from till I asked Ma if she knew anyone staying at
Leicester and then she told me that you were at a school there. I had no
idea you could draw so nicely and I would much rather have a
Valentine sent me like that drawn by hand, than I would all those old-
fashioned things you see in the windows. I wonder they do not bring
out something new in Valentines, seeing how they have improved
Christmas Cards.

It was very kind of you to take so much trouble to draw it and send
it to me and I will keep it in remembrance of you. I remember we used
to be always quarrelling, but that is ever so long ago and I hope it is all
forgiven and forgotten; it is on my part, I know.

I have not seen you for such a long time now that I expect I should
hardly know you if you were to visit us again. Sarah says you have
grown very much, even taller than your mother. I know I should feel
awfully insignificant beside you.

I must now conclude and get your address from Sarah and then it
will be about time for post.

With love, and a wish that for one brief moment we might be
situated as the little boy and girl in the Valentine,

I am
Your affect. cousin
Herbert

---

through God's grace that you could be reformed; and he asked Mr Cole to
assist him, so he was really begging. Mr and Mrs Cole, Ernest Lanham and
Minnie Moody stayed to tea so we were a pretty large party.

21st A beautiful day. Melksham concert. Harry and Ernest Lanham went over early
in the afternoon to do some tuning etc. We all started in Griffin's covered
wagonette at a quarter to seven; I rode outside with Griffin. The concert went
off pretty well, but the first violins made rather a muck of it in two or three
pieces ... Wrote a letter to Blanche Pelham.

22nd A fine day. After shop went to the Baptist Chapel and heard a lecture with
'dissolving views' of the children of the London streets.

24th A beautiful day ... Had a letter from Ernest Lanham in the afternoon and
answered it in the evening. Wrote another note to Blanche Pelham and Clara
wrote and enclosed my two letters.

26th (Sunday) A very stormy day. Got up at 7 o'clock and practised on the violin and then went down to the church with Harry and blew while he played for an hour and a half and then came back to breakfast. Had a letter from Blanche Pelham ... In the afternoon there was a grand funeral at the church; young Watts. He was killed at Swindon station and more than a hundred guards and porters came by train and followed. All the choir that were there walked down to the grave behind Mr Linton and sang a hymn. Wrote a letter to Blanche Pelham and sent it in the evening.

27th Clara didn't go to school as it was wet. Harry, Lewin, Clara and myself went over to Melksham to help at the concert at the Free Hall. After we got there Clara and I went to Burgess's and had some music ... When we had been there some little time in walked Wilfrid; he had walked over with Clara's shoes and gloves which she had forgotten. So he stayed and went to the concert with Mrs and Miss Burgess and stayed at Burgess's all night. The programme went off very well; Clara's song was encored.

MARCH

7th (Tues.) Fair Day; it wasn't a very large fair. Wrote to Ernest Lanham and sent him a blue silk tie for a birthday present ... Lewin's new printing press came. Went down to the Fair with Sarah, Clara, Emily and Jessie Light for a short time ... Music with Sarah.

9th Clara had a letter from Blanche Pelham and in it one for me ... Very good practice at Melksham; went to Burgess's afterwards; had a suspicion that something was 'up' between Miss Burgess and Mr Brereton.

10th A fine day. Went to Bath in the morning by the 11.50 train. Lewin and Minnie Moody came with me. I went to Mr Winkworth's to have my tooth seen to, but he didn't do anything to it; he said it was only a little cold I had taken. Afterwards walked about Bath looking in the windows. Harry, Clara and the Wests came in Griffin's brake, and we all came down to the recital by Charles Halle and Madame Norman Neruda; it was splendid and I enjoyed myself thoroughly. We started for Corsham directly afterwards and got home at 6.30. Lewin and Minnie came home by train. A lot of Corsham gentry were there. After I had some tea I went up to Pickwick to the band practice; they played very much out of tune as usual.

11th Framed 'Love's Young Dream' by T. K. Pelham and put it up in my bedroom.

12th (Sunday) A fine day ... Had a letter from Blanche Pelham ... After church in the evening went up to Miss West's and stayed there to supper; we had some pleasant conversation. Harry and Miss Simmonds played piano duets. I wrote in their text books.

13th A beautiful day. Wrote a letter to Blanche Pelham. Played the violin at the last Pickwick entertainment in the evening, but it was a wretched programme; the only thing I cared for was Mrs Farnoll's song, 'Darby and Joan'. Went in Miss West's afterwards and had some music.

14th A beautiful day ... In the evening the anniversary of the Corsham Branch of the North Wilts Liberal Association was celebrated by a Soirée held at the British

Schoolroom. The room was prettily decorated and on the platform was a nice lot of flowers. It went off very nicely. Mr Hancock read a very nice piece. Mr Stantial gave us an account of the Reform Bill of '32. Mr Baines gave a recitation, 'The Kings and Queens of England', and Miss Simmonds, Harry, Lewin and I gave 'At the Ferry' ... 'March of the Flambeaux', and 'Pirates of Penzance'. Harry and Clara sang 'When the wind blows in from the sea', and Ma, Clara and Sarah sang a trio, 'Thou art lovely, O Night'. There were capital speeches by Mr Fuller, Mr Eaton Young, Mr Hancock and Sir Thomas Frasergrove. Mr Mayo took the chair. The room was full to overflowing and altogether it was a successful evening.

16th A splendid day. Harry, Lewin and I went to Melksham in the evening and we had a very good practice; went in Mr Burgess's afterwards and had some tarts. There was a grand concert given by the Jubilee Singers (negroes) at the British School in the evening.

17th Had a letter from Blanche Pelham in the morning while in bed and read it. Had a postcard from Ernest Lanham to say he was coming home next week. Mrs and Miss Simmonds came in the shop and wished me goodbye; I was very sorry they were going. Miss Simmonds is a jolly girl and I like the old lady very much ... Another beautiful day ... Lewin went to Lacock in the evening to preside at the harmonium at the Good Templars' entertainment.

19th A beautiful day ... Practised Haydn's 'Creation' after dinner with Clara and Harry. Wrote a letter to Blanche Pelham (four sheets) ... Went down to blow for Harry before evening service. Met the college girls in the coach road.

21st A very cold windy day ... Harry, Lewin and I went to Trowbridge by the 4.30 train to practise for 'The Creation'. Harry borrowed a cello from Millington and I took my violin ... Mr Millington played first violin and also Mr Stoddart of Bradford. One other gentleman played second violin with me, and there were three cornets, harmonium, piano, double bass and 3 cellos. I liked the singers very well; most of the ladies very goodlooking. After class we went to Mr Daniels' and had a good supper; we then all had a turn at music, after which Mr Daniels conducted prayers, and then Harry, Lewin and I slept together in the spare-room bed.

22nd Woke in the morning about five o'clock and listened to the trains coming and going from Trowbridge station. We were up before seven. Mr and the two Miss Daniels were down to give us our breakfast and after thanking them we departed. Had a little more breakfast when we came home.

23rd A dull day and rather cold ... Had a letter from Blanche Pelham ... Harry, Lewin and I went to Melksham in the evening. Miss Burgess told me that the copy of the 'Pirates' that I sent her was opened at Bath and my note found in it, and she had to pay 1/9d. Had a very good practice. There were a lot of wires strung across above our heads which greatly improved the sound. Mr Harris and Mr Evans were sent away from Mr Hulls' for getting drunk while in charge of the boys.

25th A dull day, wet in the evening. Martin went to Bath in the morning, to the hospital to see the doctor, as he had been suffering from a stone in the bladder for some time. Received news of Longfellow's death in the paper ... Martin came back in the evening and told us he had been operated upon; it was very painful, he said.

28th A dull day. Blanche Pelham enclosed a letter for me in the letter written to Clara ... Trowbridge concert in the evening; our brake started about 5.15; it began to rain when we started but soon stopped and cleared off nicely for the rest of the evening. The hall was well filled and I enjoyed myself immensely, especially in the solos ... Watched A. W. Wood, leader of the first violins, as much as I could; he is a splendid player. Got home about 12.30.

29th A fine day (latter part). Wrote a letter to Blanche Pelham. Ernest Lanham came in the shop in the morning and talked. Went to practice in the evening ... Lizzie Gilbert's last night at the class.

APRIL

1st (Saturday) A fine day ... Mr Burgess drove Miss Burgess over in the afternoon to stay over Sunday. Harry Goold came in the evening to stay for a few days. Ernest Lanham lent me 'Thirteen at Dinner'.

2nd (Palm Sunday) A beautiful day. Got up at 7 o'clock and practised on the violin for half an hour, then went down to the church and helped Harry tune till breakfast. Had a letter from Blanche Pelham ... Went out for a walk with Harry Goold, Ernest Lanham and Wilfrid after dinner, and then Harry Goold and Sarah went to Jessie Light's to tea. Miss Burgess went to church in the evening. I showed her our seat and took her out for a short walk afterwards. Had some music in the evening.

3rd A beautiful day ... Martin cut the lawn ... and Miss Burgess, Minnie Moody and some of our people played croquet. Miss Burgess went back by the 4.30 train. Minnie was here to tea and supper. Wilfrid's birthday; we all subscribed and gave him a 'Stainer' violin with bow and case ... After shop Wilfrid, Ernest (Lanham) and I set up three fire balloons. Two of them went splendidly but the third caught as soon as it went out of our hands. Had some music afterwards.

4th A beautiful day. Had a letter from Blanche Pelham. In the afternoon had an hour's violin practice and after tea had a trio with Harry and Clara. In the evening had my first shorthand class; Jennie Amoore and Winnie Burchell were there besides all our people and also Aunt Lena. Afterwards went for a walk with Ernest Lanham and Wilfrid up to the Golden Gates and back; it was a splendid moonlight night.

5th A beautiful day ... Made some fire balloons; I cut out the word 'Farewell' and put on one of them, intended for the college girls, and in the evening Ernest Lanham, Wilfrid and I went down to the tanyard and lighted it, but it soon burnt and so we set up another; it went beautifully and when it was up very high it burnt; we then went on to Broadstone and emptied the rest of the methylated spirits on the Broadstone and lit it just as we thought the college girls were coming, but we didn't know whether it was they. Got home at eleven.

6th (Thursday) A beautiful day ... Finished four more balloons ... Harry, Lewin, Ernest Lanham, Clara and I went to Melksham by the 4.30 train; we were delayed more than an hour at Chippenham through extra traffic – Bank Holiday Good Friday. There was not a very good attendance at the class but we had a very good practice, and then after going in Burgess's to see the hot cross buns in course of preparation, and having a cup of coffee each, we started to walk home; it was a splendid moonlight night; we got home about 12.30 well laden with hot cross buns.

7th (Good Friday) A splendid day ... In the afternoon Harry and I went up in the cricket field and had a very good game. The others played croquet; Ernest Lanham too; Ernest stayed to tea and went to church with us in the evening. After practice we intended to set up a fire balloon but it was too windy. I walked down with Ernest and brought back his 'Airs from Patience' arranged for the violin. Clara had a letter from Blanche Pelham and there was a note for me enclosed.

8th Another beautiful day ... Wrote a letter to Blanche Pelham.

10th A splendid day. Ernest Lanham, Wilfrid and I went down to Bath by the 10 train and stayed there all day, coming back by the 6.30. We first walked about Bath and then went to the tepid swimming baths and enjoyed ourselves immensely there; I practised diving for the first time; took two or three headers from the top step of the diving board. After a little refreshment we went up to the Sham Castle; a very nice part of Bath and commands a good view of the city ... Went to West's Dining Rooms for tea and saw a party from Melksham there, amongst them being Miss Burgess and her brother. Saw Sarah and her sister Blanche at the station and Sarah came in the same carriage with us ... Music in the evening. Set up two fire balloons and they went capitally.

12th A wet day ... Melksham concert in the evening. Harry and Ernest Lanham went over in the cart with the piano and then Fred came back and took the harmonium and Lewin and I went with that ... Went to Burgess's and had a wash etc. in Albert's room. The concert went off very well. It took from 8.15 to 10.30, there being a good many encores. Charlie Hulls came and played first; he came over with Ma, Mrs Alfred Cole, Sarah and Clara in Mr Griffin's brake. There was a very poor audience, owing to the wet weather I suppose.

17th A stormy day ... Mr Granter of Prospect Place drowned himself in the morning in Mr Freeth's pond.

18th A fine day ... After practice went down to the British Schoolroom where the 'Blue Ribbon Army' were holding a meeting. Minnie Moody pinned a blue ribbon on for me; the room was full ... We were talking about Ernest Lanham at supper and he was in the parlour and heard it. He told Ernest and Clare, who were in the parlour with him, not to tell anyone he heard; but Clare didn't hear him and told us afterwards; but we didn't let him know we knew he had heard us.

19th (Wednesday) A fine day but rather dull ... Wrote a letter to Blanche Pelham ... In the evening held my third shorthand lesson, but it was rather small, Emily and Clara being away; Aunt Lena didn't come, nor Ma, and Sarah and Jessie Light went away soon after they came in. Afterwards Ernest Lanham came in and we had a spree, Ernest with Harry's cheap 'cello' and I practising on my violin.

20th (Thursday) A beautiful day ... Harry, Lewin, Sarah and I went to Bradford in Merrett's trap in the afternoon; we got there soon after 3.30 and had a short practice of some of the things. We stayed and listened to the practice of the trio by Mr Waite and Messrs Millington and the duet by Mr Waite and Mr H. Millington. Went to tea at Mr Beavan's and then we all went for a walk and had a good view of Bradford. We made our 'toilet' in Harry's room and then went down to the hall. The room was very well filled and the concert passed off very well; I couldn't get on very well myself as we hadn't seen some of the music at all ... After the concert had some supper at the Beavans and then home Atworth way; it was a nice starlight night. Uncle William came in the evening.

24th [At Bristol, for a violin sale.] ... Went down to the Colston Hall where I met Harry, and after he had fetched a young lady of his acquaintance we all went together to the 'Monday Pop' and enjoyed ourselves immensely. Mr Waite led the first violins. After it was over and Harry had taken the girl home we went to Mr James's to sleep. Wrote a letter to Blanche Pelham enclosing a programme.

27th A fine day ... Mr Freeth and Mr Brinkworth came over to our concert. The room was pretty well filled. The platform was badly arranged; we had to stand down on the floor on the level of the audience. We played Mendelssohn's Wedding March in honour of Prince Albert's wedding ... Blanche Pelham was at the concert.

28th A fine day ... Played one of Mozart's trios with Harry and Clara in the afternoon ... Got Sarah to give me a piece of lace out of the shop and enclosed it in an envelope to go with the note for Clara to take out to Blanche Pelham for a birthday present.

29th Blanche Pelham's birthday. Clara took out my little present and I received a note back expressing her thanks and saying that she would wear it on Sunday. A very rough windy day; a lot of trees were blown down.

30th (Sunday) A stormy day. Went to church morning and evening. Blanche Pelham was there and I saw that she had it on (the lace) ... The afternoon was so wet that we couldn't go for a walk, and so Ernest Lanham came up and he and Harry and I played one of Beethoven's trios in the kitchen, and Ernest stayed to tea. After church in the evening I walked down to Mrs Lanham's behind the girls, and Blanche looked back two or three times and smiled. Had a talk with Caleb Davis afterwards and then came home. Ernest came with me as far as the Salvation Army Chapel where they were making a beautiful row.

MAY

1st (Monday) A beautiful day ... Grandma's 73rd birthday. I went up to see her in the evening and took my violin and played to her. She was rather low-spirited as Mrs Hulbert was not expected to live. Ma was with her and after supper I came down with her. Katy, our servant, went away for good in the evening.

6th ... Miss West brought some of Prince Albert's wedding cake for us to taste.

8th A beautiful day ... Blanche Pelham came in the grocery shop with two other girls and the pupil teacher about tea time and I went in and saw them. Had a game of croquet with the newly painted balls after tea; our Ernest won. Ernest Lanham did some printing for Lewin up to 9.30 and I watched him, and then we set up a fire balloon.

9th A fine day ... Clara brought me a note from Blanche Pelham with some of her hair in it, and I wrote her a long letter in the evening but could not persuade Clara to take it with her in the morning as she had promised Miss Stone not to; so I puzzled my brain to think of some way of sending it, but couldn't. My 6th shorthand class in the evening. Jennie Amoore and Winnie Burchell were present. I enjoyed it very much; I like the class more as I go on; getting more used to it I suppose ... Ma went to Bowood in Mr Mayo's carriage with Mr Moody and some more.

10th A fine day ... Lizzie Gilbert's birthday. Asked Clara again to take my note, but she wouldn't ... Went up and watched the cricket match for an hour in the afternoon; Ernest Lanham was up there and we walked round the field together and saw the girls come by soon after.

13th A lovely day ... Sent some golden chain (laburnum) to Blanche Pelham by Clara ... Edwin and I had the shop to ourselves in the evening. Ernest Lanham brought me Nicholl's 'Esoteric Anthropology' – he got Mr Lucas to take it. I did not regret my investment as I saw it was a very useful book.

17th A fine day ... Sent some flowers to Blanche Pelham by Clara. Went up Paul Street for orders in the morning ... Went to the annual meeting of the 'Institute'; Ernest Lanham, Bryant and I were scrutineers.

19th A beautiful day. Went out for orders in the morning. Played battledore and shuttlecock with Wilfrid on the gravel ... Had a game of billiards with Ernest Lanham in the evening. Herbert Hulls went to Plymouth with his father on his way to Australia, and we heard that he cried like a child.

20th A beautiful day. Sent a bouquet of flowers to Blanche Pelham by Clara. Ernest Lanham was not up all day and in the evening I had a note from him informing me that he had been very unwell all day; I sent a note back by the servant telling him I would go and see him tomorrow.

22nd A stormy day; some thunder and flashes of lightning and very heavy rain. Mr Moody gave me an old lawn-tennis bat; I asked him the other day if he thought there was one about which the young Mayos had done with. Wilfrid and I played 'lawn-tennis' on the gravel at intervals in the day ... Lent Ernest Lanham some 'diet' books, etc.

29th (Whit Monday) (Croquet and cricket most of the day.) A beautiful day ... Ernest Lanham, Wilfrid, Sarah, Emily, Nellie Beavan (who came in the morning and went to the tea-meeting at the chapel), and I, took a woman named Mrs Sheppard out to Monks in Alice's chair and rode back by turns; we met Mr Hulls with Blanche Pelham. Afterwards we had a look at the comet and then set up my last fire balloon; it went up capitally.

30th A splendid day. Wilts Friendly Society's Fete. Went to morning service; the choir followed behind the band from the Avenue gates singing a hymn and the band played the other hymns in the church. We shut shop at 2.30 ... Went up to the Club field; there were a good many people there. I had about a shilling's-worth at the coconuts (proprietor Tom Ketwell) and listened to the brass band (Melksham) and soon after seven I came away ... Lewin acted as steward of the Society and marched at the head of the procession.

31st A delightful day. Sent a rose to Blanche Pelham by Clara. In the afternoon I took Alice's chair up to fetch Grandma; we took her into the chapel yard and then into Mr Mayo's garden and through the greenhouses and then home. After a little rest in the passage I took her up to the 'Hare and Hounds' and back accompanied by Aunt Lena, and she was spotted by several friends and acquaintances who wished to speak to her; she slept here all night ... Went a little way up Stumps Lane with Harry, Aunt Polly, Emily, Clara and Wilfrid to have a look at the comet. It was much brighter than on Monday night. Lewin and Ernest Lanham walked to Melksham to get their hair cut, and from there to Lacock and then home.

JUNE

1st (Thursday) A rather uneventful day. Three scaffold poles were erected before the Market Place preparatory to building the Town Hall.

2nd A fine day, rather sultry ... After church went up to the Mens' Institute where I was amused for some time by the witty conversation between Arthur Kinneir and Ernest Lanham.

3rd A fine morning but turned off wet ... Ma was very ill with quinzy all day. Grandma still making her stay with us up in the spare room.

5th A stormy day ... I had my shorthand class in the evening ... afterwards we all sang 'Now the day is over' for Grandma's benefit.

6th A stormy day ... Went to the choral festival practice at the British Schoolroom in the evening. Miss Stone and six of the girls were there including Blanche Pelham. Clara played the piano and there was a very good attendance. Most of the members of the choral society and Corshamside choir were present, as well as our own choir ... Ma still on the sick list, but much better; Grandma still our guest.

10th (Saturday) A stormy day ... Harry and I went over to Chippenham to play Chippenham Club at cricket. Chippenham won the toss and went in first and made 78, and Corsham followed on and made 58, to which I contributed a 'duck'. Chippenham then went to the wickets and made 27, mainly owing to Ketwell's bowling ... Corsham had about 50 to make which, chiefly through Harry and Tom Ketwell, we managed to get within a minute or two of 'time', Harry making 26 not out and Tom ... I had my hair cut in the dinner hour and had my dinner at Fisher's. Bought a pair of flash gloves at the hair-cutter's. Gave Clara some flowers to give to Blanche Pelham in the morning.

11th A fine day. Went to church ... Blanche Pelham was wearing the flowers I sent her. Went up to the cricket field where the 'Hallelujah Army' were holding a meeting, but they had finished when I got there.

12th A fine day except for one or two short storms ... Lewin and Minnie came home in the evening and brought their photographic proofs; I was much pleased with

75

Lewin's photograph and Minnie's too, the positions were both very nice. Lewin brought Ma some spoons and a revised edition of the Testament. Went to the Festival practice at the British School in the evening. Miss Stone and the girls were there. We had a very long practice, from 8 to 9.45; I enjoyed it very much, but hadn't much chance to look at Blanche Pelham.

13th A fine morning, but in the afternoon it turned off wet and kept on raining most of the evening. Choral Festival Day ... we shut up soon after 2 o'clock. Went down to church at 2 to the rehearsal and afterwards we went in the Riding School and put on our surplices, then we all got in order at 3.30 and marched into church singing a hymn; the church was crowded. The service went off very well. One of the choir boys fainted and was taken out by Mr Fearnside. The Claremont girls sat in our usual seats and I had a good view of Blanche Pelham. After the service went up to the tea tent and took my violin; enjoyed the tea very much and the concert too, although we had to stand all the time – there was such little room on the platform. Mrs Gardner's song was a failure. The Claremont girls were at the concert. Mr Alfred Humphries came here to dinner; he came from Wootton Bassett for the Festival. After all was over Ernest Lanham came home with us and Minnie sang two or three songs accompanied by Lewin. Then had some supper and to bed.

16th Had a letter from Ernest Lanham asking if I could not go down and stay with Mr James (in Bristol) while he was there; so after talking it over I asked Dad, and he said write and ask Mrs James if she could accommodate us (as I meant to take Wilfrid as well) which I did. Dad was not very well all day.

19th Got up and did a little business, but not a great deal as I was preparing for my holiday at Bristol. Wilfrid came down with me to the station and carried my portmanteau (a new one for the occasion). When I arrived at Montpelier I saw Ernest waiting for me, and he carried the ferns which I had brought for Mrs James ... (Later) Ernest called for me and after walking about the streets we went to the Museum and enjoyed ourselves very much ... After tea I went down the Cheltenham Road and called in at P——'s where Ernest was talking to a Miss Stevens to whom he introduced me ... then off to the Colston Hall to the 'Monday Pop'. We sat in the gallery and had a good view of the orchestra. I believe I enjoyed it more than the last; Miss Hardy's singing was excellent and Mr Waite's violin obbligato to her 'Serenata' was really splendid. The hall was crowded.

20th (Tuesday) Had a jolly bath in the morning in Mr James's lavatory. Mr James went off to business after breakfast and his brother to Ilfracombe. Went down to Ernest after breakfast and then we walked about together seeing the shipping ... and coming back through Redcliffe St I called on Willie Moody and talked to him for a bit ... and walked about with him during his dinner hour. In the afternoon went up to Prospect House, an untenanted house of Mr James's. The late tenants had left it in great disorder. Mrs James showed me over ... Mrs James went out to tea so Gilbert and I had it all to ourselves. After tea we called on Ernest and he showed us the bakehouse and poultry, and then I had a tune or two on his fiddle, after which we took tickets to Clifton by train and went to the Zoo. I enjoyed the band (Bristol Artillery) very much and we saw most of the animals; the lions and tigers roared, the first time I had heard them, and made the whole house vibrate. At about 9 o'clock I went to the entrance and met Willie Moody, and then we three walked about together till the fireworks began; they were very beautiful. After walking home I felt very tired and was glad to get to bed.

21st ... Met Willie Moody in his dinner hour and went with him to the Victoria Coffee Tavern where he had his dinner, and then we went to a public house to see a grand organ musical-box style; it plays 72 pieces and cost £2000 ... After dinner I called on Ernest but it came on to rain so we could not go out ... so while Ernest was making himself useful to Mrs Lanham I talked to Miss Knight who was staying with Mrs L, and helped her stem some gooseberries; tried to get her to play the piano while I played the violin, but she wouldn't ... In the evening Ernest and I went to the new theatre to see 'Patience' and enjoyed it immensely; we sat in the gallery and had a good view both of the orchestra and the stage ... I didn't get home till nearly 11.30.

22nd Had a capital bath in the morning. A wretched day, raining nearly all the time ... After tea called on Ernest and we went to the old theatre to see 'The Gay City' and 'Brum'; I think I liked the last best, it was so ridiculous, but both of them were very nice. It was the first time I had seen girls dressed in tights and I thought they looked very nice. In 'Brum' they brought in something in favour of Bradlaugh, and one old man in the audience got up and spoke against him, but I couldn't hear a word he said as they all clapped and hissed and cried 'Turn him out!' and 'Sit down!' till he was at last obliged to, as he couldn't get a hearing. We sat in the gallery again and had a very good view, but they were very noisy up there.

23rd ... Met Willie Moody ... and went in Redcliffe church for a few minutes and had a look at it; it is a very beautiful church. I couldn't hear the organ play though. After that I walked to Bristol Cemetery; it is a very large one and a lot of splendid monuments there ... Came back for Willie's dinner hour ... went down Old Market Street and had 2 or 3 turns at the shooting gallery; I had a bull's-eye once ... After dinner went with Gilbert to school; it was a great fag up there but a very nice place. Called for Ernest coming back but he wasn't there; Miss Knight said he had gone down town, so I went to meet him; I soon saw him, and then I went in one of the steam ferries and he walked by the river to meet me. I liked the ride very much. We walked along by the river and came up the Zig Zag. I called for Gilbert at 5 o'clock and we went to the Downs along the sea wall; very pretty views. Soon after 7 we went to meet Ernest by the Museum and then to the Picture Gallery and enjoyed ourselves very much. I saw Mr Pelham's two pictures; the price of one was £60 and the other £120. Afterwards we went to the Promenade and sat down for a short time and then home after a good day's walking.

24th ... Went with Ernest by train to Clifton and walked over the Downs and saw the steamers going up the river; we went down the Zig-Zag, and on the way I saw a man (blind) reading by feeling the letters, and also a man sketching. We went to the Cumberland Basin and watched two or three large ships tugged out, and then home. It was showery ... In the evening ... talked to Miss Stevens a long time ... Ernest waited till Miss Stevens was going home and walked with her; I went down to the Croft and met them and talked for a bit and then we parted, Ernest to take Miss Stevens home and I on the pretence of looking for Ernest ... went and talked to Miss Hopkins till Ernest came back, which was nearly an hour.

25th (Sunday) ... Went to the Cathedral in the afternoon ... While waiting for the gates to open I happened to see Miss Gertie Churchill and so we went in together; it was a splendid service ... Walked home with Miss Churchill.

26th Went down town after breakfast and called at the Shorthand Institute in Cumberland St to ask their terms for teaching shorthand for Mrs James. I had quite a talk with Mrs Hunt (the professor's wife) who seemed a very sensible person; her little girl, 8 years old, received Mr Pitman's certificate ... To Mr B's warehouse and asked for Mr Chivers according to Mr James's instructions, and he told some clerk (a very nice fellow) to show me over; he was more than an hour as they are very extensive premises and I saw everything. I offered him a shilling but he wouldn't take it ... Went home, had dinner, then called for Ernest to go with me to the Children's Hospital etc., but he couldn't come so I went alone. I was the only visitor but the nurse showed me over. Some poor little children were very bad, but others were sitting up playing with their toys. I put sixpence in the money box and the nurse gave me a report, and then ... I went on to the Blind Asylum to hear their open concert, and enjoyed it very much, especially the Overture to Semiramide played by two young men on the piano ... Went for a walk with Ernest after tea and then went to meet Willie Moody in Redcliffe Street. We engaged a boat for an hour; Willie rowed and I steered; I enjoyed it immensely. Willie dropped an oar, but we managed to get it again. It was a splendid evening, which made it doubly enjoyable. After landing ... we were joined by a lodger friend of Willie's (a soldier), and after promenading a little I went home, after spending a most enjoyable day.

27th A beautiful day. Had my last bath at Mr James's. After breakfast ... Willie and I and a boatman that he knew took a boat for a little more than half an hour; Ernest wouldn't come ... Wished Willie goodbye ... After dinner I went down the Cheltenham Road and saw Ernest talking to Miss Stevens, so I went in too and we had quite a lark till old Dr Doosh came along and then we bunked ... Wished Miss Stevens goodbye and Miss Hoskins, not forgetting Mrs Lanham ... then after tea wished Mrs James goodbye and after thanking her for her kindness and hospitality I departed, accompanied by Gilbert. Ernest was at the station with a hamper for his mother and wished me goodbye as the train went off. At about seven o'clock I arrived home, after having spent an enjoyable visit, with just one penny in my pocket. Had a little music with Sarah in the evening.

JULY

3rd (Monday) A beautiful day. Got up early and went down to the Weavern with Wilfrid, Ernest and Clare; the water was very cold and we didn't stay in long. While we were dressing Fred Bryant and Cooper (Randall's office) came along; they had already had their bathe and so we walked back with them. We found by them that we were an hour later than we thought, and instead of being 5.45 it was 6.45; the watch that Dad lent me for the occasion must have slipped back an hour.

4th A dull morning and turned off to rain in the afternoon and evening. Dad, Ernest and Clare went to London by excursion train at about 5 o'clock in the morning. Emily's birthday; I gave her some toilet soap ... Went up to talk to Grandma a bit after supper, and at 11 o'clock Wilfrid and I went down to the station with umbrellas for Dad, Ernest and Clare; they were the only passengers. They hadn't had any rain in London.

6th (Thursday) A stormy day ... While I was in the shop in the evening in walked my second self, no less an important personage than Ernest Charles Victor Lanham. I hadn't expected him so soon, so I was taken quite by surprise. We talked over events till shop was shut ...

8th A stormy day ... Sent some flowers to Blanche Pelham by Clara.

10th A stormy day ... Fred Bryant called for me at 4.30 and we went down to the Weavern together. On our way there we saw a squirrel in the fir-tree plantation, but though we tried hard we could not catch it. The water was very high and the stream strong when we got down there and we couldn't go in where we intended to, so we got in at the old place; it was a little too cold and the stream too strong to enjoy it very much, but still we felt very nice afterwards. Coming back through the plantation we again saw the squirrel in the very same place and had another chase for it; I managed to secure it and was putting it in my towel when it got out again and we thought we had lost it, but at last I saw it in the grass and grabbed at its tail and stuck to it. I put it in my coat pocket and brought it home and showed it to all of them, and then put it in a cage with some hay and nuts. We passed the Claremont girls in Pickwick Road. In the evening read everything I could see about squirrels, but couldn't find exactly what I wanted.

11th A stormy day. Found the poor squirrel (dead) on coming down in the morning; I suppose it must have died of fright. I cut it open but couldn't see anything the matter with it. I was very sorry as I meant to take it back where I found it as soon as possible ... The bombardment of Alexandria began in the morning and continued all day. I peeled the potatoes for dinner (the first time I had ever done such a thing).

12th A beautiful day ... Choir treat. Our destination was Badminton; we started at 10.30, Ernest Lanham, Wilfrid and I up on Mr Griffin's box. We had a jolly ride there and then walked about the grounds a bit till dinner time. After dinner all the little choir boys went and bathed in the brook and we watched them; had a look at the Hermit's Cell and then on to the stables and kennels to see the horses and dogs; after that we were shown over the house ... Lewin, Ernest Lanham, Wilfrid and I played rounders just outside the garden and we were soon joined by the other boys and had a very good game. We were called to tea after some time and then we had a recitation by Mr Duck and a comic song by Mr Sainsbury and a recitation by Mr Osborne ... then rounders again till it was time to go home. We were the last to start but we cut across the Park and got first and kept it all the way; the three other brakes went through Pickwick but we went through the town and went up Pickwick Road, turned and waited for them and then came first through the town (double cunning) ... We had splendid weather all day.

14th A dull day and a little rain ... It seems pretty well decided that Harry will go to New Zealand.

15th St. Swithin. A very wet morning but turned off fine for the rest of the day. Harry, Lewin and Ernest Lanham went to Bedminster to the cricket match. W. G. Grace played against us and made 63; Harry caught him off Mr Abbot's bowling ... Printed Blanche Pelham's name on two dozen slips of paper to put in books.

17th A very wet day ... After shop I went down home with Ernest and had some black-currant pie and then we went round the Cleeve smoking cigarettes, and went along to the Hallelujah Army tent and listened for some time ...

18th A beautiful day. (Cricket match.) Ernest Lanham and I went down to the Weavern soon after four o'clock; it was rather cold but we got out two or three times and ran about to keep ourselves warm. After shop we had some 'Patience' with Clara and then Ernest Lanham and I went for a walk and had a smoke or two ... Edwin made a speech down at the Hallelujah Army tent.

24th A fine day ... In the afternoon went to Beccles Wood to see what sort of a place it was (for bathing), but found it a most filthy place with a lot of mud ... and weeds over half the pond, so gave up all thoughts of bathing there and came back, but it was too late to go to the Weavern. After shop went down to the Hallelujah Army and listened for a time with Ernest Lanham, and then we came home where Ernest was having a birthday party; after supper we joined in their games ... I gave Ernest a 2s knife.

26th A fine day ... While I was out in the garden heard a violin being played down in the park, so went ... and found Fred Hulls playing his, with about half a dozen other fellows round him ... Had a look at the photographs of the girls at Claremont, and Ernest Lanham and Clara quarrelled over them.

27th A fine day but a little rain in the evening ... I took Grandma to Mrs Wray's in the chair after tea, and from there to Mr Mayo's to see the garden, and then took her to her 'country residence' ... Aunt Lydia came back with with me and I got in the chair and guided while she pushed; we took Martin in at the chapel gates and drove him up to his door, and then I pushed Aunt Lydia the rest of the way. Clara went out to the school in the evening as the prizes were to be given away; she received three certificates. Blanche Pelham had a prize for perseverance in music, failing to get one in any other branch of study through illness, as she couldn't attend the exams.

29th A beautiful day ... Had a ride up and down the town on Stanley Porter's tricycle and enjoyed it immensely.

AUGUST

1st (Tuesday) A fine day but rather dull ... Clare's birthday. Wilfrid and I gave him a text book. He had the two young Pyms to tea and also Stanley Porter ... In the evening Ernest Lanham and I walked down town with the two young Pyms and Stanley Porter and saw a harp and violin just about to commence operations outside Mr White's, so we listened till they had finished. They played some of 'Patience', and I enjoyed it immensely.

3rd A fine day ... In the evening went up to Mr Freeth's to fetch Sarah home and stayed there talking to Gertie Light for some time ...

5th A fine day ... Had a letter from Blanche Pelham.

8th A beautiful day. Had another letter from Blanche Pelham in the morning and wrote a long one in return in the afternoon.

9th A beautiful day. Cricket match with John Fuller's eleven. They went in first and made 137 and Corsham made 130, losing the match by 11 runs. Lewin went round for orders instead of Martin and Willie Moody went with him; he came back in time to go in and bat for Corsham. John Fuller objected to him going in ... but Lewin told him it was no good, he should go in, and go in he did, but he only made 6 ... Mr and Mrs Kenway and their children went up to watch the match with Ma and Mrs Alfred Cole, who came back to tea with us.

11th A beautiful day. Mr and Mrs Kenway and their children went to Bath to have their likenesses taken; Ma and Harry went too. Harry had his taken but not Ma ... Found a big spider and brought it up as a curiosity to Ma, Emily etc. Mr West put up the blinds in the shop in the afternoon and evening, so we didn't put up the shutters but rolled the blinds instead; it saves a lot of trouble and looks much better.

13th Stormy ... Had a letter from Blanche Pelham and answered it ... Ma, Dad, Mr & Mrs Kenway and the three children went to Bromham in the afternoon in Allway's wagonette.

16th A dull morning but turned off beautiful by dinner time ... The town was pretty well decorated for the Flower Show. We put a lot of flower pots all along our ledge, and two flags the other side of the house. We shut shop at 2 o'clock and I went down at once. Dad was in a way about Bartlett's Steam Circus that Mr Carter had let have his field ... and went to see Stokes to see if he could stop it, but there was no time ... I heard the first two things on the programme outside, and then went in the field for a shilling. I enjoyed the Coldstream Guards' Band immensely and listened to every bit of it. Had some tea on the field and after the band was gone walked about the field talking to people from Calne, Melksham etc. that I knew, and then walked about for some time with Sarah Goold, Jessie Light and Nellie Ward. The fireworks were very good and a fire balloon went up splendidly. Mr and Mrs Kenway and their children, Alice and all our people were down there.

17th A fine day ... Ernest Lanham, Wilfrid, Ernest and Clare and I drove in our trap to Lacock in the afternoon and had a jolly bathe, then all had tea at the Coffee Tavern which was a real lark, and then home.

23rd (Wed.) A stormy day. Sunday School (Church) treat held in Mr Balch's field by Mr Mayo's. The Chippenham Workhouse Fife and Drum Band came and marched at the head of the procession. Ernest Lanham and I ... had some tea in Mr Mayo's coach-house ... Harry, Amy Coxall and Clara came home by the 4.30 train ... We were all quite astonished to hear that Harry and Amy were engaged; he had written to Dad in the morning to tell him about it, but Dad kept it quiet, only telling Ma, so it came like a thunder-clap upon us. We were all glad to hear it, though very sorry to think that Harry will be going away.

25th A very wet day, but it cleared off late in the evening to a splendid moonlight night ... Went down to church to blow for Harry for about 2 hours in the afternoon; Amy and Clare came too ... Harry played at the service in the evening. Amy, Minnie and Katy Moody were here to tea. After practice in the evening Ernest Lanham came in and we had 'Voices'; Harry played the cello and Lewin the piano. After supper Sarah, Ernest, Wilfrid and I went for a walk up Pickwick Road and had a cigarette each.

30th A splendid day ... Chippenham Flower Show. Sarah, Emily, Jessie Light and I went over by the 4.30 train and went to Fisher's to tea and then into the field. I didn't go into the tents but listened to the band and talked to people I knew ... Ernest and Clare walked over in the afternoon and saw Dr Jay and his children perform in the water ... Went to Mr Brinkworth's to supper. It was a splendid night. When we had got about half way between the Chequers and Cross Keys we heard a woman screaming, and so Wilfrid and I ran back and saw a hansom cab and a man and woman by the side of the road, and a woman in the cab crying and wringing her hands; the man was swearing at her and telling her to hush up; I asked her what was the matter twice, but she gave me no answer and so we went back. Lewin and Minnie were passing at the time, and from what Lewin said when I got home I collected it must have been a case of rape.

SEPTEMBER

5th A wet day ... Had a letter from Blanche Pelham and answered it. Went to the Church of England Temperance Meeting in the evening; took my violin and played the hymns with Fred Hulls. Clara and Sarah sang duets after supper.

6th A beautiful day ... Margaret Balch was married to Mr Callingham; I blew for the hymns and psalms and Ernest Lanham for the Wedding March. Mr Moody gave me another racquet ... it was very much warped but otherwise not much damaged; I put it in some water when I got home and then pressed it in Lewin's press ...

7th A beautiful day ... Lewin went to Bristol to have his first lesson with Mr Riseley ... Wilfrid and I had a game of 'tennis' on the lawn ... Wilfrid and I went down to Mr Lanham's after shop; Bertie Elliott was there and we four went out for a walk, out to the 'Seven Stars' and along 'Squitters' Lane' and down Lacock Road; Ernest Lanham diverted us with his wit all the way ...

8th A splendid day ... A man in the employ of Mr Chapman at the station was charged with having stolen a half-sovereign and he flung a ruler at Mr Chapman's head for suspecting him; he was taken into custody.

12th (Tuesday) A fine day ... A cricket match between Mr Mayo's eleven and Mr Spackman's was held up in the cricket field; we picked up on the ground. I won the toss and we went in first and made 114; Wilfrid made 47 and I 10. Willie Shannon went in with me and made 20. They followed and made 56 just saving the follow-on. We went in again and made 76 of which I made 28 and Wilfrid 14. They made 94 second innings, leaving us the victors by 40 runs. Lily Beavan went back to Bradford in the evening. Ma, Aunt Jane and Uncle Laurie came from Exeter by the same train that Lily left. In the evening we had some glees in the drawing-room.

14th A very cold morning but fine. Got up at 6.30 and went down to the church with Lewin to blow for him; we stayed till 8.20; he practised pieces for Mr Riseley. Uncle and Aunt Laurie, Ma, Aunts Emily and Lena, Clara and Clare went to Farleigh Castle in Mr Griffin's wagonette; they started soon after 11 and got back at 6 o'clock. It was fine all the time and they enjoyed it immensely. Ernest went to Bath with Fred Cole and some more of his companions. I had 'tennis' with Wilfrid on the lawn in the afternoon ...

15th Lewin's birthday. Mrs Draper of Calne sent him some of his favourite cakes for a present ... Minnie and Katy Moody were here to tea and played croquet with Aunt and Uncle Laurie ... Clara went to Portskewitt; Sarah telegraphed for her Thursday to come and help nurse Ethel as she had bronchitis.

16th A beautiful day. I drove Uncle and Aunt Laurie and Aunt Polly right round Castle Combe after breakfast. We started at 9.30, went down to Ford and from there to Castle Combe and then back through West Yatton where we called for Mr Hulbert's butter and regaled ourselves with milk and biscuits; we got home just before dinner – about 3 hours' ride and a jolly one too.

18th A fine day. Miss Simmonds washed the grocery shop out ... I drove Uncle and Aunt Laurie and Aunt Lena to Monks, Neston, Atworth, Whitley and back through Velley in the afternoon. Dad, Ma, Uncle and Aunt Laurie went to Mrs Cole's to supper. Ernest Lanham was here to supper and we had quite an interesting talk together afterwards, chiefly about London life, actresses etc ...

19th A wet dull day ... Aunt and Uncle Laurie, Dad and Ma, Aunts Emily and Lydia, Ernest and Clare went for a long drive in Mr Griffin's wagonette. They went to the White Horse and along to the Monument, then went on to Beckhampton and Devizes and then to Bromham where they stayed some time and had tea. They came home about 11.30.

20th Another damp day. Clara had a letter from Blanche Pelham and I opened it to see if there was an enclosure for me and there was, so I wrote to Clara and enclosed it. Ernest and Clare came in the shop and helped us, and Edwin and I taught them some of the 'tricks of the trade'. Uncle and Aunt Laurie, Ma and Mr Moody drove to Lacock to see the Abbey ...

21st (Thursday) A fine day ... Uncle and Aunt Laurie went to Box with Fred in the trap with the Box goods. Lewin went to Bristol for his third organ lesson. I went up to the Justices' meeting at the Methuen Arms with Ernest Lanham ... after dinner and stayed all the afternoon. There was a Salvation Army case on there which occupied a long time. The Salvation Army had engaged a good barrister from London who conducted their case well, and reproved Mr Rook, one of the magistrates, for a sneering remark to one of the witnesses. The Bench decided against him (Captain Sutton), and so the barrister told them he should apply at a higher court. The Salvation Army had a procession in the evening and a lot of roughs hooted at them, but Dad went down to the chapel with them and soon stopped it. Ernest Lanham, Wilfrid, Sarah and I called for Jessie Light after shop and went past the 'Seven Stars' for a walk.

22nd A fine day ... Went up to the Court with Uncle and Aunt Laurie, Minnie, Ma and Aunt Lena in the afternoon to see over it. I had never been into some of the rooms and enjoyed it immensely. We went into the gardens afterwards.

23rd A fine day ... Went down to the church for an hour in the afternoon and helped Lewin tune. Violin and harp in the street in the evening; listened for some time ... Edwin's last day in the shop.

24th A beautiful day ... Went to church morning and evening. Saw Blanche Pelham, beautiful as ever ...

25th A fine day, but for a short storm about dinner time. Our first day without Edwin, but with the help of Clare and Ernest I don't think we shall miss him a great deal, except that I shall have to stay more in the shop as I can't leave Martin by himself as I did Edwin. Uncle and Aunt Laurie went back to London. Uncle gave Wilfrid and I half a sovereign between us to go to Harry's complimentary supper, and pocket money besides ... Mr Hulls spoke to Ma about me going up to teach some of his boys the violin.

26th Had a letter from Clara in the morning with the enclosure for me ... Mr Hulls came down about tea-time and settled for me to go up tomorrow. A wet stormy day. Drove over to Melksham Forest with Aunt Sarah, Aunt Lena and Clare in our trap in the afternoon ... stopped at Burgess's for some refreshment; introduced Aunt to Miss Burgess ... heard that Mrs Burgess was very ill. We got home just in time for tea ... In the evening had some music with Aunt Sarah and Sarah ... after supper went up to Grandma's with Aunt Sarah, Emily and Sarah and then we walked up to the top of Pickwick Road arm in arm. It was a splendid moonlight night.

27th A fine day. Went up to Mr Hulls' at 9 o'clock to give Brooks his first (violin) lesson, and then went round for orders (Edwin's round). Ernest Lanham came with me. Lewin and Ernest Lanham went down to meet Harry in the afternoon. Church practice at 6 o'clock for the Harvest Festival; Harry played the organ. After practice we went up to the Methuen Arms where the supper was given to Harry, Jim Balch and Albert Feaviour as they are going to New Zealand. About 80 were present; Mr Linton in the chair as President and Mr Yockney vice-president. After a number of toasts ... songs were given by Mr Osborne, Mr Smith of Hartham, and Mr Brown at Pickwick and Mr Rogers; Mr Balch Senior and Mr Feaviour also spoke, to make up for their sons who failed in that capacity, especially Albert Feaviour who made a very short and amusing speech. After it was over Ernest Lanham, Wilfrid and I walked up Pickwick Road and back to help digest our supper; it was a splendid moonlight night.

29th A fine day ... Went down to Mr Alfred Cole's and brought up an old clarinet, but couldn't get much sound out of it.

20th A dull day ... Harry was collecting the music to take to New Zealand and putting it in his box a great part of the day. I bought four 'Bath Heralds' with the account of the supper in it and sent one to Miss Simmonds, Miss Burgess, Joe Ward and Frank Wheeler.

OCTOBER

1st (Sunday) A stormy day. Went to church ... I walked up the avenue with Katie Rowell and had a good look at Blanche Pelham; she was dressed very nicely ...

2nd A stormy day ... Went over to Melksham in the trap in the afternoon with Ernest; called for Jessie Light and took her too; passed the schoolgirls twice, once before I got to Prospect and then after I had Jessie with me; the second time I had a look at Blanche Pelham and we exchanged smiles as Miss Stone was on in front ... Uncle William came by the 8 o'clock train and slept with Harry.

4th A fine day. Harry went to Mrs Kenway's to wish them goodbye ... In the afternoon ... I contrived to go to Mr F's with some biscuits and intended to go from there out to Claremont to keep an appointment I had made with Blanche Pelham to see her out there, but as I met her with the other girls in Pound Pill I came back ... After supper had two rubbers of whist with Uncle William and Dad and Ma; I and Dad won one rubber and Ma and Uncle the other.

6th Albert Feaviour and Jim Balch came in to wish us goodbye. There were a good many people down at the station to see them off. A dull day.

8th A dull day ... Harry's last day (Sunday) at church ... he and Lewin played a duet on the organ going in in the evening.

10th A dull day ... Went up to Mr Drew's in the afternoon and paid all our subscriptions for the choral society. Bought our music too, and in the evening we practised it with Lewin.

11th A wet miserable day ... Went my round of orders in the morning. First choral class night in the evening. Mr Bell conducted and Lewin played the piano ... It seemed awfully funny without Harry.

17th (Tuesday) A dull day but no rain ... Lewin drove to Trowbridge after dinner as he was engaged to play at a concert there, and Ernest Lanham and I went with him; we walked about the town while the rehearsal was on, and then all went to Mr Daniels' to tea, and had fun with the parrot, and Florrie Daniels played one or two pieces on her violin, Lewin accompanying her on the piano. She played very well indeed considering she had only been learning about six months; Willie Millington is teaching her. I enjoyed the concert very much ... We passed the Ladies' College out at the Harp & Crown going, but Blanche Pelham was not amongst them ...

21st A dull damp day ... Poor Stephen Fry died about two o'clock in the afternoon.

24th A very wet and rough morning. The water came into some houses in Church Street, and down at the station it was nearly up to the platform. I went down to see it. The water was falling in about a dozen streams over the aqueduct and looked very pretty. A train came in while I was there; Mrs Amoore went to London by that train and wished me goodbye; Jenny and Alan are going soon. They are going to live at Ealing ... Our first entertainment in the evening ... the girls were there and we had a pretty full room. It was a splendid moonlight night and after the entertainment was over ... we set up a fire balloon, but it burnt very soon. Clare played the triangle in the first piece. Jessie Light gave me a birthday card.

25th A beautiful day. Wilfrid and I went to bed by turns so as to be awake to see the comet, and at about four o'clock we both went down to Ernest Lanham's and woke him up and walked out together as far as Claremont, but it was too cloudy to see the comet ... In the evening we were all invited to go into Mr Linton's to see the testimonial and purse presented to Harry; there was a good company there; we had refreshments and then music. Harry, Lewin, Ernest Lanham and I played several pieces and we all sang several of our old glees. Miss Olding and Miss Pym also sang songs. Mr Linton in presenting the testimonial made a very good speech, to which Harry responded as well as his very bad cold would allow him. After we came home Harry read to us all a splendid letter to him from Aunt Clara at Nottingham, which made most of us more or less dewy.

26th A fine day ... Harry's two boxes were nailed down and the address painted on them and sent off by train to London. Harry had a farewell bachelor party in the evening. The guests were Mr Osborne, Mr John Burraston, Mr William and Alfred Cole, Mr Lane, Mr Brinkworth, Ernest Lanham, Mr William Bromley. Mr Lane brought two violins and I played on one of them. We had a good supper, music, cards, and after supper we handed round cigars. We didn't break up till 1.30.

27th A wet day ... Harry went about wishing friends goodbye, and went with Clara out to Claremont in the afternoon and wished Miss Stone goodbye; he asked Miss Stone and four girls – Blanche Pelham, Lizzie Gilbert, Florrie Cotton and Ada Simpson – to put their names in his text-book, which they did. Harry played at church in the evening ... Had a last tune or two on Harry's fiddle. Some of us put together and gave Harry 15s for his purse.

28th (Saturday) A damp showery morning. Harry departed from Corsham for the last time. Lewin, Wilfrid, Clara, Ernest, Clare and I went to see him off by the 10.43 train. John Burraston, William Bromley and Mr Abbot were there. He kept up very well, but of course must have felt it after living all his lifetime in Corhsam. I didn't like to think that it was the last time I should see him for years ...

30th A wet day. Locked up some of Harry's things that he had left. In the evening went down to Ernest Lanham's; he had a fire in his bedroom and we went up there and had it comfortable; about 9 o'clock Wilfrid came and we had coffee and cake; came away about 10.30.

NOVEMBER

1st A very rough wet day ... Dad went up to London in the morning and stayed to see Harry off, and Mr Alfred Cole went with him. In the evening went to the choral class; Clara played the piano, but before she could do so the piano had to be forced, as Lewin hadn't given her the key ...

3rd A very wet windy day ... Went down to the 5.45 to meet Dad and Lewin. They arrived safely. Lewin brought my watch chain from Mr Laurie's and a splendid chain it was too, and also my music stand ... We suppose Harry fairly launched for New Zealand and think he is having a rough time of it.

5th A very windy day ... Alice's birthday; gave her a shilling. Went to church morning and evening and wore my grand chain.

6th A fine morning but a very wet afternoon and evening. We received a letter from Harry to say that he had been in his berth 30 hours! owing to the rough weather, and that he liked the clergyman, his companion, very much. Went down to Bath to get a York ham for the Court; had a tooth stopped at Mr Winkworth's and had my hair cut; looked in on Edwin for a few minutes.

7th A fine but rather dull day ... Took my locket to Rogers' to have Blanche Pelham's photo put in. Shooting party at the Court; Colonel Methuen at home.

8th A fine day but cold ... Went to practice at the Methuen Arms in the evening. Didn't enjoy it a great deal; seemed to miss Harry more every time; have no faith in Mr Bell's management. Very busy in the drapery shop with 'Dorcas'.

9th Splendid weather but very cold air. Lewin came into our room about 5.30 and woke us to see the comet; it was much plainer that I had seen it yet; everyone in the house, Alice included, saw it ... Went to Bible Class in the evening and enjoyed it ... Still busy in the drapery with Dorcas.

11th A very fine day ... Did a good deal of copying music in the shop all this week.

14th A very cold east wind blowing today ... In the evening ... we all sang glees in the kitchen together. Dad very bad with an attack of bronchitis. Heard from the papers that the 'Chimboroza' had reached Naples yesterday morning.

15th (Wednesday) A splendid morning but turned off dull in the afternoon and rain in the evening ... Went to class in the evening; it gets worse and worse every time; the basses were very rough.

21st A fine day but dull ... Our second entertainment came off in the evening. Mr Newnham's song I enjoyed very much; it was encored and he sang 'Polly' in reply. Mr Linton's reading was very good. Mr Drew's song was a regular mess. Arthur Hulls has a good voice, but I don't like his style; some persons at the bottom of the room were rude enough to hiss him. Our two pieces went off pretty well, but I was rather nervous at taking my part alone as I had been accustomed to have Harry for company. Dad not much better.

22nd A very windy day. Dad buried Mr George Taylor; he went to Chippenham by train and from there to Littleton Drew in the hearse and then had to wait on the hearse an hour; it didn't do his cold any good. Went to practice in the evening; enjoyed it better than any previous one this session.

28th A fine day ... Had a letter from Harry by the middle-day post in shorthand addressed to Lewin; he read it out at dinner-time; it was very interesting. Wrote to him in shorthand ready to enclose with the others ... Ernest Lanham, Wilfrid, Clara and I had violin quartets in the drawing-room.

29th A fine day ... Went out to Velley in the evening to an entertainment. Called for Jessie Light and took her with me. I enjoyed it very much. Miss Clutterbuck's violin solo was very good, and also the quartet for men's voices; it all went off very well. Ernest Lanham and Wilfrid came too. Went to Mr Freeth's for some supper and then home.

30th A fine day ... Went to Mr Hulls' invitation concert in the evening at the British School, given by the young ladies and the boys; it opened with the Overture to Zampa by Blanche Pelham and Lizzie Gilbert, Miss Bradbury and Ada Simpson. Then a song by Blanche Pelham entitled 'After' which I enjoyed immensely; I was agreeably surprised in her voice ... Lizzie Gilbert played a pianoforte solo, 'Voices', which showed capital execution; Ada Simpson sang 'Message'; she has a very good voice but spoilt the song by getting too sharp. She was encored and sang it all again. All the girls gave two part-songs and the boys sang 'Jack Frost'. There were two plays, or parts of plays; a scene from Colman's comedy 'The Poor Gentleman' and four scenes from 'Julius Caesar' which went off pretty well with the aid of some prompting. The school room was crowded. Took Jessie Light home with Ernest Lanham afterwards.

DECEMBER

3rd (Sunday) A dull damp day. The Archbishop of Canterbury died in the morning and the communion table was put in mourning; Lewin played the Dead March from 'Saul' coming out.

6th A fine cold day ... Saw the transit of Venus about 2.30 capitally by means of a piece of coloured glass.

9th A fine day ... Finished 'Vanity Fair'. Went up to the Institute after shop and borrowed the Christmas numbers of the Graphic and Illustrated London News till Monday. Ma's birthday; we all subscribed and gave her a white wool shawl which she liked very much.

12th (Tuesday) A cold day; hard frost again; rime on the trees looked very pretty. Had a very good slide down the gardens, but hadn't much time to enjoy it ... Went to the entertainment for the 'Institute' in the evening and played a duet with Ernest Lanham, and the 'Lovers' Waltz' with Lewin and Ernest Lanham. It was a terribly poor room; neither Mr Hulls' boys nor girls were there. It was about 50 I think; but we enjoyed it nevertheless. Had two letters from Harry by midday post and read them at dinner time; capital letters they were. They stayed so long at Aden that he had time to write two while he was there. There was some skating down on the Pond today ... but it wasn't exactly safe ... when anyone fell down they made a hole in the ice.

18th A dull day ... Mrs Taylor's concert at Chippenham in the evening ... There was a capital room and the concert went off fairly, but Mr Lane, Ernest and I didn't get on very well as we had had no rehearsal or seen the music ...

19th A dull day ... Trowbridge concert in the evening. Lewin went over in the afternoon ... Miss Olding and her sister, Emily, Minnie Moody, Clara, Wilfrid and I went in Mr Griffin's covered conveyance ... The concert was quite a success and the large hall was packed, about 800 altogether. The platform was capitally arranged; everyone's name marked on his (or her) chair and plenty of elbow room.

20th A dull foggy day ... Went to class after shop; the singing seemed very mediocre after Trowbridge.

22nd A fine day but rather dull ... 'Iolanthe' came by post ... Had it through in the evening with Clara; first impressions very favourable. Framed one of the new almanacks and put it up in our bedroom.

23rd A fine day ... Very busy day especially towards night. We had the Chinese lanterns lighted in the window in the evening. A turkey came from Sarah.

24th A fine day ... Wrote to Blanche Pelham and sent her a pair of kid gloves; received a pretty card from her in the morning. Went up to Grandma's to tea and read her Harry's letters. The choir sang some carols after the sermon in the evening.

25th Christmas Day. A very dull day; drizzling rain. Went to early service ... the Colonel was there and a good many besides. Afterwards tuned five reeds ... Enjoyed my dinner very much – turkey and plum pudding. Ernest Lanham came up in the afternoon and we had music and Nap and Proverbs; he stayed to tea and we had some singing, and whist, and finished up the evening with some choruses from 'Messiah'.

27th A very damp windy day ... Carol entertainment at the British School in the evening. The room was nicely decorated by Mr Abbot a few days ago for the boys' treat and breaking-up, so it came in nicely for us. There were as many there as could be expected on such a night ... Our 'Pastoral Symphony' went off pretty well. Sarah came back from her visit to Bath; she went to see 'Iolanthe' on Tuesday with her brother Willie and sister Blanche.

28th (Thursday) A dull day but not much rain ... There was a 'Christmas Tree' treat at Pickwick School in the afternoon and Ernest and Clare went to it ... Went to the meeting at the chapel in the evening and played my violin in four choruses: 'And the glory', 'Glory to God', 'Lift up your heads' and 'Hallelujah', and Mr Davies the lecturer made a reference to me, saying that he used to play the violin; the choruses went very well and there was a vote of thanks to the choir at the close. Wilfrid and Clare sang and Lewin played the harmonium. Had a letter from Blanche Pelham in the morning thanking me for the pair of gloves that I sent her; but from something in her manner of writing I concluded we had been found out, and was very much annoyed to think how unpleasant it must have been for her, and all through me.

29th A damp day ... Wrote a letter to Blanche Pelham enclosing it in Clara's. Duets with Clara in the evening.

NOTES FOR 1882

January 15th The coach road: branch to the lodge near the cross-roads near Lacock road.
29th Jessie Light, at Prospect, another cousin on the Goold side.
February 14th Daisy Goold: first mention of the half-cousin he was to marry. The Valentine is still extant.
24th Ernest Lanham was staying in Bristol.

March 11th T. K. Pelham: Blanche's father, an artist. See June 23rd.

12th Text books: autograph albums.

April 1st Harry Goold: half-cousin, and brother of Sarah. He later married Jessie Light.

5th Broadstone: An unusually large paving stone on the footpath over a culvert. A Corsham saying ran that the Devil turned it over at midnight.

May 1st Mrs Hulbert: neighbour, connected with Spackman family by marriage.

June 16th Wilfrid stayed at home because of his father's illness.

20th 'Lavatory' Herbert would have used a hip bath in his bedroom at home, where there was no bathroom.

22nd Bradlaugh: Liberal M.P.

July 24th Beccles Wood, near Biddestone.

August 3rd Gertrude Light (Jessie Light's sister) kept house for John Freeth (Goold relative by marriage) at Prospect.

11th Mr West: carpenter.

September 7th Organ lesson.

October 24th Birthday: his eighteenth.

25th and November 9th. 'The Comet'. Known as 'The Great Comet', this was the third and most brilliant to be discovered that year. It was clearly visible in daylight to the naked eye. Its orbit is so large that it may return in 1000, 10,000 or 100,000 years!

October 25 Aunt Clara: Daisy Goold's mother.

November 3rd Watch-chain: Uncle Laurie was a jeweller.

8th Dorcas: clothing club.

29th Velley, i.e. Claremont.

December 6th Transit of Venus: not a common event. The next is due in June 2004.

During this year Herbert acquires ten violin pupils. The family is increased by the temporary adoption of the three small Kenways after the death of their mother Sarah, Herbert's half-sister.

JANUARY

1st (Monday) Not a very nice day for the first in the year. Had some violin practice in the morning. Dad, Lewin and I helped to pack Harry's box up and valued all the articles to insure them against risk. Lewin, Clara and I went up to the Court at nine o'clock to the Servants' Ball. There were a good many Corsham trades-people there. Mrs Dickson and her two daughters and son were present and also a lady friend staying with them and most of her servants. Lord Methuen led off with Mrs Ladd in Sir Roger de Coverley, and I joined in it and got on pretty well for the first time. The two Miss Sanfords, Mr Prior Goldney and the Colonel also took part in it. Clara danced a polka with the Colonel. I made a fair start with the polka, but that was all I could manage except the round dances; I enjoyed those last very much. Cook's band from Bath were engaged and played very well. The gentry went to bed about 2 o'clock, but the others kept it up till after five, and then the rain detained us some time. I enjoyed my first ball very much, considering the little I knew about dancing. I couldn't get to sleep when I got home, through excitement I suppose. Before leaving Lord Methuen wished us all a happy new year.

2nd A bright day but very showery. Didn't get up till 9.30 and went without any breakfast ... Measured and weighed myself; height 5ft 5in. and weight 126 pounds.

3rd A much finer day. Had some piano practice in the morning. Went my usual round of orders. Went to Choral class in the evening and enjoyed it very much, though not in a musical sense. Saw an old photograph of Harry and Charlie Osborne with their violins and John Burraston with his flute up at Mr Abbott's; I had never seen it before. They were all taken very well. Blanche Goold came to see Sarah in the morning; she looked very pretty. Harry's box was soldered down and his name painted on it. Miss Blandford died.

5th A stormy day ... Ernest and Clare went to Bath with Fred Cole and Frank Ryall and messed about together.

7th (Sunday) ... Clara had a letter from Blanche Pelham with a note enclosed for me; was not altogether pleased with its contents.

9th A dull day and very cold; slight fall of snow in the evening ... Went up to Miss West's after shop to learn a little dancing. Wilfrid, Emily and Clara came too ... We had Sir Roger de Coverley, the polka, Schottische, Galop, Varsovienne, Swiss dancing and laughing and conversation, enjoying ourselves immensely; came home about ten o'clock.

10th A dull damp day ... at the Methuen Arms in the evening and enjoyed it very much, chiefly through Mr Drew in his witty and sarcastic remarks about Mr Bell.

11th (Thursday) A dull damp day ... Eva Neate came to tea and after shop we had some music beginning with Iolanthe and Patience and ending with some choruses from the Messiah; Eva sang 'Secret Sorrow' and I played the violin accompaniment. She also sang 'Rejoice Greatly' and 'On the Banks of Allan Water' and 'At the Ferry'. Uncle and Aunt Rowell were here and Aunt Lyd came down too.

16th A fine day ... In the evening went up to Jessie Light's and went with her out to

Corsham Court

93

Corsham Parish Church

the Chapel Knapp entertainment ... Mr Linton got me a chair by the side of Jessie. Miss Clutterbuck didn't get on so well with the violin solo as she did last time; she didn't tune her violin properly. The school children's pieces were very amusing, especially the smaller fry who broke down in their encore and were smartly disposed of by Mr Linton amid the laughter of the audience. Had some supper at Mr Freeth's and then home, 11p.m.

18th A dull day ... Went to Bible class in the evening at Mr Pickett's and enjoyed it very much ... Ernest Lanham went over to Chippenham for his exmination for the bank in London.

22nd A fine day but not much sunshine ... Went up to Miss West's in the evening with Wilfrid and we had some dancing; we improved in the quadrilles, but I had nearly forgotten the Schottische and the Polka; soon got into it again though. Two nieces of Miss West were up there.

24th Went to the concert in the evening at the British School; it went off fairly and there was a crammed room in spite of the wet and windy weather. The platform was very wretched; I couldn't find a place to rest my 'obbligato' bit for Eva Neate's song, and at last had to engage Mr Brinkworth to hold it up for me. Mr Hulls was hissed by Childs' fellows when he had finished his song, owing to the county court case I suppose.

25th A beautiful morning but very dull in the afternoon and rain in the evening ... Ernest and Clare went to Mrs Moore's to tea at the invitation of Fred and Stanley Porter. Ernest Lanham brought us the welcome news that he had passed his examination for the bank.

28th A splendid morning. Wilfrid and I got up at 6.30 thinking it was 7.30 and intending to go to communion service, but as it was so early we went for a walk down to Mr James Pictor's house and took Jack with us; got back about 9 o'clock with a good appetite for breakfast ... Went for a walk down the park in the afternoon with Ernest Lanham and Wilfrid and saw the island in the pond with most of the trees cut down; it looked so funny. Went up to Grandma's to tea and after talking a bit read her a story from Chambers's Journal.

29th A very wet and windy morning ... Miss Stone came here in the evening and had a long talk with Dad and Ma in the parlour about her dismissal by Mr Hulls ... Went up to Grandma's to take Lewin some presents as it was his birthday. Annie Chapman was talking to Grandma ... I took her home across the fields.

30th (Tuesday) A short storm of snow after breakfast, but it soon cleared off. Miss Clutterbuck came in in the afternoon and asked me to go out with my violin on Monday. Miss Stone was in again in the evening; she had been out to Claremont to pick up her things ... Went down to Ernest Lanham's in the evening for some music and a little supper; he came up with me and we had some more music.

31st A cold day but no rain for a wonder. In the evening Ernest Lanham, Lewin and I went up to the Methuen Arms to have a practice with Dr Nealand for the concert; we had the overture to 'Cloches de Corneville' through twice, and 'Don Giovanni'; then Miss Olding sang 'Braga's Serenade' and I played the violin obbligato; I was very much pleased with it ...

FEBRUARY

5th A beautiful day ... Went out to Miss Clutterbuck's at 11 o'clock for the first time. Got on pretty well, though she knew more of the second position than I did. I took out Berthold Tours's book and we played several exercises from that. One of her sisters was in the room all the time, and when I was going asked me my terms; I told her 30s a quarter ... We heard from Harry mid-day – he sent us a very interesting log book with the names of all the passengers and his notes on some of them.

6th (Evening) Practised for the Reading ... It was our most successful entertainment; a capital room full and a very good programme. Miss Addie Sainsbury sang very much out of tune, but not very loud so it was not very noticeable ...

7th A beautiful day. Mr Hulls paid me for instructing Brooks with a cheque; (my first cheque). Amount 'one pound four shillings'.

12th A very rough windy day and a good deal of rain ... Went out to Miss Clutterbuck's in the morning; Mr Fowler's coachman lifted me as far as the gate of Mr Clutterbuck's park. Had our practice in the dining-room this time, and got on very well ... There was a Church of England Temperance Society Tea Meeting at the British School Room in the evening; I went down with Ma but it was so crammed and so hot that I didn't like to go in ... A good many couldn't get seats for the tea. The Colonel took the chair and I heard his opening speech from the door.

13th A fine day ... After shop went up to Miss West's and had some dancing; Wilfrid came too, and Mrs Dunne came over and Polly West and Jane Smith joined in.

14th A very windy wet day. Had a valentine sent me with 2d to pay (Corsham postmark), but didn't take it in ... Clara had a valentine from Stanley Hudson.

15th Played marbles in the shop in leisure moments with Ernest Lanham and Ernest and Clare.

16th (Friday) ... After practice went up to Mr Freeth's for Sarah; Ernest Lanham preceded me and we had an animated discussion on the Church of England Temperance Society meeting on Monday night and other topics, Ernest being very eloquent.

18th A fine day ... In the afternoon went out to Pockeridge with Sarah and Ernest Lanham and talked to Gertie and Jessie Light at the door for some time ... Lewin went to Hartham church and was not particularly edified.

20th A dull damp day ... Went to a lecture (with magic lantern) at the British Schoolroom in the evening and enjoyed it very well; the lecture was on Ireland in connexion with the Irish Church Missions. Ernest Lanham came in afterwards and we had a very amusing conversation, Ernest being 'wound up'.

MARCH

1st A fine day ... Sarah went away by the last train (to Bath). Jessie Light, Minnie, Emily, Clara and I went down to see her off; I got her ticket for her.

4th (Sunday) A beautiful day ... Went for a walk with Wilfrid in the afternoon along the Chippenham road and round to Biddestone and then home. Dad, Aunt Wild, Ma and Emily went for a drive in the trap through Neston Park to

Box and Rudloe Firs and home. Got Lewin to write for some music for Ernest Lanham and Clara for their respective birthdays.

6th A fine day but a very cold wind ... Day of the Devizes concert. Started in Mr Griffin's brake at 2 o'clock so as to be in time for the rehearsal; it was a very cold drive. After rehearsal I had some tea at the Bear with the rest and then strolled about Devizes with myself; then soon after 7 o'clock made my way to the orchestra and took my place. The hall soon filled and looked very nice. They took £120; about 1300 present. 'The Creation' went off fairly except the last chorus which was nearly a break-down, but we 'righted' and finished very well ... The drive there and back was the great drawback to our enjoyment, being so cold. My hat blew off once going and once coming back.

7th Fine but very cold ... Our fair day; no cattle at all and only a few horses, but plenty of shows etc ... Class in the evening; the poorest attendance we ever had; 3 basses, 2 tenors, no altos and 7 trebles; however we struggled through.

8th A cold windy day and two short snow storms ... Cricket meeting at the Methuen Arms ... After a great deal of pressing – there being no other – Dad consented to Lewin and I being joint secretaries.

9th Fine but cold ... Gave Paul Pym his first lesson (violin). We received a bulky letter from Harry in the afternoon.

12th A fine day ... Went to Dr Newnham's (missionary) meeting in the evening and was dressed as an Arab with a long pipe, to illustrate some of the Eastern costumes; Fred Bryant, Fred Cole, little Bromley and another little fellow were also dressed up.

14th (Wednesday) A fine day ... Called at Mr John Burraston's to see a cello; he offered it to me for nothing, bow as well, and I was therefore highly delighted. After practice I went up for it and brought it home with me, after thanking Mr Burraston profusely. A good deal of repairing to do to it before it will be playable.

15th ... Lewin and I drove over to Melksham in the evening for a practice for the concert. I enjoyed it immensely. Lewin conducted. After the practice we went to Mr Ainsworth's and had some supper; Miss Burgess was over there and sang a song, and Mrs Ainsworth and Lewin played a piano duet. I went to fetch the horse and we started back about 11 o'clock; nice moonlight night.

17th ... Ma made me a baize bag for my cello.

19th Took my cello down to Bristol by the 2.22 train; Mr Jones said he would do it up for me, and the bow too, for 6s 6d; he showed me over his shop ... very nice old man ... After tea (at the James's) called for Ernest Lanham and went to see 'Elijah' at the Colston Hall; enjoyed it immensely ... It wasn't over till 11 o'clock. Saw Harry's girl while going to see 'Elijah'.

20th A dismal day. Got up at about 6.45 and had a bath in Mr James's lavatory, and after a good breakfast with Gilbert and wishing Mr and Mrs and Alice James goodbye at their bedroom doors we started for Montpelier Station in nice time for the train and I got home at 20 to ten; went round for orders at once.

23rd (Good Friday) A beautiful day but a very cold wind. Got up before 8 o'clock and went for a walk out to Monks with Wilfrid, Ernest and Clare and came back with a good appetite for breakfast (hot cross buns) ... After dinner went up to Jessie Light's and asked her to come for a walk with us; I brought her back with me and we (Miss Wightman, Emily, Clara, Wilfrid, Jessie and I) went up to Rudloe Firs and had a view of the country; I went part of the way home with Jessie ...

26th (Ernest Monday) A stormy day, snow etc. ... Decided to go down to Bristol and stay the night with Ernest and bring back my cello in the morning ... After tea we went to the theatre (old) to see 'Not Guilty' and 'Ali Baba' and enjoyed it very much. There was an enormous crowd ... Slept with Ernest for the first time in my life.

APRIL

3rd (Tuesday) A beautiful day ... Mechanics' Institute Soirée at the British School. Our first instrumental piece went very well, but in the second my E string broke and I had to stop; had to tune in the middle of the piece too. The two vocal quartets by Mr Brinkworth, Eva Neate, Lewin and Clara I enjoyed very much. I made a very good tea down there ...

5th (Thursday) A very nice day. Ernest and I walked to Corsham (from Melksham) after breakfast in an hour and ten minutes. Drove over to Melksham at 4.30 in Allway's wagonette: Eva Neate, Minnie Moody, Clara, Clare, Ernest Lanham and I. (I had asked Jessie Light to go with my ticket but she couldn't, so Ernest and Clare cast lots, and it fell to Clare.) We had a very good rehearsal and the concert went off capitally. There was a very fair attendance. I liked Miss Taylor's voice very much. There were a great many encores ... Nice drive home.

7th A fine day ... Letters from Harry to Lewin, Clara, Dad, Emily Cole, Cousin Mary (Eastbury) and Aunt Clara (Nottingham). Harry wanted to know if I was ready to go out and accept an engagement as violin *primo* at the Theatre Royal, Napier!

17th A rather dull day ... Cousin Bessie and Mrs Booth her sister came here with two children each in the afternoon and had tea; the children amused themselves with violins and cello; they all went back to Wootton Bassett by the 7 train after Lewin had taken them to the church and played the organ. In the evening ... helped with the 'Corsham Orchestral Society'! Ernest Lanham came too; I played the cello in one piece.

18th A very windy morning and a nice drop of rain in the afternoon and evening to lay the dust. Mr Sainsbury brought a parcel for us from Harry: views of Napier, newspapers and books. Finished 'The Miser's Daughter' lent me by Minnie ... Went down to the 7 train to meet Aunt Lena who was coming home after her long stay with Sarah at Portskewitt.

19th A beautiful day. Cello practice and violin too ... Ernest had our stilts lengthened to fit ... I had to get on our big door to get on them.

20th A beautiful day ... Went round the town asking tradespeople to close their shops at four o'clock Wednesdays, and all consented except Henry Balch, and

Mr Child said he wouldn't close earlier than five. Ernest Lanham prepared a preliminary notice for the windows.

MAY

7th (Monday) ... Letters from Harry; doing very well out there; earned £21 in the first six weeks ... Tried a hot air bath on going to bed; not very successful though.

10th A fall of snow early in the morning and very cold all day. Dad a little better.

14th (Whit Monday) ... Cleaned my cello with soda water; I did it in the printing room while Ernest Lanham was printing ... Went out to Miss Clutterbuck's for the 12th time ... we tried through the piece they were going to play at the concert two or three times ... Polished my cello after dinner, then went down to Ernest Lanham and took some music; we had some piano and violin duets and then I came back and went to the tea-meeting at the Baptist Chapel; I enjoyed it very much; didn't stop to the meeting but came home and went up to the Independent Chapel with Ernest Lanham to hear the 'Corsham Amateur Orchestral Society'. It was rather better than I thought ... Went down to Ernest's; Gertie and Jessie Light were down there. Afterwards went to the chapel [Baptist] and heard Mr Lee and Mr Hurlstone speak.

15th A beautiful day ... We pulled down the blinds and put up the door shutters about 3.30 and then we went off to the Bazaar. I enjoyed the band very much ... Saw a great many people I knew, amongst them being Mr and Mrs Pitman. The Scotch pipers were very nice to look at but I didn't care for their row ...

17th A splendid day ... Lewin and Ernest Lanham were very busy preparing for the Town Hall concert all the morning ... Mr Hulls paid me a cheque for 30s (for violin teaching). Mr Millington came about 5.30 and we had a band practice at the Town Hall. He had 'Tancredi' much faster than I thought we should have it. Lord Methuen made a short speech on opening the Town Hall and so did Colonel Methuen; Mr Linton also spoke, thanking Lord Methuen and the Colonel for their share in the work ... The glees and band pieces went very well. I didn't care much for any others except a cello solo by Mr Dundas. The trio by Colonel Methuen, Mrs Cotton and Mr Dundas was a regular failure; they began three times and then it didn't go very well; I didn't care for the music of it either. The Colonel's solo was better, but he didn't come up to my expectations.

20th (Sunday) A fine day ... Had Colonel Methuen's trio through with Ernest Lanham and Clara in the afternoon; it wasn't so very difficult ... Ernest and Clare went to Mrs James Cole's to tea.

21st A fine day ... Went out to Miss Clutterbuck's for the 13th time. We were alone this time and she was much more chatty than when two or three of her sisters are with us ... Dressed the butter-house window.

23rd A beautiful day. Practised violin in my bedroom in the morning as the drawing-room and parlour were undergoing spring-cleaning ... After 4 o'clock Ernest Lanham, Wilfrid, Ernest, Clare and I drove to Lacock in our trap to bathe. We had a capital bathe; I enjoyed it immensely; and we went to the Coffee Tavern and had tea … Annual meeting of the Mechanics' Institute in the evening.

27th A fine day … Went up to the chapel with Alice and stayed to morning service and sat with Dad … Wilfrid and I went up to Grandma's to tea … Tried to get some sound out of Lewin's clarinet and managed nearly an octave.

30th (Wednesday) A beautiful day … Wilfrid, Ernest, Clare, Ernest Lanham and I went down to Lacock again in the trap; the water was a little colder but very enjoyable, and we had a good tea at the Coffee Tavern. Got home about 7.30. Cousins Clara and Mary came by the eight o'clock train and we had some violin quartets in the drawing-room.

31st A fine day … Cousins Clara and Mary went to Box with Fred in the trap in the afternoon; Clara went with them. Had some more music in the evening with Ernest Lanham and Cousin Clara; the Colonel's trio, one of Dancla's duets, the Russian March, Overture to Tancredi, Incidental Music and Graceful Dance with Lewin.

JUNE

1st (Friday) A beautiful day. Cello and piano duets with Cousin Clara after breakfast. Went down to the Town Hall with Cousins Mary and Clara in the afternoon and then went on to Mr Mayo's garden and Mr Moody showed us round. We went on to the Court and had a view of the pictures, and then I got Mrs Ladd's permission to go along the private walk to the Dry Arch. It was a lovely walk, the Park was at its best. I had never been before. We got home just in time for tea. Went to church practice in the evening; Cousins M. and C. went to evening service and stayed to the practice afterwards. We had some Iolanthe and Patience after supper.

3rd A beautiful day. Cousins Clara and Mary went to church both times and sat in our seat. In the afternoon we (that is, Cousins Clara and Mary, Lewin, Minnie, Ernest Lanham, Wilfrid, Clara and I) went down to Weavern for a walk. We went through the woods. After church in the evening Cousins Clara and Mary, Ernest Lanham, Wilfrid and I went up to Prospect Place for a walk, and after supper we had some of the Mendelssohn vocal quartets.

4th A beautiful day … Brought two ferns from Mr Moody's for Cousins Clara and Mary. Went down to the 4.32 train to see them off; Lewin and Minnie came and Clara too.

7th A fine day … The annual choral Festival was held at St Paul's, Chippenham, in the afternoon. Our choir started about one o'clock in Mr Griffin's brake. Lewin, Ernest Lanham, Mr Tucker and I had a practice in the school room there for our instrumental pieces; Mr Clark allowed me to play the Amati he had in his possession. He was rather cheeky to Ernest about his bowing; one would think Ernest was a paid member of his band to hear him talk. The service went off as well as could be expected and the concert ditto; we played the Incidental Music to 'Henry VIII' …

10th (Sunday) Ernest brought us the sad news of Sarah's death while we were lying in bed in the morning. Mr Kenway had telegraphed. She died about 7 o'clock in the morning. Dad and Ma drove down to Bathampton to catch the 2 o'clock train for Bristol. Very heavy thunderstorm about tea-time ... Had some violin duets with Wilfrid.

11th A fine day ... Dad came back from Portskewitt in the morning, and Ma with the three children by the 4 o'clock train... Maitie, Katie and Ethel seemed quite happy, not realising their great loss.

12th A fine day. Went round for my orders today as Sarah was to be buried Wednesday. The coffin came by the 4.30 and Martin and three other men went with the bier to fetch it; Dad and Lewin went too ... Mr Kenway came by the 7 train and slept in the spare room. He brought the engraved plate for the coffin and a splendid wreath.

13th A beautiful day. We closed shop about 11 o'clock and got ready for the funeral which was at 12. Before we started we all sang a hymn round the coffin; Lewin played the harmonium and at the last verse I believe he was the only one singing. Mr Kenway and Dad walked first, Lewin and Mr Alfred Cole next, Wilfrid and I and then Ernest and Clare. There were splendid wreaths sent by different people. There was no pall; the coffin was simply put on the bier with the wreaths on top. Seventeen sat down to dinner afterwards. In the afternoon did some scrap pasting, and after tea went up and watched the Box cricket match. Corsham won again ...

20th A wet day ... Made three wooden tables for Maitie, Ethel and Katie.

21st Ethel's birthday (6 years old). The Sunday Schools had their annual treat in the afternoon, preceded by a flower service at church; most of the children brought flowers – they were for the hospital. The Chippenham Drum and Fife Band came over and headed the procession through the town; they looked very nice with their new flags and banners and flowers. At 7.30 the church choir and the teachers had tea at Mr Linton's; there was music on the lawn afterwards. Miss Olding sang two songs, Frank Sainsbury one; we had two glees and Lewin and I played 'Iolanthe'. Ernest Lanham walked in while we were playing; he passed 2nd out of 29 and is going back on Saturday. Very short notice, but he couldn't help it. Walked down home with him afterwards. Ethel, Maitie and Katie had a bazaar up in the nursery.

22nd A fine day but rather dull. Ernest Lanham came up to tea and we enjoyed ourselves with the three children, Maitie, Katie and Ethel; they sang together and Clara played the piano ... I gave Ernest three pieces of music as a present on his leaving Corsham.

24th (Sunday) A fine day ... Went out for a walk with Maitie, Katie and Ethel in the afternoon; Wilfrid came too. The children were rather quarrelsome and they spoilt the pleasure of the walk ... Tore up a lot of old letters etc.

25th (Monday) A beautiful day ... Set up a balloon for the benefit of the three children; one of them burnt but the other went capitally and we went down the park and found it again. Ethel was afraid and wouldn't see it.

JULY

9th A fine day ... Lewin, Wilfrid, Ernest, Clare and I drove to Lacock after tea to bathe; we tried these swimming collars that Lewin brought home from London and they answered very well.

11th A stormy morning but broke off fine in the afternoon and evening ... Martin went for the Pickwick Road orders and I for the Hastings Road, to get it done soon as it was to be the School Treat in the afternoon. Wilfrid, Ernest, Clare and I walked out about 4.30; first played cricket and then had tea, afterwards football, then swings, French tag, Jolly Miller, and a large party of us went down in the quarry; we had stove lamps and it was very jolly. Walked home with a large party, Miss Addie Aust and Miss Churchill.

12th ... Harry Amoore landed in England on Tuesday morning, was brought home and lingered till this afternoon when he died; all the family were with him. He was a mere skeleton.

13th A stormy day ... Poor little Bertie Cole died in the afternoon from the effects of his accident on Friday (cut hand).

16th Mrs Pym complimented me on her son's progress with the violin; she said he did me great credit.

18th A fine day ... Wilfrid, Ernest, Clare and I went to Lacock to bathe after shop in Mr Merrett's pony trap; we came back Gastard way and had some tea and bread and butter at the Gastard Coffee Tavern ... Good Templars' Meeting; Mr Joseph Malins was there. I enjoyed his speech immensely. A great deal of the Yankee style about him.

25th A beautiful day ... Our club played the school ... we all went to Mr Hulls' to dinner and a capital good spread it was too ...

28th A fine day. Cricket match with Lacock ... In the evening Amy Coxall and her brother Percy came to Corsham. Percy slept with me and Wilfrid slept with Lewin.

29th (Sunday) A fine day ... Percy and I talked a lot in bed, and then I got him to have a sponge bath. Before breakfast Percy, Wilfrid and I went up to the chapel with some flowers for Sarah's grave and then on to Grandma's with some fish for her breakfast. Music (vocal quartets, Mendelssohn) in the evening.

31st A fine day ... Percy, Wilfrid and I went down to Bath by the 12 train and came back by the 7. We saw the Abbey, then had a good hour's row on the river ... we had nearly two hours in the baths and Percy enjoyed himself to the utmost. We had a very good tea at Westley's. Amy and Clara went to Velley to a tea fight.

AUGUST

1st (Wednesday) A fine day. Percy, Wilfrid, Ernest, Clare and I went to Lacock after 4 o'clock; the water was rather cold and we didn't stay long. We went on to Melksham and had tea at the Coffee Tavern ... on to Burgess's and bought some cake for home. Got home about 8.30 and I went to the British School Room where Mr Newnham was holding a temperance meeting, and listened to Archdeacon Crawther, a black man, talking for a bit ... About 9 o'clock Percy, Amy, Wilfrid, Clara, Ernest and I went for a walk together up to Rudloe Firs and enjoyed it very much.

2nd A fine day. Percy, Amy, Clara, Ernest and I went to the quarries in the morning; we went in at the tunnel and came out at Number 7. We took some cakes with us and had lunch down in the quarry and got home in time for dinner. After shop Percy, Wilfrid, Lewin and I went down to Mrs Alfred Cole's to supper; Amy, Clara and Minnie went to tea. I took my violin and played one or two pieces, and we had songs from Minnie and Amy, and after supper some of 'Patience' and 'Iolanthe'.

3rd A fine day. In the afternoon Percy, Amy, Clara, Jessie Light and Mrs Wall, and also Katie Moody and Maitie, went to the Court to see the pictures with me. We walked in the park as well.

5th (Sunday) ... In the afternoon I took Alice up to Grandma's with Amy and the three children ... then Amy and I went to the church and Lewin played some pieces on the organ; he went soon afterwards and I blew for Amy; then we had a stroll in the park.

6th (Bank Holiday) A wet morning, but broke off before breakfast and remained tolerably fine till about 9, when it came on to rain again. Our Grand Amalgamated Fête was held in Mrs Thomson's field. The three societies paraded the town to church, with the Cirencester and Swindon Bands, and after service went round Pickwick. Amy, Minnie, Aunt Lyd, Mrs Cole and I went together to hear the speeches after dinner; the Colonel made a very good one. We made a very good tea and then I went home to fetch Alice in the chair and the three children, and took them about the field; Dad took them home about 8 o'clock. I went with the rest to the Christy Minstrel affair, but it wasn't very first-class and we came out before it was over ... The fête was fairly successful I think.

8th A very wet day ... Our intended drive to Bradford or Castle Combe was of course postponed. I had a note from Ernest Lanham in the morning, brought up by their servant, to say that he had come home as he was too ill for work, and asked me to lend him a fiddle. I went down there to tea after four o'clock and found him very weak; we had a capital evening of music. Miss Wall is a very good player.

12th (Sunday) A fine day. Percy went back home by the 2.35 train ... Miss Wall and Ernest Lanham came to tea and we had plenty of music ... We had some choruses from the Messiah, and after supper Miss Wall and I had 'The Holy City' right through. Lewin and Minnie picked up a hedgehog in the park and brought it in the kitchen.

13th (Monday) A beautiful day, the hottest we have had I think. Had a talk about bicycling with Dad at the dinner table; I asked him if he had any objection to my buying one, and he advised me not to buy one, and then ensued a long argument for and against, which ended in my giving up the idea for the present.

14th A fine day with a very rough wind, blowing up the dust unmercifully ... Started on Martin's round of orders soon after twelve with Fred to tell me the houses and got back about 4.30 (Martin was on holiday). Took £7 odd ...

16th A fine day but terribly windy, blowing up the dust in one's eyes. I went up the Lane for orders in the afternoon. In the evening Wilfrid and I ... went over to Chippenham in the trap to see 'Iolanthe'; I bought two sides of bacon at Edmunds' and he offered to put up our horse in his stable, so I gladly accepted.

We enjoyed the entertainment very much; the room was very full. We had a nice moonlight drive home.

21st ... There was a practice in the drawing-room for the 'Vicarage Gathering' in the evening. When it was over Emily, Wilfrid and I went down to Mrs Cole's to supper and then went for a moonlight stroll down Pound Pill and up Station Hill.

22nd The 'Parish Gathering' came off in the afternoon ... Went there about 4.30 and made a very good tea and soon after the concert began. The Pickwick Handbell Ringers gave one or two performances. There were about 150 there. Our 'Tancredi' went very well and so did 'Pirates'. Ernest Lanham and I drove Mr Baker home.

23rd A beautiful day. In the afternoon Amy, Aunt Lyd and I drove to Box with the goods and we came back Neston way, which made a very nice drive ... Gave Jessie Light her fourth lesson in the evening; Miss Wall was up there and we had a nice chat afterwards and some supper. Wilfrid called in while we were at supper; he came up with Amy and Emily and they went on to Claremont, but Wilfrid got very comfortable in Mr Freeth's armchair so stopped, and they (Amy and Emily) after waiting outside some time went home; so you may be sure we got it sharp when we arrived home.

25th A lovely day. Ma went to Chepstow ... Harry's letters arrived and Amy and I read them together. Mrs Alfred Cole came up in the evening to help in the shop.

26th A fine day. (Sunday) ... Had some bowling on the lawn after dinner. In the afternoon Amy and I and Wilfrid went out in the park and laid down under a tree for some time, and then home to tea. Amy went off to London by the 7.20 train; I stayed away from church and went down with her and also Emily and Aunt Lyd ... Had some music with Miss Wall at Mrs Lanham's.

29th A fine day. Wilfrid, Ernest, Clare and I drove over to Chippenham Flower Show in the afternoon. We went first to see Dr Jay's performance with his children, which was very good, and after a little refreshment went to the field. The Coldstream Guards soon struck up 'Zampa' and I listened attentively ... Came out of the field about 8.30 and went to the Market Place to see the fireworks. Lewin and Minnie came home with us in the trap, so Israel fancied himself with six in the trap.

SEPTEMBER

3rd (Monday) We were all up by six o'clock ready for our trip to Bournemouth. It was very stormy but after we got there we didn't have a drop of rain all day. We all had our lunch at the public house opposite the station, and then went to the harbour and engaged a sailing boat. There was hardly room for us all, so Wilfrid and I and three more were towed behind in a boat; it was very rough and I enjoyed it immensely. The men had to carry us pick-a-back on shore and it was amusing to see one of them stagger under Mr Hatherley. We walked all along the sea coast to Bournemouth, and about four o'clock had a good tea in the refreshment house. After tea we all went on the Pier and Wilfrid and I played cross-touch with the boys, and afterwards we all had an easy stroll round Bournemouth to the station. It was a long ride home but we passed the time pleasantly away with singing rounds and short naps etc. We reached Bath at 11.40 and Lewin, Wilfrid and I had a cup of coffee at the refreshment bar; Mr Griffin put us down at Mr Linton's at 1.30 so we had a jolly long day. We made an awful row down Pickwick Road and the town, ending up with three cheers for the Colonel and Mr Linton.

5th A fine day. After 4 o'clock Wilfrid, Ernest, Clare and I went up to the cricket field and had a game of cricket until nearly 7 o'clock. After some tea I went down to Mrs Lanham's and had a last hour or two of music with Miss Wall as she was going home in the morning.

12th A fine day ... I took Maitie back to school at Bath by the 2.22 train. We had a nice walk up to the school and then I came back into Bath and had my photograph taken. Had a tepid swimming bathe, and Fred and Stanley Porter came with me as they had already got tickets to go ...

16th (Sunday) My 'proof' came in the morning; I was not altogether pleased with it but still it was better than I expected. A beautiful day. Wilfrid and I took Grandma out for a ride in Alice's chair in the afternoon down Lacock Road; Aunt Lyd and Emily with Katie and Ethel came too.

18th A beautiful day ... Mrs Franks came here in the morning with her two sons Fred and Frank; they stayed to dinner and tea, then Mrs Franks took Frank to Mr Hulls'. They brought us a nice pair of fowls and eggs ... Young Thomas at the Bank fell off his bicycle at the Chequers and broke his arm ... Went up to Miss West's and had a nice evening of music; Clara came afterwards and had some duets with Miss Simmonds.

19th A rather dull day ... About 3 o'clock Emily, Clara, Wilfrid and I started for Bradford in the trap and got there just in time for tea. We tried to get a boat to have a row, but the only one available was three quarters full of water and holes in it, so we gave it up and went for a walk instead; afterwards had some music, supper and home.

26th ... I put the cello in order for Wilfrid and the viola for Ernest.

27th A stormy morning ... Drove Mrs and Miss Simmonds and Frank West to Neston Park in the afternoon. After tea they came down here and we had a capital musical evening. I played Hummel's trio and Haydn's trio with Miss Simmonds, then she played duets with Clara; afterwards we had choruses from 'Messiah', and 'Patience' right through.

29th ... Wrote letters to Harry Goold, Sarah Goold and Ernest Lanham and sent photos in them. Gave Mrs Alfred Cole a photo, and Miss Simmonds.

OCTOBER

1st (Monday) ... Town Hall concert. We had a very full room, much fuller than at the opening. People couldn't get in even for standing room. Mr Brinkworth read a very amusing piece and also a song; Miss Pym's song was encored and also Eva Neate's. My piece would have been very well but for my wretched strings getting flat owing to the hot room. Wilfrid and I had our tea at the Coffee Tavern together; they did a very flourishing trade.

2nd A fine morning but rain in the afternoon ... Lewin, Minnie, Clara and I drove over to Melksham in Merrett's trap to help at the temperance entertainment. We had tickets sent us for the tea in the school room and regaled ourselves there on arrival. We had a very good meeting; I was actually encored twice and responded both times. The first time I have ever been encored. Clara was loudly applauded for her song, and she played two pianoforte duets with Lewin ... Went along to Burgess's and had a bun; saw Mrs Burgess – heard Miss Burgess was engaged.

3rd A very wet day ... Had a letter from Percy Coxall; he told me that Blanche Pelham was asked in church.

4th ... Wet and windy ... Finished Cobbett's 'Advice to Young Men'.

5th A fine morning, wet in the afternoon ... Went to the confirmation service at 12 o'clock and blew for Lewin; Ernest and Clare were confirmed and a great many others. The Bishop gave a very good address. Dad's breathing very bad.

6th A fine day ... Went over to play some trios with Miss Olding ... She told me that Miss Greaves (a lady staying with Mr Newnham) said I ought to go to Leipzig and study the violin under a master; (she saw me play at the Town Hall).

9th ... Went up to Jessie Light's for shorthand after tea ... Came back with Mr Freeth to the Liberal Meeting at the Methuen Arms; Mr Fuller explained the Agricultural Holdings Act. Very well attended and a good meeting.

10th A foggy morning but turned out beautiful for the rest of the day ... Went down to Mr Alfred Cole's sale about 2 o'clock; Mr Alexander was auctioneer, a very witty fellow. Dad bought a sponge bath for Ernest and Clare for 9s ... Went to the first Choral Practice at the Town Hall at 7.30; it went off very well and Lewin made a very good opening speech. Joe Ward came down and listened with Dad. Mr and Mrs Cole slept here. After supper we had 'Iolanthe' through in the drawing-room, then I played some Gavottes with Clara.

21st A fine day ... Dad, Ma, Uncle William, Clara and all of us were at church in the evening, it being Mr and Mrs Cole's last attendance at church, and Mr Linton preached a sort of special sermon which I managed to scribble down somehow.

22nd (Monday) A beautiful day ... Mr and Mrs Cole looked in to wish us goodbye in the morning; Lewin, Wilfrid, Clara, Emily, Uncle William and I went down to see them off. Wrote out Mr Linton's sermon of the night before. Went down to the Town Hall with Uncle William before dinner and showed him round.

23rd A wet morning, fine the rest of the day. Went down to the station with Uncle William to see him off by the 7.30 train; he gave me a bob for going with him ... Got Mr Linton to correct my transcription of his sermon. Went to the Town Hall at 3.30 and tried through the 'Serenata' with Miss Olding; Lewin played the piano. Mechanics' Institute Entertainment in the evening; I played two Gavottes with Lewin. Wilfrid and Clara did very well with their duet. The room was only about half full.

24th My 19th birthday. Had a jolly letter from Miss Simmonds. Wilfrid, Clara, Ernest and Clare gave me a phonetic dictionary – I was delighted with it ... Sent my first contribution to the 'Bristol Mercury'.

25th ... Went to Bible Class at the Town Hall. Arthur Hulbert pitched 'Son of My Soul' too high and then started it lower after we had sung two verses. Wrote a letter to Sarah Goold in the evening with an enclosure for Daisy.

27th Mr and Mrs Alfred Cole's sailing day.

29th Dad sent Mr Webb (of Calne) a cheque for £3.4s 0d for my new violin and the book I had of him.

NOVEMBER

5th (Monday) A beautiful morning but very wet in the evening. Dressed the grocery window. Went over to Miss Olding's and had some music with her and her sister; afterwards went over to Miss Sainsbury's to learn chess; Mr Mark played against Miss Sainsbury and I, and after a game of $2\frac{1}{2}$ hours' duration we won. Wilfrid came soon after I did and watched our game. We had refreshments – tea and cake etc. Jessie Light was here to tea ... Alice's birthday (24). Gunpowder night, but perhaps chiefly owing to the wet night, very little was done towards commemorating it.

7th A fine morning but turned off rather foggy towards dinner time. Clara, Wilfrid and I prepared for our little trip to Portskewitt. We went by the 10 train; Caleb Davis and Fred Wheeler went down in the same carriage ... It was rather foggy going over the river and we couldn't see much. Mr Kenway was at the station to meet us and we went to his office. He took us over the works in the afternoon, and then we went to the school room where the concert was to be held. Most of the performers were rehearsing and we were introduced; they had a splendid 'grand' there and Madame Brett was playing on it – a very good player. They were rehearsing till nearly 8 o'clock; Wilfrid and I were beginning to feel hungry, having tasted nothing since 12.30 ... Then we went to Mrs Tiddy's (where Clara was staying) for supper and some music ... Wilfrid and I went to the 'Black Rock' Hotel to sleep.

8th (Thursday) Early in the morning we went to Mr Kenway's lodgings to breakfast and woke Clara up ... About 10 o'clock Wilfrid and I went to the station and took tickets for Chepstow, and on arriving there walked to Tintern; but owing to the stupid directions of a woman, we went up over the hills instead of keeping to the turnpike road, and wallowed through farmyards, ploughed fields etc. but managed to get to Tintern at last. We had some dinner at the 'Beaufort Arms' and afterwards had an inspection of Tintern Abbey. We walked back to Chepstow by the turnpike road, and the views of different coloured trees made it quite a pleasant walk despite the dirty roads. We had a hasty walk round Chepstow Castle and got the train to Portskewitt just in time. We had a jolly tea at Mr Kenway's lodgings and then brushed up a bit for the concert. We had some difficulty in finding our way to the concert room, and when we did arrive we were in a fine state – dirty shoes, splashed trousers and wet coats and hats and in a chronic state of perspiration; however it didn't prevent us enjoying the concert very much ... Clara accompanied Madame Brett (or Brent).

9th Got up early and went to Mr Kenway's lodgings for my violin and music; he told me he wished Clara to stay and go back with him the next day ... We got on top of the steamer and had a capital view all round. I enjoyed my violin in the train on the way to Bristol ... Got home about 11 o'clock and related our adventures to them all ... Made out a catalogue of all my music.

12th A fine day ... Went down to Mr Mayo's and took down a letter for him in shorthand and then transcribed it ... Lewin, Minnie Moody, Clara, Eva Neate, Wilfrid, Clare and I went to Lacock in the afternoon to help at the concert ... The long programme went off very satisfactorily. Mr Brinkworth's reading was very amusing again, and his duet with Eva Neate from Mendelssohn's 'Lobgesang' was lovely; also 'The Angel' by Eva Neate and Clara. I sang in 'I love a lass', which was encored ... Got home about 11.45.

13th A fine day ... Our entertainment (in the Town Hall) was quite a success; the room was full ... our instrumental pieces seemed to take pretty well. After it was over Mr Kelly, Mr Brinkworth and Mr Burbank (Chippenham reporter) came here to supper and we had some music; Mr Kelly sang ... Mr Brinkworth read 'Old Mother Hubbard' and we had some glees.

14th A hard frost again ... Finished my job for Mr Mayo; he gave me 4s for it. Went over to Melksham by the 4.30 train to band practice ... went to Burgess's and had buns, gooseberry tarts etc; Miss Burgess sang one or two songs ... Walked home; met Wilfrid just past Shaw. It was a lovely moonlight night.

17th A very wet morning but fine later ... 'The Violin and How to Master It' came in the morning and I was glad to find it a good tutor, better than Tours. My contribution to the 'Bath Herald' re the entertainment was inserted. Miss Perrin engaged me for lessons and agreed to buy Barnes's violin. Fanny Olding also engaged me for lessons. On reckoning up found I had 10 pupils (4 ladies).

18th (Sunday) A fine morning but dull in the afternoon ... At evening service we had a sermon by a Mr Phipps, of very high church narrow views to judge from his sermon, as he said that for a young man, on being married, to go to chapel because his wife did was actually sin ...

19th A fine morning but wet in the evening ... There was a practice in the drawing room at 7.30 for the cricket concert. Afterwards went to Miss Sainsbury's with Wilfrid to play chess, and stayed till 12 o'clock; Mr Linton, Mr Mark and his friend Mr Ffoulkes were present.

22nd Heard the Colonel was to be married to one of the Miss Sanfords.

25th A wet stormy day ... My Kreutzer studies came, also 'Invitation to the Waltz' by Weber ... Finished 'Sybil' by Lord Beaconsfield ... Missionary sermons and collections at both services. Minnie Moody away at Melksham all day and Lewin roaming about like a fish out of water.

27th A fine day ... Bertie Wild came over from Chippenham for the concert ... I was miserably unlucky right through the concert; first of all I couldn't find my obbligato to Eva Neate's song, but after she had begun I found it ... In the 'Waltz' (Weber) my strings were terribly flat and the E string squeaked fright-fully. I substituted a wire, but couldn't get it in order for Miss Olding's song and so didn't play. 'Iolanthe' went very well ...

28th A fine day. Drove over to Melksham with Miss Burgess about 4.30 in the trap.

Had tea and some music with Rosie ... Afterwards went to the Free Hall with Harry Ainsworth to see the drawings. There were several by the Miss Clutterbucks, Miss Fowlers (etc), some of them very good. After that went to the band practice and found them much improved, a good deal better in tune. Looked in at Burgess's and had a cake or two, and then home which I reached at 11.45. Thoroughly enjoyed myself.

DECEMBER

2nd (Sunday) ... Decided to try two meals a day, leaving out dinner.

7th A fine day. Had a capital walk to Rudloe with Paul Pym. Had a letter from Ernest Lanham, a good long one. Experimented with making rosin, and it turned out very well for the first trial.

9th (Sunday) A fine day but dull ... Ma had a lot of presents. 49th birthday. Wilfrid and I went for a jolly walk in the afternoon, down Collett's Bottom, up to Rudloe and home ...

10th A damp stormy day ...In the evening went to the entertainment at Corsham-side ... It was a success and the room crowded. I liked the first dramatic piece entitled 'A Fair Encounter' by the two Miss Clutterbucks. Our trio scraped through somehow, and the 'Serenata' went very well. The second dramatic piece was very good but not so good as the first ... I came home in the cart which came over for the piano.

11th (Tuesday) A windy day ... Town Hall concert. There was a stage fitted up for 'The Merchant of Venice' and the balustrade taken down. The entertainment went off very well; Arthur Hulls made a very good Shylock, and young Pym played his solo much better than I expected; Lewin, Clara and I played some music behind the scenes between the acts. The room was well filled. Had a little refreshment in the Coffee Tavern afterwards.

13th Dropped my violin out of the trap on the way to the concert, unnoticed by me. Luckily Jessie Light picked it up at Prospect, and I recovered it. Borrowed one from Mr Lane.

17th A fine day but very cold ... Harry's letters came in the morning; one (each) for Dad, Lewin, Alice, Wilfrid, Clara, Ernest, Clare and myself, and we each read each other's at breakfast time; they were very interesting and amusing, es-pecially Alice's. Dressed the butter-house window for Christmas.

20th A dull day ... Katie and Ethel went to Bath to their aunt's to spend Christmas; Clara went with them. Went up to Jessie Light's in the evening and gave her a shorthand lesson; also talked to Mr Freeth on the Allotments Act ...

23rd (Sunday) A fine day. Helped Lewin tune the organ ... Went up to Grandma's with Amy (Coxall) after supper as she wanted to wish them goodbye. Sang some carols in the drawing-room afterwards.

24th A damp dismal day ... Amy, having wished everyone goodbye, proceeded to the station followed by a small cavalcade; she went off in very good spirits. Wilfrid, Ernest, Clare and I went down to Bath by the next train ... I had a tooth stopped and then we all had a jolly good tepid bathe, only one fellow in besides us all the time. Afterwards walked about Bath and looked at the shop windows, some of them very brilliant ... Mr Lanham put a note from Ernest into my hand at the station; on opening it found that Ernest was coming by the 5.45 ... The concert was a success; all the carols went fairly and there was a full room. Ernest Lanham came in afterwards and we had a long talk. Uncle and Aunt Laurie went to the concert.

25th Christmas Day ... Morning service with the anthem went very well. Wrote an account of the carol concert for the Bath Herald and Bristol Mercury. Ernest Lanham came to tea and we had some duets; Clara played the piano. Minnie and Katie Moody came up after tea and we had a jolly game of 'Forfeits' in the drawing-room; afterwards us four boys and Ernest Lanham played Nap till 1.30. A wretched damp foggy day.

26th A second edition of yesterday with the weather ... Ernest Lanham came up in the afternoon and we played Nap in the parlour ... Went back with him and had a good talk with him and Mrs Lanham, then Ernest and I went up to Grandma's and had a game or two. Lewin and I went to Dr Kemm's to play dance music at 8.30 and we were there till 3 o'clock; never had such a spell of fiddling before; I enjoyed it though. There were about 50 guests.

27th ... After shop in the evening I was initiated into the mysteries of a 'secret society' in the parlour and soon found it out. Miss West came down to teach us a little dancing and we tried her, but it was a long time before she could make any sense of it. Then had some dancing in the kitchen.

28th (Friday) Servants' Ball at the Court in the evening. Wilfrid, Clara and I, with Miss West, went up in Banks's about 8.30. Lord and Lady Methuen, the Colonel, Miss Sanford, the two Miss Sanfords, Mrs, Miss and young Dickson, Johnnie Fuller, Prior Goldney, Mr Linton, Mrs Kemm, the two young Pyms and others constituted the 'gentry', and they retired about 1.30. The Colonel danced with his intended; the two Pyms took it in turns to dance with Clara. I danced in about 16 dances with about 20 different partners, and took part in everything except the waltzes, lancers and Varsoviennes. Miss Campbell of Hartham I danced with once or twice and had a nice talk with her; she reminded me of Lizzie Gilbert. We stayed till about 5 o'clock. The band was very fair; violin, cornet and harp.

31st A dull day ... Jessie Light came up in the evening and played whist; Wilfrid, Ernest, Clare and I played nap after shop ... then we indulged in some dancing in the kitchen till the old year had 'kicked the bucket'. Clara taught me the Varsovienne. Wilfrid and I went home with Jessie Light and I took the 'bull's-eye' as it was very dark. All decided not to lay supper in the New Year; a great improvement. (Priest-craft.)

NOTES FOR 1883

May 30th Clara and Mary: two of the Eastbury family. Their holiday was well filled.

June 10th Sarah Kenway, his half-sister. Some trains from Corsham must have branched off the main line at Bathampton. Hence the family often take trains only partway to or from Bath.

August 29th Israel: the horse, so called because he transported them to practices of 'Israel in Egypt'.

September 3rd Trip to Bournemouth: a choir outing.

18th Mrs Franks: of the Butler family, cousins at Bromham.

October 10th Mr Alfred Cole's sale: Alfred and Emily Cole had decided to emigrate to New Zealand; but see May 16th, 1887.

29th He had sold his old violin for £2 – what he had paid for it.

The entries are becoming fuller, perhaps because he was reporting for local papers as well as taking shorthand notes for individuals. Daisy Goold appears in the distance!

JANUARY

1st (Tuesday) A cold north-east wind... The Sunday Schools had a treat at the Town Hall in the afternoon: tea and magic lantern entertainment, at the expense of Miss Bella Dickson. Lewin and I played with the choir boys in one or two carols. A present was given to each child and also to the mothers.

2nd A very foggy damp day. All in our house went up to the chapel to tea instead of having it at home; our own people filled the chapel except two. Very sad accident in the field opposite Mr Luchford's: Mary, the oldest Court servant, found drowned in the pond in his field; supposed, it being a dark night, she lost her way and fell in. Heard that Mr and Mrs Shewring were going through the field and heard some noises, but thought it was sheep. No doubt it was the poor girl crying out, but not distinct enough to excite suspicion.

3rd Damp and milder. Went to see the pond that Mary Elms was drowned in in the morning. Never knew there was such a pond there. Jenny Amoore came to tea; after shop we had dancing in the kitchen and then I went to the 'Oak' with her.

5th A dull day and a good deal of rain. Mary Elms was buried in the afternoon; Lord Methuen followed her to the grave with a young man staying at the Court. All the servants followed. There were a great many people present. A fox was sighted in the park just before the funeral; I saw it scamper off in the direction of the pond, the first time I had seen a fox wild.

6th (Sunday) A rough wind and some sunshine ... Went for a walk with Wilfrid and Clare in the afternoon to the pond where Mary fell in. Mr Linton made a reference to the drowning in his sermon; I took it down and copied it out for those to read at home.

8th A wet morning but cleared towards evening ... Had a letter from Ernest Lanham describing the first night of Gilbert and Sullivan's 'Princess Ida' ...

9th Mr Baker and Miss Neale were married at the Independent Chapel in the morning; Dad put down some carpet for them. I looked in and saw the latter part of the ceremony.

10th A fine day. Clara went to Bradford to stay with the Beavans for a few days ... Went up to Hartham in the evening on the fire engine, to have a look at the Fancy Dress Ball. Watched the guests out of their carriages first, and then when they had put up the window, watched the dancing and saw all their costumes. The band was capital and I could easily hear it from outside. Had some supper and some coffee; went through the rooms and saw the decorations etc. before the guests arrived. The supper was splendid. Came home in Mr Bromley's trap about 4 o'clock.

13th (Sunday) A fine day. Us four went to early service and I collected; went to morning and evening service. Went up to Jessie Light's in the afternoon and gave her a shorthand lesson and then Wilfrid came up and we walked with Jessie to Pockeridge ... Mr Kemp's (curate) banns asked in church.

17th ... Went to the soirée at the Town Hall in the evening. The room looked very nice, decked with flags, and the floor was nicely prepared ... Eva Neate sang two songs, one of them encored, and Clara and Minnie sang a duet. I danced everything except 2 sets of Lancers, 21 in all; danced with both Miss Lewises.

The dancing was kept up till 4 o'clock. I enjoyed myself thoroughly; it was a success in every way.

21st Dressed the grocery window ... General Tom Thumb was advertised to come here, but failed to turn up in the evening; the coach drawn by 3 goats came down the town mid-day.

24th In the evening we had a dancing class at the Town Hall and got on very well; there were 31 there; Clara, Lewin and I took it in turns to play. Afterwards went in the Coffee Tavern and had some refreshment ...

25th A stormy day; in the afternoon there was a flash of lightning followed by thunder and then snow and rain, a regular mixture ... Dad went to Bath in the afternoon and while he was away, Ma got Mr Cole's men to put a gas bracket behind his kitchen chair, and then we surprised him at tea time.

31st A very wet day ... About 4.30 started for Langley Fitzurse in the trap, to practise with Mr Clark; took Mr Brinkworth up at Chippenham. It was a very unpleasant drive, fearfully muddy. We had dinner with Mr and Mrs Clark and Miss Spencer of Chippenham, who took second violin in the Gavotte for 4 violins. Went to the schoolroom at 8 o'clock to practise the choruses with the choir. Started for home a short time before eleven. Mrs Clark is a very nice lady, not at all uppish.

FEBRUARY

6th (Wednesday) A fine day. Went for orders in the morning. Met Mr Thomas by the 4.30 train; Mr Brinkworth and Mr Freeth came afterwards (for the concert). Mr Freeth had grown a beard and looked very peculiar ... The room was comfortably full, with a quiet, orderly and attentive audience. The cantata went off very satisfactorily and also the miscellaneous part; there were refreshments provided in the interval by the Coffee Tavern.

7th A fine day. Hired Merrett's trap and pony to go to Langley; started soon after four and picked Mr Brinkworth up at Chippenham. We had dinner at Mr Clark's with three clergymen and three ladies in evening dress – tableau!!! The concert went off about as well as I expected; a very full room; a good many from Chippenham.

11th (Monday) A stormy day ... Walked out to Chapel Knapp in the evening to an entertainment; it was awful fun. Some gentleman staying at Mr Clutterbuck's conducted two toy symphonies and it was the greatest fun watching him; he had a stick about as long as a yard measure and brandished it about like a maniac. Talk about fancying himself! He gave a whistling solo.

12th A fine day. Went down to Box in Mr Mayo's carriage with Mr Mayo and Mr Bromley to hear Mr Handel Coysham at the Schools in the evening. Enjoyed Mr Coysham's speech immensely; it was 'Gladstone and the Legislation of the Past 50 Years' ...

13th A fine day. Had a letter from Sarah Goold in the morning and answered it in the afternoon, sending her some snowdrops at the same time. Also sent some to Florrie Simmonds as a Valentine.

14th A splendid day ... Went to the dancing class in the evening; there were 60 present. I played in one or two pieces.

17th (Sunday) A wet day ... Wilfrid, Clara, Ernest, Clare and I went up to Grandma's to tea and sang her some carols, Holy Messiah and Mendelssohn's quartets. Aunt Jane and Emily came up too, so we had a large tea party. Went up to Jessie Light's afterwards and corrected her shorthand exercises.

19th A wet drizzly day ... Lewin had 'Princess Ida' come by post and tried a little of it after breakfast. Went to the Men's Institute Entertainment in the evening; played two trios with Mr and Mrs Clark of Langley and a trio with Lewin and Clara, also played the accompaniment to the 'Children's Home' sung by Mrs Clark (with cello, piano and harmonium as well). Nellie Beavan walked from Bradford and got here about tea time and went to the entertainment. Had some dancing afterwards in the kitchen. Letters from Harry and Mr & Mrs Cole.

20th February 1884

Dear Daisy
Please accept these few snowdrops as a Valentine. I am rather late, but perhaps you won't mind that. I am afraid when they reach you they will be rather faded but I hope not.

We received letters from Harry and Mr & Mrs A. Cole last night. Harry has told us what he did in his Christmas holidays, but he has not written much as he is busy seeing about a new house. Mrs Cole is putting his present house in order. He says he has had no 'woman' in the house since he has been there, and of course without that very necessary appendage his house must be in an awful state.

I have sent you a programme of a little entertainment we gave last night. Please show it to Sally.

I have not received that long-wished-for photo yet, Daisy. Mind you do not forget me. Love to all my cousins both great and small (of course including my valentine) and also to Aunt Clara and Uncle. How I should enjoy a visit to Nottingham.
Yours ever
Herbert

21st A wet day ... Went to the dancing party at Mrs Frank Baines's with Lewin, Emily, Minnie, Aunt Lyd, Clara, Ernest, Clara, Ernest, Clare and Wilfrid. It was very jolly; we stayed till after 3. Several gentlemen from Melksham were there.

22nd Mr Moody lent me Mark Twain's 'A Tramp Abroad' and I devoured some of it in the afternoon ... Nellie Beavan walked home, Emily and Clara going part of the way.

25th Busy today dressing the shop windows. Went to the Soirée in the evening. Clara, Lewin and I played 'Iolanthe' and Eva Neate sang two songs, one of which was encored. There were a good many from Chippenham and Melksham, about 130 altogether. I danced all except the Swiss Dance and I couldn't get a partner for that one. The band was much better than last time. We kept it up till nearly 4 o'clock. It was very convenient having the passage into the Coffee Tavern ... Cousin Fred Orders came here in the morning and was present at the dance; played whist with Dad most of the time.

26th (Shrove Tuesday) A beautiful day ... Ernest Lanham was up in the morning. He was obliged to leave London for his health. Went to the Coffee Tavern with him and Wilfrid in the evening and talked some time. Had a letter from Daisy Goold.

End of February

Dear Daisy

What a pretty bunch of flowers at the commencement of your letter! I am glad the snowdrops reached you in pretty good condition, as Nottingham being a day and a half's post from here I was rather anxious about them.

I really could not give you an answer about coming to Nottingham. Of course I should be only too delighted to come, but I do not know what the decision of the Supreme Court would be. It would have to be in August or about, when Mr Hulls' boys have their holidays, as I have to go up there twice a week to teach violin and shorthand. I must get you to ask Aunt Clara to write to the guv'nor about that time. Not a word about your photo, Daisy. I hope you are not going to disappoint me.

Harry did mention in one of his letters that there was a young lady out there that would just suit me, but that was his view of the matter, you see; besides she may be married a long time before I get out there. [letter unfinished]

27th Aunt Polly Hawkins said goodbye and departed from Corsham, seen off by a host of relatives and friends.

28th A fine day ... Wilfrid, Clara and I went to Mrs John Baines's to a party, rather smaller than Mrs Frank's, but it was very enjoyable ... We had 12 dances and I played Sir Roger for them at the close. Clara sang 'Awake, awake!' and I played the violin obbligato. We came home about 3 o'clock.

29th A frost and a lovely morning ... Cousin Mary and Bessie from Eastbury walked over here from Chippenham and stayed the night. I took them to the Court and Town Hall in the afternoon and we went in the Coffee Tavern ... and played some jolly games of draughts and 'Go-bang'. Afterwards we sang our class glees in the parlour.

MARCH

2nd (Sunday) A beautiful day. Went up with Alice to the chapel in the morning; went to morning and evening service at church. Ernest Lanham sat with me. Went down with him after church and he showed me an account of Pelham's failure in the 'Globe'. Had some music with Clara after dinner; Ernest Lanham came up and we went down to the church with Lewin and Minnie and Lewin played several pieces. Afterwards went up to Jessie Light's with Clara and Ernest Lanham, stopped talking there some time and came back with Ernest to tea; had a look at some of Ernest's actresses and his three-quarter size violin. After church in the evening, Ernest Lanham, Emily, Clara and I had a very interesting talk in the parlour, touching on actresses, doctors and their prescriptions, love and other matters.

3rd A very wet day ... Clara and I went to Mr William Neate's to tea and we had some music ... and several games of cards, amongst them 'Cheating' and a new way of playing 'Old Maid'. In the first one we had some rare fun out of old Mrs Baines. Mrs Frank Baines and the two Miss Holmes were there. Just imagine, at a card table with six ladies.

5th Clara's birthday, 17. Gave her 'The Other Life' in shorthand. Jessie Light and Minnie and Katie Moody were here to tea and also Ernest Lanham. After tea we played Old Maid (new game) and then I went over to Miss Olding and played some trios till class time. Ernest Lanham came to class and sang tenor. After class went in the Coffee Tavern a short time and then back home to cards again. Went up with Jessie Light about 11 o'clock; splendid moonlight night.

6th A fine day. A good many fair vans located in the market place. In the evening went over to Melksham with Mr Mayo's carriage to a political lecture and took notes for practice. Very good lecture; gave the political history of England from the time of William the Conqueror. Afterwards called in at Mr Burgess's ... Heard Rosie was to be married in Easter week, and Albert off on a voyage to Australia in May.

8th (Saturday) A fine day. Gave Ernest Lanham a phonetic dictionary as it was his 21st birthday. He was very pleased with it.

9th A fine day ... Went out for a walk with Ernest Lanham and Wilfrid and we went in to Mr Lanham's to tea. Tried on Ernest's dress coat and waistcoat, hat and masher collar to try the effect; immense!!! After evening church there was a practice at the Baptist Chapel for the 'Holy City' on Monday; Dad gave me the wrong latch key and Clare and I couldn't get in the house, so after trying for about a quarter of an hour, sent Clare up to the chapel and Dad came down and let me in.

11th A fine day ... Had a long and deep game of chess with Ernest Lanham in the shop and finally won. Went to the Liberal Soirée in the evening. Lewin, Clare and I played two pieces, Overture to Tancredi and Caliph of Bagdad, and I played 'Tarantella' by Raff as a solo. I took notes of the speeches. Miss Burgess sang two songs and was much applauded. Miss Alding sang, and a lady staying at Mr Mayo's; Mr Boyle also read an Irish piece very nicely. The refreshments were served very well. Afterwards wrote out part of my report up to one o'clock.

Old Market House, Corsham, with stocks

15th A lovely day. Wrote in Miss Holmes' confession album ... Martin and I
      drowned poor Jack after dinner; Fred took him up to Mr James in the morning
      but he said he was too far gone, so we put him out of his misery and buried him
      by the arbour in the lawn ... Minnie Moody sent me up some stewed apple and
      cream for tea; enjoyed it muchly. 11s 11d –worth from the 'Bath Herald'.

22nd A fine day. Finished my Turkish bath in the evening and tried it before I went to
      bed, and it was very satisfactory. Ernest Lanham had a telegram consigning
      him to the tender mercies of the town of Swansea, first train Monday morning.
      Went down to the Coffee Tavern with him about 8.30 and played a game of
      chess, which he won. Went up to fetch Grandma in the chair in the afternoon;
      brought her home and established her in the nursery.

24th A beautiful day ... In the afternoon went up to Grandma's to help take away
      the furniture with our cart ... Went to Mrs James Cole's to fetch Alice in the
      chair, and stayed and played whist with Mrs Cole, Fred Cole and Wilfrid. We
      played Nap too. Ernest Lanham departed for Swansea.

26th A dull day and cold. Had a letter from Ernest Lanham in the morning and on
      reading it found that Swansea was much worse than he had imagined; he sent a
      sketch of the country which was very amusing.

28th A dull day ... Went to Trowbridge by the 2 train and to the Daniels'. Tried our
      concert pieces through and then to the rehearsal. While there heard that the
      Duke of Albany (Prince Leopold) had dropped down dead. Hills Hall was very
      prettily decorated ... the concert went off very well. Our instrumental piece
      'Guy Mannering' was encored and we did part of it again. My solo passed off
      all right. The Dead March was played by Mr Giddings at the close of the
      concert – and wretchedly played too.

29th (Saturday) In the morning after breakfast had a little music with Florrie and
      Louie Daniels and then went down town and had a shave, shampoo and crop
      at Woodwards; was back just in time for the train. Stopped at Bath and went to
      a concert at the Assembly Rooms in the afternoon to hear Mr Carrodus the
      violinist, and enjoyed it immensely. There was a fine cello player, too, Mr
      Whitehouse, and Miss Shackell, a handsome girl, sang two songs ... Home on
      the 6.35. Found Ernest Lanham at home and went to the Coffee Tavern with
      him and played him a game of chess and beat him.

APRIL

8th   A fine day ... Put my cello in order. Had two games of chess with Clare after
      shop and lost both of them. Went up to inspect Grandma's new house after tea
      and was more than satisfied with it. (South Avenue)

11th (Good Friday) A lovely day ... Went up to the chapel in the afternoon with
      Wilfrid to Phemie Osborne's funeral and helped sing, at the grave. There were a
      great many people present ... Clara, Wilfrid, Ernest and Clare and I sang some
      of the old glees in the parlour after tea.

12th A fine day ... Ernest went to Chippenham in the morning to get some funeral
      cards for Lewin; he couldn't get them at one place and didn't try another,
      coming home without them, so Clare went next and went to another place but

because the printing was not exactly the same he thought that would not do, and likewise came without them; I followed on and brought them back, but when I got home found I only had 25 instead of 50 of them (I clearly asked the man for 50). Of course there was a good deal of joking about the matter.

14th (Easter Monday) A cold stormy day. Dad, Emily, Clara, Wilfrid, Ernest, Clare and I drove to Bromham House in Allway's wagonette; we started about 9.30 and the ride was very enjoyable. We had a little lunch at Bromham House and then walked to the place of the sham fight, but we were too late for the fight – one of the men was wounded and the fight stopped in consequence. Had a good lunch under a hayrick and then walked back to Bromham House where we had a good tea and a little singing. Dad's breathing came on rather bad as we were starting for home – it was none too good today; in spite of all drawbacks however we enjoyed ourselves, especially the drive home; we sang glees a great part of the way. Some eccentric man called here while we were gone and asked Ma for a box to put flowers in; Ma soon got rid of him, and he went to the Court and tried to see the picture galleries, but Mrs Ladd wouldn't admit him – 'he had better look at Mrs Dickson's'. He introduced himself to Mrs Dickson and dined with her and the Miss Dicksons, but they suspected him and sent him off by Mr —— to the station.where he decamped without a ticket, having no money.

15th A dull day. We got Grandma up into her new house in the evening and she was very pleased with it.

17th (Thursday) A cold windy day. Emily, Clara, Minnie and I drove over to Melksham in the morning to see Rosie Burgess married; the chapel was full and the ceremony passed off nicely; Rosie was nervous and her words were scarcely audible. We took some of the inevitable rice with us and distributed it.

20th A fine day ... Clara, Wilfrid, Ernest, Clare and I went up to Grandma's to tea, the first time in the new house, and we sang 'The Silent Land', 'Good Night' and 'Dream baby, dream'.

26th A nice storm of rain in the afternoon ... Dad went to Calne to bury Mrs William Spackman.

28th A dull day and stormy ... Mr Kenway and the three children came in the afternoon, and so did Uncle William. Mr Kenway went up to see Grandma before tea. Ernest Lanham came home from Swansea in the evening and came up to see us; told us he was back at Chippenham for a time. Clara and I went over to Mrs Moore's in the evening and had two or three trios (Haydn) over with Mr Ward. Walked down with Ernest Lanham when I came back.

MAY

4th (Sunday) ... Ernest Lanham looked in in the morning; he walked back to Chippenham about 12 o'clock; I lent him 'Old London' to read. Went for a walk with Wilfrid in the afternoon and passing by Grandma's went up and talked to her and Aunt Sarah (or rather Aunt Sarah talked to us!).

8th A fine day; whitewashers about the house; had meals in the parlour.

11th (Sunday) An exquisite day ... Thomas, Wilfrid and I went to Colerne for a walk in the afternoon; went up to the top of the tower and had splendid views; Thomas played the organ. Heard Vaughan say the Lord's Prayer in an intoning voice which was very amusing ... Ernest Lanham was here in the evening.

13th 'Old May Day'. A fine day again. Uncle John and Lewin went with Mr Moody to Mr Gladstone's house at Bowden Hill in the afternoon in Mr Bromley's pony trap. Uncle John, Aunt Margaret and Aunt Sarah were here to dinner, tea and supper. Went to the Band of Hope Service of Song at the Independent Chapel in the evening and made a short report.

14th A dull morning and afternoon but brighter in the evening. Went up in the cricket field soon after three o'clock and played till six o'clock; Uncle John played, and Wilfrid, Ernest, Clare and several more; afterwards went over to Mrs Moore's and played some trios with Mr Ward and Mrs Porter and had a little supper; Mrs Porter a very fair player. Spring cleaning; drawing-room and parlour in confusion. Very bad news of Aunt Polly from Mrs Coxall; she was taken with delirium after sea-sickness and we suspect that she is dead.

17th (Saturday) A fine day. Went down to Bath to play for Chippenham against Bath Association; made 8 and caught 3 ... There was a circus in the field and some of us went in; it was pretty good, especially the shooting of some man who shot a pipe out of a girl's mouth and a glass ball from her hair from 10 or 12 feet distance. I went to Whatley's where Jessie Light was and had some dinner, and talked to her and she introduced me to a friend.

21st A fine day. Had some violin and piano duets with Clare in the afternoon, and at 4 o'clock went up in the cricket field and played till 6.30; Uncle John played and we picked sides. Ernest Lanham came over from Chippenham on the tricycle with 4 other fellows and two girls and went in the Coffee Tavern; they didn't stay long. Wilfrid and Clara went to Chippenham to have their photos taken.

26th A fine day ... Had a little ride on Fred Cole's tricycle ... Heard that Uncle John had let Uncle Laurie in for a considerable amount.

27th A fine day. Had two games of billiards at the Court in the morning with Mr Joliffe; the first game he gave me 40 and beat me; the next game 50 and then I beat him. Went over to Chippenham in the evening by train and went to the May Fair; heard the Toy Symphony, and Mr Brinkworth gave 'Mrs Watkins' Evening Party'. Talked to the Miss Belchers some time. Ernest Lanham was there. Walked back at 10 o'clock and Wilfrid and Thomas met me half way.

31st Finished 'Guy Fawkes' and got 'Star Chamber' (Ainsworth) at Mr Mayo's ... Uncle Laurie came in the evening; walked from Chippenham.

JUNE

1st (Whitsun Day) A beautiful day. Went down to Bath in Merrett's trap in the morning to meet Jessie Light; it was a nice drive, but I had the misfortune to let the pony down about by Alexandra Terrace coming home and hurt one of its knees.

3rd A fine morning; some rain in the evening ... Took Mrs Porter and Mr Ward and Joe to the Court in the afternoon and we had a good look at the pictures; I went in some rooms that I had never been in before. We shut shop at 5 o'clock and a good many tradesmen did. Jessie and Fred Goold called here in the middle of the day ...

12th A lovely day. The Annual Choir Festival was held in the church in the afternoon; we closed shop at 2 o'clock. There was a hurried rehearsal at 2.15. The service went off very satisfactorily and there was a very large congregation. Ernest Lanham came over from Chippenham. Tea was held in the Riding School and over 500 sat down. At the concert in the Town Hall there was a crowded audience; the programme was rather poor; it was terrible hot work playing. Wrote out reports for the Mercury and Herald afterwards.

15th (Sunday) A fine day ... Thomas, Wilfrid and I went for a long walk in the afternoon; walked through Hartham Park from the Golden Gates. Thomas came in the drawing-room in the evening and played the piano and I the violin in 'Sacred Songs for Little Singers'. The new curate performed for the first time – Mr Chugg.

18th A beautiful day. A deputation attended on Lord Methuen asking him to present a petition to the House of Lords for the Franchise Bill; the petition was in the hands of a reporter who didn't turn up in time, so they had to imagine it ... Wrote to Mrs Cole at Auckland.

20th A beautiful day ... Dad let the field adjoining Ash Villa to Mr Balch for the hay, and as they were haymaking there, Clara, Minnie and Katie Moody, Emily, Clare and Alice went down and had tea amongst the hay; I went down for about an hour before tea ... Finished Mark Twain's 'Prince and Pauper'.

24th Lily James's brother died after a long illness ... Went up in the cricket field after tea. Mr Chugg the new curate was there and he bowled very well, better than he batted. Had our shorthand class from 9 to 10 and afterwards Clara and I played some of 'Princess Ida' and Wilfrid sang.

25th A lovely day. Sunday School treat in the afternoon ... in Mr Clutterbuck's grounds, Monks Park. We had a nice tea on the lawn. I swung a good many children and organised the races; Ernest and Clare went for races. We came home in Griffin's brake about 7.30. There was a Primitive Methodist meeting in the British Schoolroom in the evening and I looked in; wrote accounts of the treat and the meeting for the papers afterwards.

26th A fine day. The banjo came mid-day for Ernest Lanham and I had a look at it and sent it on to Ernest.

JULY

2nd (Wednesday) Another lovely day. We had tea on the lawn and Grandma came down; Minnie and Katie Moody, Aunts Lyd and Anna. Afterwards Wilfrid, Ernest, Clare and myself drove off to Bath to see 'Princess Ida'. We called on Jessie Light and she introduced us to one of her friends, Miss Copeman. Jessie came to the theatre with us and Miss Millwitter, another of her shop-mates, came at 9 o'clock. I went out and brought her in. Wilfrid and I went home with them at 10 o'clock (after the first act) and came back and saw the finish. We enjoyed it very much. It was a beautiful night; we walked all up Box Hill coming back and reached home before one.

3rd A fine day ... Dad had letters from Harry and Ma one from Amy; Harry very busy as usual and spoke about Clara and I going out.

8th A fine day. Mrs Ladd spoke to me about lodgings for her sister who wished to visit her for a few weeks, and I saw Aunt Lyd about it; Mrs Ladd came up and saw the rooms, and finally Aunt Lyd let her the bedroom only, 5s a week. Went down to Ash Villa and picked strawberries after tea with Emily, Clara, Minnie and Katie Moody. Had some 'Princess Ida' again afterwards.

18th (Friday) A fine day ... After tea I went down to Ash Villa and picked some raspberries; caught Mr Coates' eldest son picking gooseberries. Went down to young Pym's and saw their carpenter's house and tools.

19th A beautiful day. Lewin and I went to Bath to play against Lansdowne. I called in at Mr Whatley's, saw Jessie and bought some buns for lunch. Lansdowne won the toss, went in and were in most of the day, making 555; they had a very strong team ... Saw Ernest Lanham in the evening and he gave me one of his photos.

20th A fine day. Ernest, Wilfrid, Clare and I went to the Weavern in the afternoon to bathe. After Church in the evening went down to Ash Villa and picked some fruit, and then Wilfrid and I went up to Mr Freeth's and talked to him and Gertie Light for some time.

21st A fine day. Dad went to London to the Hyde Park demonstration against the rejection of the Franchise by the House of Lords.

23rd Excursion to Weymouth. A stormy day. Lewin, Clara, Wilfrid, Ernest and Clare, Minnie and Katie Moody, Amy Davis, Emily, Nellie Beavan and I kept together most of the day. Ernest Lanham put us in a first-class carriage at Chippenham. Mr Brinkworth came with us and we had a jolly party. When we got to Weymouth we bathed, Lewin, Mr Brinkworth, Wilfrid and I having a machine to ourselves, and afterwards went to Portland in the steamer; it was nice weather going over but coming back pouring rain, but it didn't last very long. We saw the convicts quite close, and had some fun on the pebble beach; got back to a good tea at Weymouth and afterwards 11 of us had a donkey ride together. Nellie Beavan's and mine wouldn't go the first time in spite of all our endeavours, but the second ride was better. I engaged a boat for an hour afterwards and we had a capital row, each of us taking an oar in turn; we saw a race between 4 boats. Saw Mr and Mrs Stantial down there. About 50 went from Corsham. We had a 2nd class coming home and played nap and whist. Got home about eleven after a very jolly day.

31st A fine day. Went for orders up the lane in the morning. Lewin and I took Mr Cole's piano up to the Miss Perrens' and brought back their old one, a very high-standing one. The Walford family (hand-bell ringers) visited Corsham and gave an entertainment in the evening. Us 4 boys went and Clara and Ma, and enjoyed it very much. The eldest Miss Walford is a very nice girl; she came round with her photo and I bought one. Wilfrid, Clara, Aunt Lyd and I went for a little walk afterwards. Lovely moonlight night.

AUGUST

5th A fine day ... Clara went to Bradford on a week's visit to the Beavans, and there was some unpleasantness at the station because a man objected to her entering his carriage; Mr Lanham however was equal to the occasion and gave Clara a second-class carriage.

6th (Wednesday) A fine day; splendid weather. Wilfrid, Ernest, Clare and I read from the Pilgrim's Progress on the gravel before breakfast; it was quite pleasant in the sun. After four o'clock, Wilfrid, Ernest, Clare, Fred Cole, Will Bromley and I went to the Weavern and had a jolly bathe; Thomas came down just as we were dressed and Wilfrid and I waited for him, then we went into Mrs Poulsom's and had some warm milk and bread and butter.

13th A stormy morning but fine the rest of the day. Wilfrid, Emily and I drove over to Bradford in the trap in the afternoon and fetched Clara back. Got there about 4.30 and after tea we sang a few glees, and then went for an hour's walk. After supper we had quadrilles in the kitchen till ten o'clock and then we started for home ... Clare, Ernest, Wilfrid and I went down in the yard in the morning and threw buckets of water over each other instead of our usual bath; it was capital fun.

15th A fine day ... Went down Station Road in the evening where a travelling company with a woman 7ft 6in. high and 'Tom Thumb and his wife' were to be seen, with the usual shooting galleries etc. Had a long talk with Ashley Cooper walking up and down the town.

17th (Sunday) A lovely day ... Wilfrid and I and Ernest and Clare and Thomas went to the Weavern in the afternoon, but we found our usual place frequented by a lot of boys and tried to find another place; we decided on the piece of water by the house, but as soon as we got in we had to shunt, by Mr Poulsom's orders, and went to our old place; the other was too near the house I suppose. Ernest Lanham was here today. Wrote to Sarah Goold.

19th A beautiful day. Packed up our old piano in its case to be sent to Wallingford, and installed the new one it its place. Clara went to tea at Mrs Neate's with Ada Ayliff, May Lily and Maggie Elliott; Ernest and Clare went down after tea and Wilfrid and I after shop; we had some jolly games such as acting verbs, and consequences. Home about 12.

21st A fine day. Uncle and Aunt Rowell, Aunt Lena and Clara drove to Castle Combe in the morning ... We had tea on the lawn ... we took the harmonium down and went through the lancers and quadrilles after tea.

24th A fine day ... After dinner Wilfrid, Clara, Emily and I went down to the station to meet Sarah Goold and Mr Beilby, but they didn't come. Stayed in all the afternoon and read 'Broken Bonds' ... Went down with Emily to the 7 train, to meet Sarah and her sweetheart; they came this time, and of course we had a lot to talk about all the evening; we had some choruses from the Messiah too.

25th A fine day but much cooler. Took Mr Beilby and Sally down to the church in the morning; Clara came too and played the organ. We went in the Town Hall and Coffee Tavern too; after dinner we had some 'Princess Ida'. Clara, Emily and I went to see them off by the 3.45 train. Mr Beilby, though not goodlooking, is a very nice fellow.

SEPTEMBER

1st (Monday) A very wet day. Colonel Methuen's birthday. Mervyn Comber and Monty came in in the evening and we had a liitle 'Princess Ida'. At 9.30 I went up to the Court and fiddled for the servants who were having a sort of jollification; I sat on a stool on top of a table. Mr Otway, the gardener, played a polka while I danced. Some fellows sang some songs. We kept it up till one o'clock. I went down to the station to meet Sarah Goold in the evening and brought her up.

2nd A stormy day. Dad and Ma went to Stonehenge with Mr Neate's party in the wagonette. Sarah helped Wilfrid in the shop. Ernest and Clare played in the juvenile cricket match in the cricket field and Clare made 59 ... Had a talk with Sarah in the kitchen after shop, mostly about Aunt Clara's children.

September 1884 (enclosing a photograph)

Dear Daisy,
I was delighted to receive your little note and fervently hope it will not be the last. But I was very sorry to hear you haven't a photo for me. I should have liked one 'muchly', but I must wait patiently. As for being unwilling that you should have mine, you mistake me altogether. I wonder that you care to have it, but if you ever see the beautiful original himself the photo will appear perfectly insipid. You will no longer care for it, but let me convince you that you are perfectly welcome to it and I shall be looking forward to my share of the 'exchange'. Mind it is a good one, Daisy, Cabinet, life-size if you can.
Sarah has been telling me of a certain young lady who has been amusing herself with letter-snatching. At home? Oh! no. In church, of all places, if you please. Things are getting worse and worse. I must commission the clergymen of your church to deliver a 'special' to young ladies on the modern vice of letter-snatching in places of worship. Perfectly serious I assure you.
Well, goodbye,
   with kind regards
    from
     impudent
     Herbert

3rd A fine day. Choir treat. Started by the 7.20 train from Corsham. The Chapel Knapp choir men came with us and Mr Chugg. Arrived at Gloucester about eleven and went straight to a hotel to luncheon which was relished very much. Went to the Cathedral and had a look round; heard the organist practising (Mr Williams). Grand old place. We went down in the vaults beneath. Just outside the cathedral we saw the place where Bishop Hooper was burnt in the reign of Queen Mary. Started about one o'clock in the steam launch down the canal for

Sharpness Pound ... passed several large ships being towed up the canal. Had a jolly tea at Sharpness; we saw the Severn Bridge. Played nap on the way back – John Burraston, Lewin, Wilfrid and I; I won 6d. Hadn't much time to stop in Gloucester when we got back; the town looked very nice with the shops lighted up. Got to Chippenham about 10.30 and went home in Porter's brakes, kicking up a nice row as we came into the town and cheering the Colonel and Vicar on arriving at the vicarage.

4th Very busy today, chiefly in preparing for my holiday. Mr Osborne wrote an account of the trip and sent it to me; after curtailing it a bit I sent it to the Herald office.

5th (Friday) [Visit to Mr Porter's, Street, Somerset] Was up at 5.30 and got my breakfast, then drove off to Melksham bound for Street, accompanied by Wilfrid and Mr Thomas. It was a splendid morning. I had to wait an hour at Wells and had a look at the exterior of the cathedral, which I like better than Gloucester. Fred and Stanley Porter came to meet me at Glastonbury and we drove in the brougham to Mr Porter's. After dinner Fred, Stan and I went to bathe, and I enjoyed it muchly ... The gardener, who had been to India for several years, gave interesting anecdotes about snakes and other animals he had killed. Had some music in the evening. Dropped a postcard home.

6th A very wet day. Played music and chess in the morning. Mr and Mrs Porter and I drove to Wells in the afternoon and went to the service at the cathedral; it was very good singing; the anthem was capital ...

7th (Sunday) Fine day, very windy. Went to chapel in the morning; very good sermon. Joe, Mr Evans, Fred and I went for a walk in the afternoon to Glastonbury Tor; it was a capital breeze up there and a splendid view ... Had a postcard from Lewin who informed me that he was going to be married in November.

9th A dull wet morning, but broke off to a beautiful afternoon ... Went down to bathe ... saw several fellows fishing there and we saw one catch a large carp, which weighed 6½lbs ... Stanley and I went for a walk up Buckley monument; it was a splendid view up there, even better than the Tor I think. Fred Porter's birthday; I gave him a shilling towards his bicycle. In the evening we bought some crackers and squibs and had a spree in the garden. Stanley made a balloon and it went off splendidly. We had some fun with the mask too.

10th A dull day, misty rain falling all morning. Joe took Fred and me over the factory; it was very interesting. Afterwards Fred and I walked to Pidwell to Mr Porter's and we had bagatelle ... and played tennis which I enjoyed very much; the first game I ever played ...

13th A beautiful day ... Mr and Mrs Porter, Joe, Fred, Stan and I started for Cheddar about one o'clock in the wagonette; it was a lovely drive there. The cave ... was a grand sight; I thought the best was to see the reflection of the stalactites in the water, the reflection being as clear if not clearer than the original. We had a capital tea in the Gardens Hotel; Stanley amused himself with a boat on the pond. After tea all except Mrs Porter walked through the cliffs and climbed them; at the end we had a splendid sight; the sun was just

Flemish Buildings, Corsham

setting and tinged the clouds with the most beautiful shades. We enjoyed the sight for some time and then descended. After an enjoyable and rather noisy drive back of nearly 3 hours, stopping at one of the villages for some peppermint and ginger beer, we reached home, having spent a jolly day.

15th A fine day. Fred, Stan and I went to Burnham and had a good day's outing. Went on the beach first and watched them shipping cattle over to Cardiff; it was cruel work ... Went for an hour's sail and took turns at the oar ... Had a bathe and enjoyed it very much, the only drawback being the absence of any towels; however we made shift with our bathing drawers and handkerchiefs ... Got back about 6.30. Went to Open Lodge in the evening and helped with the string band; it was very laughable.

16th (Tuesday) A fine day. Finished 'First Violin' in bed in the morning. After breakfast I went down to the Bowling Green factory and Joe showed me round; Fred came. It gave me a good idea of how paper is made. Bought a pair of boots at the other factory, hygienic shape. About 3.15 Mr and Mrs Porter, Fred and Stan, Mrs Walker and I drove off to the station at Glastonbury, I homeward bound and Fred and Stan off to school; I had spent a very pleasant holiday ...

17th A fine day ... About 5 started for Lacock in our trap to bathe. The water was pleasant and afterwards we had a capital tea in the Coffee Tavern ... Sarah and Polly Goold came by the 4.30 train and stayed here the night.

18th A fine day. Sarah and Polly Goold went to Chippenham to have their photos taken. They both went to Bath by the 7 train. Polly wished us goodbye as she would not see us again.

19th A beautiful day. Went to church practice in the evening. Clara played through Spohr's 'Christian Prayer' and Handel's 6th Chandos Anthem (our choral class pieces) and also 'Rebecca' (Barnby) ... Ma went to Bath with Maitie and Katie and I went to meet her in the evening; Sarah came up with her. Sarah and I had a talk in the evening and she told me a good deal about Mr Beilby. Wilfrid and I slept in the spare room as our room was delivered over to the whitewashers.

20th A fine day ...Sarah Goold went back in the evening; Emily, Clara and I went down to see her off for the last time.

27th ... Clara went to Bath with Katie Moody and saw Sarah married; it passed off very well.

28th (Sunday) A fine day ... Clara, Ernest, Clare, Wilfrid and I went to Hartham Church in the afternoon; it was Harvest Thanksgiving and the church was crowded and several couldn't get seats. Wilfrid and I went for a walk to Collett's Bottom instead ...

29th (Michaelmas Day) A fine day ... Atworth Harvest Festival; Mr Sainsbury asked Lewin to give a concert over there, so we went in Mr Clarke's and Mr Allway's conveyances at 6.30; Ma, Lewin, Clara, Wilfrid, Ernest, Clare and I, Mr Barnes (Henry), Mr Hulls, Caleb Davis, Miss West and Fanny Alding. While the tea was on some of us went and had a look at the church; it was very nicely decorated with every conceivable variety of fruit and flowers and vegetables. The concert went off very well, 'Three Doughty Men' being vociferously encored. The room was a wretched one for sound as it was a very low ceiling. It was a splendid moonlight night and after a good supper we drove home and were much amused at the swaying of the conveyance; it was like a boat on a rough sea.

30th A fine day. Our first entertainment in the evening; there was a very good attendance. Sarah's wedding cake came, a large quantity for us to distribute.

OCTOBER

1st (Wednesday) A beautiful day. I went down to Bath by the 2.30 train. Went and talked to Jessie Light and the other girls at Whatley's and had my hair cut ... Met Wilfrid, Ernest and Clare at the baths (they came by the 3.45), and after some tea at West's we had a jolly long time of it in the baths; I managed to swim on my back a little.

3rd ... Masons making doorways in our garden wall.

4th A beautiful day. Watched the eclipse (moon) in the evening. Read my diary for 1877; some of it very interesting.

8th A foggy morning. Got a white muffler at the shop and wore it; found it very comfortable ... Edwin Lee came over and brought his present for Lewin's wedding, a very handsome cheese cover, ditto water bottle and three jugs, pretty pattern ... he had a look at the other presents down at Mr Moody's.

9th A very wet morning. Wesleyan chapel harvest festival in the evening; I went up and had a look at the decorations and made notes. Played a solo down at the Town Hall in the evening at Mr Newnham's temperance meeting, and wrote out an account of both meetings in the ante-room after my piece. Had a discussion on theology in the kitchen afterwards, Dad holding (as usual) Bishop Colenso's opinion with regard to the Bible.

10th A stormy cold windy day. All of us busy in changing the bedrooms; Wilfrid, Ernest, Clare and I to sleep in Emily's room, Emily and Alice in Lewin's room, and Lewin in the spare room for the present.

11th A fine day, very cold. Hung my pictures in our new bedroom and rearranged some of the furniture to my satisfaction. Painted Lewin's bath. Ernest Lanham was up in the evening, a regular masher. Mr Kenway came and slept with Lewin in the spare room.

18th A fine day, uneventful; busy in the shop at times. The two Pyms gave Lewin a fretwork flower-stand for his wedding present. I was taken for the bridegroom by Brinkworth, the grave-digger.

24th A fine but dull day. My 20th birthday. Had three letters: one from Joe Ward with a photo of himself; a card (hand-painted) from Daisy Goold, and a letter from Miss Simmonds ... Harry's wedding cake came too; it had been delayed a long time somewhere. Lewin's cake came in the evening from Huntley and Palmer's decorated very nicely ...

25th A fine day. I went to Bath by the 11.50 for the purpose of going to a concert at the Assembly Rooms; ... it was very enjoyable; Bottesini the double bass was really wonderful. The lady violinist, Madame Anna Lang, was very good too.

They played a duet together which I enjoyed more than any other item. Bottesini's solo, 'Carnival of Venice', was very good too ... Ernest Lanham was in Bath, but went to 'Called Back' at the theatre.

27th (Monday) ... Clara and I went to Chippenham in the evening to Willie Taylor's practice; they were very free and easy compared to our singers, rather too much so; a little more seriousness would have been better ...

29th A fine day. Mr Linton invited the choral class to the vicarage in the evening to witness the presentation of a clock to Lewin on his marriage. Nearly all the subscribers were there, and Mr Linton's rooms were taxed to the utmost to find a place for everyone. First there was the presentation and a nice little speech by Lewin (previously got up), and then music of all description; I played one or two solos and we had some glees. There was no lack of refreshment and a jolly evening was spent.

30th A fine morning; Lewin and Minnie's wedding day. Went to the church at 9.30. There were a lot of people at the wedding. It passed off in first-rate order. Mr Moody gave the bride away; Willie Taylor played the organ. I followed Lewin and Minnie to the carriage and closed the door, and they had to pass through a regular shower of rice.The bell ringers had a share in the festivities. Ernest Lanham put them into a first-class carriage at Chippenham, so they had it to themselves. There were 71 presents in all. Sent accounts to the Bristol paper and to the Wiltshire Times for Mr Burbank.

NOVEMBER

2nd (Sunday) A wet day ... Willie Taylor got on very well with the organ at both services. We had a jolly afternoon; Ernest Lanham came up and we all sat round the drawing-room fire and sang glees and 'Rebecca' ... Willie played a dashing piece on the organ coming out in the evening and some people stayed to listen.

3rd A fine day, rather frosty. Went to the station with Willie Taylor after breakfast and saw him off. In the evening Clare and I walked out to Corshamside to see a dramatic entertainment; the schoolroom was crammed, a great many Corsham people being there. The first part of the programme was a one-act drama, 'The Cape Mail', the second part a comedy in 2 acts, 'The Mysteries of Muddlewits'. I enjoyed the second part most. A beautiful moonlight night. Wilfrid came to meet us.

5th ... Our practice at the Town Hall was quite laughable in the evening; there were only 15 altogether, Mrs Lanham the only treble, and no alto, a few tenors and basses and no conductor ... Alice's birthday; gave her a little box with thimble and cotton. Colonel Methuen had an accident while hunting.

8th A fine day ... Went down to meet Lewin and Minnie by the 8 o'clock train; their home was got up in fine style to receive them; we had a lot to talk about when they arrived. After 10 o'clock I set off some fireworks in honour of their arrival

9th A wet day. On coming home after early service we heard that Mr Hurlestone had died in his sleep in the night. His death was very unexpected as he was getting much better after his illness; Dad felt it very much.

21st November 1884

My very best wishes for happy returns of the 'sweet eighteen' birthday.

My dear Daisy,

I couldn't with any approach to the truth put 'little' now, as Sarah tells me you have grown so, that I should appear quite small beside you. Perhaps she exaggerates a little.

How kind of you to paint that beautiful little card and send to me on my birthday. I shall value it a great deal more as done by your own hand than if you – There, I began that sentence supposing you had painted it yourself, but you simply say 'hand painted'. I know you are very clever at that kind of work so I will give you the credit for it. I am sorry I cannot return the compliment, with some of my original work; I shall have to content myself (and you too, I hope) with a letter.

I am glad of your good wishes and shall do my best to deserve them. I hope, by the time I am 21, to be better in a good many respects than I am at present, and like a violin improve with age and use.

As to my thinking you impertinent in writing, I am sure I shall be glad of a very large quantity of it. Impertinence, instead of being one of the small vices, will become a very pleasant virtue in my sight.

So Mr Beilby and Sally are still as affectionate as ever. If it is pleasant to see them, I conclude it would be still more pleasant to *be* them. Never mind, Daisy, perhaps our time will come if we wait patiently. But I am in no hurry to marry yet. The worst of it is, you can't help falling in love, and then it is a done job. You must either marry, or be miserable for the rest of your life. But enough of this. Perhaps I didn't ought to be writing this, but they were my thoughts for the moment.

Yes, I was very glad to see Polly again, and should like to have had a longer look, but unfortunately she was soon off again. How very young she appears to be. At the very most 25.

Are you fond of skating? We are all hoping the lake will bear this winter. We have waited three years for it now. How jolly it would be if you could spend Christmas with us, and have a skate among other amusements. It would be an Elysium on earth. I have just received a long letter from Mrs Cole in New Zealand, and Harry has sent us a sketch of his rooms with every article of furniture down to the fender, tongs and poker.

Well, I hope you will rush to the postman for this, and get rewarded for once. With love to all my cousins, uncle and aunt, of course including yourself, and dear Daisy, may I venture on a little cousinly privilege, a modest x x x?

Ever yours,

Herbert

11th (Tuesday) A fine day. Willie Taylor's concert (at Chippenham) ... There was a very good attendance and the concert passed off very well; there were a good many encores. Willie Taylor played his solo well, and his duet with his sister. Lewin, Clara and I played a trio which seemed to please. Eva Neate's song 'Laddie' was encored and she responded with 'The Better Land' ... Home in Mr Porter's brake, singing old glees on the way.

13th A dull drizzly rainy day. Mr Hurlestone was buried in the afternoon; there were nearly 300 persons up at the chapel. We sang a hymn at the grave.

20th A dull day ... In the evening went up to Miss West's and had a jolly evening, dancing ... we kept it up from 8 till after eleven; there were refreshments provided by hospitable Miss West ... Letters from Harry and Mrs Cole.

21st Wrote a letter to Daisy Goold.

22nd ... We lit a fire in the shop, and I did booking out in the 'den'.

25th A hard frost, white ... Wilfrid and I ran down to the pond before breakfast and found it frozen quite all over. All in the house except Dad and Ma went to Mr Moody's to tea and we had Mr Mayo's magic lantern in the evening. It took some time to get it in order, but was very good when Lewin found out how to manage it.

28th ... Wilfrid and Ernest had their first violin lesson in the drawing room with me.

30th A hard frost, the pond frozen over again. We 4 boys went down before break-fast. It came on to snow during church and fell quite deeply ... Read 'Put Yourself in His Place' by Charles Reade all the afternoon.

DECEMBER

2nd (Tuesday) A very wet day. Put on some roller skates at the Court in the morning and tried them down in the cellars; I quite enjoyed the sensation. Our entertainment in the evening; Ernest Lanham came over and played in some instrumental pieces and also a duet with me. Mr Hulls read Sheridan's 'The Rivals' and Mr Rudge gave two very good comic songs.

7th (Sunday) A stormy day ... Ernest Lanham came up in the afternoon and we went in to Minnie's and stayed till 4 o'clock; I played violin with Lewin at the harmonium. Afterwards Wilfrid and I went down with Ernest to tea and we had some amusing anecdotes from Ernest of his experience as booking clerk; also some from Mr Lanham. Went into Minnie's after church and had some more music; stayed to supper.

8th (Monday) A dull day ... We had some good dancing in the kitchen in the evening. I played the violin up on the table.

9th A wet day. Liberal meeting in the evening; I took shorthand notes. It was very interesting ... Ma's 50th birthday. Aunt Lyd, Lewin and Minnie, Lizzie and Katie Moody here to tea and after supper we had a little dancing in the kitchen.

15th ... Band of Hope entertainment in the evening; crowded audience. Katie Moody and Fred Cole played a pianoforte duet ... Clare took part in a piano-forte duet with Una Linton and Ella Layton ... After it was over Wilfrid and I gave 'Love and War' in the dark and empty hall.

18th A very wet day. Mr Sainsbury died, aged 85, First night of the dancing class;

there were nearly 40 present although it was a wretched night; the ladies were rather scarce.

23rd A dull cold day. Very busy round for orders and in the shop. One of my customers, Mrs Maggy, showed me her photographic album and told me all about her friends; I saw some of her crewel work and her husband's fretwork. Ernest, Wilfrid, Clara and I sang some carols in the evening.

25th Christmas Day. Dull and cold ... Wilfrid, Clara, Ernest and I went up to Grandma's in the afternoon and sang some carols ... Wilfrid and I went up to Hartham in the evening ... it was the Servants' Ball. Mrs Dickson and party came down and danced a short time; I had a polka with Miss Bella Dickson. I played the violin for a good many dances; we had refreshments and a stand-up supper and had a jolly evening; came home about 3.30.

26th A dull cold day. Wilfrid and I went down to Bath by the 12 train ... went to West's dining rooms and had dinner and afterwards a tepid bathe. Went to the Pump Room concert in the afternoon and came out at the end of the first part to catch the 4 train; we had to run for it. Herr van Praag played very nicely and the band pieces were first-rate. Had a small-fry party in the evening; Agnes Bromley, Willie Bromley, Fred and Norah Cole, Frank and Maud Ryall and Katie Moody; had games and dancing.

27th A cold windy day ... Clara, Wilfrid and I drove over to Bradford in the afternoon; we went to Mr Beavan's where we found a large party: Harry and Willie with their respective girls ... and Arthur Beavan. We had some dancing after tea; (I played the violin), and also some Messiah and other vocal music; Miss Eveleigh a very good performer on the piano and a cultivated voice. We started back about 11 o'clock and arrived home soon after 12.30, having spent a very jolly evening.

31st A fine day ... After practice went up to the Court where the servants were having a kick-up and played till after eleven; Came home and danced the Old Year out and New Year in. A lovely moonlight night; bells ringing.

NOTES FOR 1884

January 24th Coffee Tavern: probably in the house next to the Town Hall (Priory Street). There was also at one time a Coffee Tavern opposite the Flemish Buildings – later Lewin Spackman's printing works.

31st Rev. Clark, vicar: see Kilvert's Diary. A good water-colour painter as well as violinist. Mrs Clark: née Awdry.

February 27th Aunt Polly ... departed: for New Zealand? See May 14th.

March 2nd Pelham's failure: presumably father of Blanche.

6th Market Place: before Town Hall was built.

15th Date ringed in black. Jack is the dog and Mr James the vet.

22nd Grandma was 'established' with the family while they moved house for her – from Stumps Lane to South Place (opposite Methuen School).

May 11th Thomas: violinist friend. There was also an Albert Thomas, assistant in the shop (January 28th, 1886).

13th John Hawkins.

26th Uncle Laurie: John's brother-in-law.

September 2nd Aunt Clara's children: the eldest was Daisy!

October 9th Bishop Colenso (1814–1883): Bishop of Natal, noted for his advanced and unorthodox views on the literal truth of the Old Testament.

Letter, November 21st 'Sweet eighteen': he should have written 'nineteen'.

Herbert has some lessons from a professional violinist and joins the Bath Orchestral Society. Partly through reporting, he is becoming increasingly interested in the Liberal cause, and in anti-vaccination. He gets about occasionally on a borrowed tricycle and 'enjoys it very much'. He and Daisy now exchange letters.

JANUARY

1st (Thursday) A little sunshine after a week's disappearance. Ernest and Clare went up to Pickwick School in the afternoon, where Miss Dickson had a Christmas tree loaded with presents for the church school children and Ernest and Clare being in Mr Linton's class were entitled to a share.

6th A fine day: hard white frost. Went to Bath in the morning to see Herr von Praag about some violin lessons ... decided to have 3 lessons (1 guinea) ... Miss Dickson gave a tea to the members of the Mothers' Sewing Meeting and their husbands and gave a dramatic representation of 'Cinderella'. I saw a good part of it in the doorway.

8th Our first soirée of the season ... Ernest Lanham drove over from Chippenham and a good many besides ... about 90 in all. I danced about 21 out of the 24 with about 18 different partners, some good and some not so good. I enjoyed a waltz with Polly Aust very much. Came home about 3.30 ... Ernest Lanham and I had a gallop together.

12th A hard frost and fine all day ... Went down to Bath by the 11.50 to have my first lesson of Mr Praag ... He found fault with my manner of holding the bow and other little details and I had a regular drumming. I played on his violin which he gave 50 guineas for.

13th Very cold all day. Felt wretched most of the day from a cold; nearly all of us more or less touchy. Practised before breakfast and after shop at night.

19th A dull day. Emily, Clara, Wilfrid, Clare and I went up to Miss West's in the evening to her party. Ernest stayed at home as his cold was bad. ... Clara and I took turns in playing for them and we had some very good dancing. Didn't go home till nearly two o'clock and it was pitch dark; we couldn't see a yard in front of us.

23rd A fine day ... Went up to Rudloe and gave lessons; there was a new pupil for me named Osborne. Mr Richards lent me 'John Bull and His Island'.

24th A wet dismal day. Went down to Bath in the morning ... Called in at Mr Pitman's and spoke to Mr Pitman. He inquired for Lewin and gave me some New Church Almanacks for distribution. Went to the pantomime 'Beauty and the Beast'; enjoyed it pretty well, especially the performance of a lady upon the guitar and banjo.

28th A wet morning. Mr Drew, Mr Thomas, Paul Pym and I practised a quartet for 4 violins before tea with a view to performing it at the town hall. We all went in to Lewin's to tea and afterwards had some music and games and some dancing in the kitchen. Maitie, Katie and Louis joined in the dances. We tried the 'Erl King's Daughter' and new glees for the class.

FEBRUARY

3rd (Tuesday) Our entertainment in the evening. It was pretty well attended ... Mrs White from Kingsdown gave two capital recitations. Mr Drew read a selection from Mark Twain's 'Tramp Abroad'. Our violin quartet went off very well, though the start was not very unanimous.

6th Went to Rudloe and saw little Bertie Shannon lying in his coffin. He looked very nice; I wanted to kiss him. The nurse who showed him to me was a very superior sort of person ...

7th Wilfrid, Ernest, Clare and I were bearers at Bertie Shannon's funeral. Mr Hulls, his sons and all the boys were present ...

11th After choral practice ... we cleared our bedroom out, beeswaxed our shoes and had a capital dance.

14th A fine day. Went down to Bath in the afternoon to have my third lesson of Mr Praag. Went to the Pump Room concert ... music not very classic, but I enjoyed the overtures to Semiramide and Poet & Peasant and Boccherini's Minuet for muted strings. Ernest Lanham was up in the evening and we went in to Lewin's and had a long chat in there. Saw Edith Goold in the Pump Room. (Paul Goold's daughter)

16th A wet day ... Cricket club soirée was a great success, about 130 there, many from Chippenham, Bath, Draycot, Sutton, Lacock and Atworth. ... I danced 24 out of 26. Sat out one of them with Willie Taylor's Miss Baker, a very nice girl. We started the proceedings with the waltz chorus 'Euterpe' and brought the people into the room. It was after 4 o'clock when the last dance was finished. I enjoyed a waltz very much with Miss Sophie West and a jolly polka with Mrs William Clark.

MARCH

8th (Sunday) A magnificent day. Albert Thomas, Wilfrid and I walked to Bath in the morning; we had breakfast and started about 8.15 and did not stop till we arrived at New Church, Henry Street, about 10.45 ... I started taking down the sermon by Mr Child but he was too fast. Mr Paul Goold was in the choir and after service we walked part of the way home with him; ... We went to West's and made a good dinner off apple tart and tapioca; after dinner we called on Henry Baggs and he took us for a capital walk to Sham Castle and beyond where we had a good view of Bath; after tea (at his house) we sang some of the 'Holy City', Mrs Baggs playing the piano. The evening service at the New Church was very well attended and the sermon was splendid; we three sat in the choir. After service we mounted the tram which took us about a mile and a half on our way ... We arrived home about a quarter past eleven having thoroughly enjoyed the day.

16th Had a letter from Daisy Goold in the morning.

18th (Wednesday) A fine day, but stormy at times. Made out a ledger account of my takings for teaching. After shop, Wilfrid, Clare and I went down to Thingley Bridge on the side of the railway looking for violets, but we did not find many. We all went to tea at the British School, Good Templars tea-meeting, and a very good spread it was. Went to the meeting afterwards at the town hall. Tom Horrocks was the chief speaker and was immensely funny. I laughed most of the time, I think. Wrote out an account afterwards.

20th Ernest and Clare carrying on a flirtation with a young lady of 12 over at Miss Southey's, from the shop doors pretty often in the day.

23rd A fine day ... Heard that Uncle John had got into trouble and been arrested at

Corsham
[*c*. 11th March 1885]

My dear Daisy
I am going to tell you about a little outing we had last Sunday. If it
should prove uninteresting you must do what Hugh Conway advises
his readers about a dozen times in 'Dark Days' – 'put it aside'. Wilfrid
and I thought we should like to hear a Swedenborgian service for once,
so we invited a friend (Mr Thomas) to come with us and we started for
a walk to Bath. It was a splendid morning, couldn't have been better
for walking. We arrived at the New Church about quarter to eleven and
went in, but there wasn't a soul there! ... The people, I find, don't
come to church so early as they do at Corsham – you see them
trooping down our avenue about quarter past ten. We had taken our
seats but a few minutes when in walked – Mr Paul Goold and took his
place in the choir. We had no idea that we should see him ... [Here
follows a fairly detailed description of the day's programme including
walk to Sham Castle, as in diary.]
    By the time we reached home (soon after eleven) we had walked
quite 26 miles. Not a bad day's work, and I don't know when I have
enjoyed a Sunday more. Oh, if we could have such soul-refreshing sermons every Sunday! ...
    How do you get on with your pupils, Daisy? do you find them
troublesome? I expect some of them try you occasionally as they do
me. Please write me a letter as soon as you can. Love and kisses to all
my cousins (there's a pleasant duty for you), and also to Uncle and
Aunt. I wish I was there to relieve you by doing it myself, and
impressing a cousinly kiss upon the lips of Daisy herself.

Ever yours
Herbert.

Manchester on a charge of fraud or obtaining money under false pretences.
Inspector Daniels was inquiring here about him. Finished reading 'Griffith
Gaunt' by Charles Reade, a splendid tale.

APRIL

3rd (Good Friday) A beautiful day. Hot cross buns for breakfast. Wilfrid's birthday; gave him Berthold' Tours tutor for violin ... In the afternoon Dad,
Wilfrid, Ernest, Clare and I drove to Marshfield in our trap. We had never been
so far on that road before and found it very interesting. We found the shafts
were cracking soon after we got there, but luckily they didn't break before we
got home. ...

Castle Combe

6th A good deal of wet in the night making the roads very dirty and we gave up the idea of going to Wootton Bassett, especially as Dad was not up to the mark. Wilfrid, Ernest, Clare and I went to Bath, to Box by train and walked in; we went in the tepid baths and enjoyed an hour there and then to West's to dinner; the place was crowded and they ran out of pudding and we couldn't have a second helping. Went to Gippet's circus in the afternoon; some of it was very good but there was the sameness common to all circuses. ... We had fun going home in the train.

14th Went down to Bath by the 3.45 train to play at the New Church Soirée ... It was held in the library underneath the church, and the room was nicely fitted up. I played a fantasy on Patience and the audience appeared to like it very well. The thought-reading was very interesting, nearly every case being successful. We had some dancing afterwards, round dances and the Swiss Country ...

20th A magnificent day. Wilfrid, Ernest, Clare, Alfred Thomas and I went down to Bath by the 5.45 train to hear a lecture by Mr Alfred Milnes on Compulsory Vaccination ... Went into the library at the top of Milsom Street and read the papers ... The lecture was immense; I don't know that I ever enjoyed a lecture more, or even music which I have heard in Bath. We brought away a library of tracts and signed our names on the piece of paper provided for the purpose. Went to West's for coffee and had awful fun there. It was a nice moonlight night and we arrived home about one o'clock.

21st (Tuesday) A beautiful day. Heard in the papers that Uncle John had 15 months given to him ...

29th A beautiful day. Went round for orders in the morning and delivered a good many tracts on vaccination and in conversation with some of my customers heard of many cases of death, disease and general ill-health arising from vaccination. After 4 o'clock us 4 and Thomas drove down to Lacock and had a bathe ...

MAY

5th A dull day and very wet. Got in a fine mess going out to Miss Fowler's in the morning. ... Mr James, having left Budgett's, called for orders on his own account.

15th A beautiful day ... Took a petition to Lewin asking him to teach us harmony, and signed by 'us 5'.

17th (Sunday) A beautiful day ... In the afternoon Wilfrid and I walked out to Velly Chapel with Mr Stewart and came back through the fields picking some cowslips on our way ...

18th A stormy day ... At 5 o'clock Clare, Fred Cole and I started on tricycles for Trowbridge as I wanted to attend a rehearsal for Wednesday's concert. Clare and I rode Paul and Guy Pym's machines. We did 12 miles in an hour and a half. While the practice was on a heavy storm came on and made the roads much heavier going back, and we reached home at 11.30. I enjoyed the novel exercise very much.

24th (Whit Sunday) A fine day. Dad and Ma and the boys went off about 5 o'clock in the morning. Ernest & Clare went on to Newbury by train from Seend, and Dad and Ma went on to Rode and Bromham where they spent the day ...

25th (Bank Holiday) A very wet mucky disgusting unfeeling hard-hearted day. Our plans for Calne were frustrated. Had a game of billiards with Uncle Rowell at the Town Hall ... in the afternoon played nap in the drawing-room ...

28th A fine day. Wilfrid and I went to Bromham after tea on Paul and Guy Pym's tricycles. We had hard work pushing up Bowden Hill. We arrived at Bromham at 7.30 and went in the fête field. A good many Corsham people were there; I had a capital set of lancers with Jane Smith, a polka with Miss Wheeler and a Varsovienne with her friend Miss Woolley. We started for home about 9.15 and arrived 11.15. It was very fagging coming home; nearly all uphill and the machines were not in good order.

JUNE

1st (Monday) A magnificent day ... In the evening after shop I went up to Mr Freeth's and had a ride on his tricycle out to Claremont twice, then out to the Harp & Crown and lastly to Cross Keys and back. It was a nice easy machine and safe. Miss (Elizabeth) Goold across the road dying.

3rd A magnificent day ... Tea on the lawn. Martin had a serious accident about 4 o'clock. He was in the soda house getting a box and fell forward on his head cutting it very badly. I went down to see him when I heard of it and stayed for half an hour with him; it was very lucky his neck was not broken.

7th (Sunday) A dull day but only a little rain ... We started for our day's outing at 4.45 (a.m.) in Allway's wagonette; Dad, Ma, Wilfrid and I, Emily and Clara. We got on the wrong tack near Holt and nearly lost the train. Emily and Clara saw us off and went on to Bradford where they spent the day. Bessie Wild was at Woodbury station to meet us and drove Ma in ... Mr Ferris (Bessie's intended) drove Ma to the station after tea; we managed to get capital third class carriages. In the morning I had a tune on my violin coming along in the train. Managed to leave one of the umbrellas in the train when we got out at Holt. Dad telegraphed for it. We sang chants and hymns coming home, which we reached about 10 o'clock.

17th After shop, drove to Lacock (cricket). After the match we had a bathe. I stayed in nearly for an hour and managed to change from front stroke to lying on my back. Quite an acquisition in the art of swimming ... Drove on to Whitley (?) to hear Mr Fuller and others at an open air Liberal meeting. Dad was there in Mr Mayo's carriage.

24th At 3 o'clock Wilfrid and I joined the party in Griffin's brake en route for Draycot. It rained all the way there. I sat on the box. We put up at the hotel and had to wait an hour and a half before the band arrived. I danced 18 out of a possible 21; the company numbered about 50. A Miss Hillyer from Chippenham was not half a bad girl. Started home about 10 o'clock. Miss West was in an awful funk because Griffin drove fast.

26th A fine day; sight of the sun again ... Went to the quarries underground with

Percy (Coxall) in the afternoon and saw the men at work there; we carried a lantern.

28th (Sunday) Aunt Lyd, Emily, Clara, Minnie, Wilfrid and I drove to Hinton in the morning in Allway's wagonette. We arrived there about 9.30 and after a little rest and refreshment walked to Steeple Ashton church to service; there is a fine organ there and the church is a good one for the size of the place. After dinner we watched Uncle Sims make his cheese. We all went to Mrs Twinney's to tea and then lay on the hay in front of the house. Uncle Sims showed us over his farm afterwards. We arrived home about 11 after spending a very enjoyable day.

29th (Monday) A fine day ... Bathed at Lacock in the afternoon ... Went to see 'Thauma' – half a living lady suspended in space – at the Town Hall; the illusion was good.

30th After shop ... went and had another look at 'Thauma' and asked the showman to turn her round and also to walk round her, but he passed off the questions, seeming not to like them.

JULY

1st (Wednesday) A splendid day. Wilfrid and I, Thomas and Clare drove down to Bath in the afternoon; Ernest and Percy went on tricycles. We went in the baths first and enjoyed an hour; afterwards had a good tea at West's and then went in the Sydney Gardens and heard the City band ...

2nd A fine day. Made a few fire balloons and set off 2 in the evening; they went very well ... Clara went on a visit to Nottingham.

14th Got up at 3.30 and was down at the station at 4.15; through some mismanagement on the part of the Bath officials our train did not come, and we had to wait till the ordinary 7.25. On arriving in London went straight for the Inventions and stayed there all day, seeing and hearing all we could; organ recitals, Grenadier Guards and the renowned Strauss orchestra. We were much amused at the affectations of the conductor. We found the old musical instrument department very interesting; some very valuable violins and cellos were on view. ... We left at 8 and had to wait nearly an hour at Addison Road for our train. Arrived at Corsham Station at 1.15.

21st Had a postcard to say Mrs Beilby had a little son and heir.

22nd Percy Coxall sent me 'The Maiden Tribute of Modern Babylon' reprinted from the Pall Mall Gazette.

27th Very hot day. Went to Weavern to bathe (with the Rudloe boys' school). After a jolly dip we went to Mr Poulsom's and had some milk, lemonade, cider, bread and butter and cheese ...

28th A fine day. Mr Chugg and I went down to Bath to buy the prizes for the athletic sports; it took us nearly three hours and then we had dinner at West's. Afterwards strolled into Victoria Park and had a cigarette. Then a dip in the tepid baths and home by the 4 o'clock train well loaded with good presents. After tea Lewin and I arranged them in the butterhouse window and crowds soon collected outside. Walked up to Prospect with Jessie Light in the evening and watched Bowood fireworks from there.

31st Had a talk with Dad about going to New Zealand; he thought it advisable to wait a bit before deciding.

AUGUST

1st (Satuday) ... Clara came home (from Nottingham) bringing Edith Goold with her.

3rd A fine day. (Fête.) Went to church to special service; the members marched in procession headed by the Bradford band. The sports went off very well. I won the obstacle prize, a biscuit barrel. Ernest won the electro silver teapot and Clare a butter dish and cup.

8–18 [Holiday at Bristol with Albert Thomas & later the Jameses.]

20th A dull morning. Our choir outing. Destination Burnham. Went up to Chippenham by the 7.23 and from there took tickets to Highbridge; chartered a brake to convey us to Burnham which we reached about 11 o'clock. A steamboat was already in the dock bound for Cardiff and we decided to have the trip ... it was a pleasant voyage. Had a dip when we got back, but the bottom was very muddy ... Had a capital dinner at the Queens Hotel and then walked to the lighthouse and went to the top of it, having a good view of the country ... Mr Clutterbuck paid all expenses which amounted to over £12.

24th A lovely day. Dad, Ma, Clara, Edith Goold, Clare, Lewin and Minnie and Fred Aust went to Bournemouth for the day; they drove to Melksham in the brake and got a train from there; paid a visit to the Isle of Wight and altogether had a jolly day ... They came home about one o'clock. Wrote a letter to Daisy Goold.

24th August 1885

Dear Daisy,
Wilfrid, Ernest and I are all alone in the shop today. All the rest are gone for a day trip to Bournemouth, Edith included. They started off in the dark about 4 a.m. in a brake for Melksham where the train starts, but it was a near miss that they weren't too late; they had to go and wake the driver up and only had half an hour to do the 5 miles. They will have a jolly day of it if the weather holds up. A good Brass Band will be with them all day, & they will visit the Isle of Wight, perhaps pay a visit to Her Majesty at Osborne. Mr Moody is going with them, & that will be an advantage, as the 'Isle' being his home he can show them places of interest. I wish Wilfrid could have gone as he has had no holiday except cricket matches and the choir outing to Burnham. That was very enjoyable, though Burnham itself is an uninteresting place; but we managed to get a trip in a steamship to Cardiff. Four hours on the water! wonderful for we inland people. We

had a bathe at Burnham too but the water is very muddy, and such slime to walk on. The water at Bournemouth will be better today, nice and blue. I expect Edith and Clara will bathe. I know Clara took an elaborate bathing gown with her, one of her own manufacture.

What a funny girl Edith is. I can't get her to accompany me on the piano. Clara tried to drag her in the other day, but failed in the attempt. 'Tisn't as if I was a crack player on the piano and wanted to criticize everything. I know very little of the instrument, and am too much occupied with my own part to notice what the accompanist is doing. She must try & overcome such timidity; it will be a bar to her progress. I know she is quite capable of playing the accompaniments, as I heard her the other day.

I began 'Charles Auckester' but I don't care a lot about it. The author is a little bit *too* ideal. I can hardly follow him (or her) in his flights of imagination. Perhaps the latter half is a little more practical; I must try again. But Spohr's life I enjoy reading very much. I knew I should. What an amorous disposition he had: Fell in love with every pretty girl he met, & got into scrapes through it too. But there are so many printer's errors in the book. One in every page almost. Perhaps it is the fault of the translator.

I think Edith is doing a little to shorthand. I suppose you haven't time to learn; but a half-an-hour a day for six months would help you on wonderfully. Most likely you could write me a shorthand letter in that time.

To return to Spohr. I see that he did not consider the violin a lady's instrument. Persuaded a lady friend of his to discontinue the study of so *unbecoming* an instrument. Opinions have altered since then. Look at Madame Norman Neruda. Who would say that the violin was not a lady's instrument after seeing her play?

Well goodbye Daisy, for the present. Love to all the household, including the 'Boss' (during her mother's absence).
Yours ever,
Herbert.

P.S. Don't be too despotic with your brothers and sisters. 'Deal gently, it is better far.'

SEPTEMBER

5th (Saturday) A beautiful day. Cricket match with Chippenham. I played and kept wicket. Chippenham made 91 and Corsham, after an exciting innings, just tied it. Arthur Kinneir in making the winning hit was caught low down at point, a lucky catch. Mrs Beilby and Emily and the baby arrived by the 7 train; Sarah not looking very well. Ernest Lanham looked up in the evening.

7th A stormy day. Edith Goold went back to Nottingham ... she was very sorry to go ... Heard that Dr Newland the cello player was dead from bronchitis. Very sorry to hear it as I contemplated having some more music with him.

8th A stormy day. The Band of Hope gave a service of song entitled 'For Christ's Sake' at the Town Hall in the evening. Clare played the harmonium and Ernest sang bass ...

10th A wet dull day ... Wrote to Harry telling him I hadn't decided about coming out to him as I could not see my way clear at present.

11th Clara told me she was going to be confirmed and leave the chapel for church.

16th (Wednesday) A fine day. Went to the meeting at the chapel in the afternoon and took Alice up. Mr Gage of Bristol preached a capital sermon against bigotry, drunkenness, immorality and scepticism. All the household were up there to tea; 210 sat down, the chapel being nearly full ... I had a talk to Miss Woolley and Annie Tinson in the interval and after all was over ... I pulled them up in the chair and they dragged me back part way. I made them pay the fare (a kiss).

19th A dull morning, fine afternoon and evening. I drove Sarah and her baby over to Bradford in the afternoon where she was going for a visit. It was a lovely drive; we got there just before tea; the Bradford Brass Band was playing, it being a children's treat; they paraded the town.

20th In the afternoon Albert Thomas and I went down to Bath by train and went for a walk with Henry Baggs up over Beechen Cliff. It was a lovely afternoon and clear and sunny, and I never saw Bath to greater advantage. After tea went to the New Church, harvest thanksgiving service ... Spoke to Mr Harbutt some time on the vaccination question.

23rd Went down to Bath by the 5.45 to the first orchestral practice. Called on Mr Harbutt and bought 'The Story of a Great Delusion', a book on vaccination. He introduced me to his wife and some friends and we had some music ... Put up at the Temperance Hotel; it was very comfortable but they charged too much.

24th A fine day. After breakfast (for which they charged me 1s 6d) I went to see Sarah at 11 Albion Place ... found her very ill and in low spirits; the doctor had told her if she were to catch cold then she would die in two or three days ...

29th Harvest thanksgiving at Box; Lewin, Clara, Wilfrid and I and Minnie went down to help at their concert after evening service. Lewin sang the Judge's Song from 'Trial by Jury' and we joined in the chorus. It was encored. I played two solos and Clara sang a song (encored). There was a capital audience and the concert was a success ... Mr Clark from Langley was there. We came home in a covered conveyance.

OCTOBER

8th (Thursday) A stormy day. Wilfrid, Ernest, Clare, Aunt Lyd, Minnie, Clara and I drove to Bath in Allway's wagonette after tea to hear 'Mikado'. A heavy storm came on as we entered Bath and we were very wet before we reached the theatre. Left our clothes at the neighbouring Coffee Tavern. The pit was so crowded that we decided to patronise the upper circle, but we could not get seats together. The opera was very enjoyable. We reached home shortly before one.

13th (Tuesday) A fine day ... Went to the inquest on Robert Shewring at the Pack Horse in the evening as a juryman, a new experience; I didn't like the formality business though.

15th A dull day. Mr Chamberlain came through the street in Mr Fuller's carriage but I did not see him ...

18th (Sunday) Ernest got in a temper with Wilfrid and knocked him down in the parlour. Wilfrid restrained himself from giving it back to him and called Dad, who merely reproved him instead of sending him to bed for the rest of the day ... Went to Grandma's to tea.

21st A wet day. Lewin, Clara, Minnie, Wilfrid and I went down by the 10 train to Bristol to hear the 'Elijah' at the musical festival, Colston Hall. Wilfrid and I went in Clark's the clothier's and I was measured for a dress suit. We had a fairly good seat in the hall ... Mrs and Miss Fuller were there ... I was really disappointed with Mr Santley, but Joseph Maas was beautiful and Miss Anna Williams the soprano was good. Madame Patti has a good voice but not so good as it was. The chorus was very fine. When it was over we went to a coffee tavern and had a good tea; I bought a mackintosh at Anderson's ... We got home about 7 o'clock. Cousin Butler and Mrs Moore were there ... just off as we arrived. Went down to the Liberal meeting at the town hall and took some notes. Rev. J. Stewart made a very good speech and Mr Hancock then explained the ballot to the electors and a mock ballot was instituted; 62 votes for Mr Fletcher and 3 for Lord Somerset.

23rd A pouring wet day. Walked to Rudloe and found my new mackintosh very useful.

24th My 21st birthday. Had a present of Longfellow's Poems from Joe Ward with a letter, and also a letter from Daisy Goold. I had a good brush and combs given me by the household, in addition to a regular outfit from Dad, a dress suit, top coat, pair of boots and mackintosh and set of bedroom wear. Received numerous congratulations and good wishes.

26th A wet morning, brighter later on ... Conservative meeting at the Town Hall in the evening; Mr Robert Atkins gave a lecture and Mr Clutterbuck took the chair. The lecturer was interrupted continually by some of the audience, the great majority present being Radicals. Mr Mayo was present and ... when questions were invited he went up amidst vociferous cheering and challenged Mr Atkins' statement that the Conservatives had passed the repeal of the Corn Laws. Mr Atkins replied that he did not say the Conservatives had passed it but the Conservative party, but of course his intention was to deceive the people ...

27th Received a pretty birthday card from Edith Goold from her place in London, and an original letter with it too. Answered it in the afternoon.

Oct 26/85

My dear Daisy,
Many thanks for your kind wishes and the share you have had in making me that handsome present which I received today. It is so kind of you all. I wish to express my gratitude in a more demonstrative way than by cold words on paper. And Clara meant to write to Aunt Clara on her birthday but quite forgot it when the day came and she says she won't write now as Aunt would think she only remembered her birthday through your writing to me. Although I don't play the piano, I shall find the book very interesting and Lewin, Clara and Clare will like to read it. I shall get one of them to play me that odd looking music at the end. I am sure it would have completed my happiness if you could have made one of my very quiet birthday party on Sunday. We celebrated it with music of course. I have received many nice presents. A copy of Longfellow's poems, & a silver-mounted walking-stick amongst other things.

Are you fond of poetry? I don't think I am, very. I fancy I like Longfellow more than any other. You can understand him better.

Please get that eccentric idea about my being a swell out of your head. 'Second thoughts' were not best for once. I hope you will not entertain any exaggerated idea as to my musical abilities, as you will certainly be disappointed. I can tell you that I am quite 'ordinary' and should have a lot to learn if I came to Nottingham. How I envy your pupils! Who couldn't get on under such circumstances? [Here follow some rather sententious remarks on Life, and a long description of 'Elijah' at Bath.]

... It was a performance I shall not soon forget, as I had never been to a festival before and had heard no *good* soloists.

Now, dear Daisy, I will end this chapter (to be continued in our next, as the penny dreadfuls say when you come to an exciting part). Mind you thank Aunt Clara and Cousin Kate for the present and kiss them both for me. As for you, as Shakespeare says, 'I'd smother thee with kisses' if I were with you.

Goodbye
Herbert

NOVEMBER

1st (Sunday) A fine day ... Went to Chippenham in the afternoon with Wilfrid to take tea with Ernest Lanham. Found that Ernest had been turning his attention to literature for a change; he wrote a very good essay on criticism ...

4th A fine day. Lewin's present to me, a rubber stamp, came mid day and I stamped some of my books. Lewin and Minnie kept up their anniversary of the wedding; we all went in to tea … First day of 'Dorcas'; I helped in the drapery.

6th A fine day … Served on an inquest at Mr Marks' in the evening on the body of the baby. I felt convinced, from the fact of its vaccinated arm being much swollen and its left side discoloured, that the child's death was caused by vaccination and I put several questions to the witnesses to try and elicit some facts confirming my opinion … but the jury would not or could not see the strong circumstantial evidence … and the Coroner (Dr Kemm) advised them to return a verdict of 'found dead in its cradle', which Mr and Mrs Marks were much dissatisfied with …

10th A dull day. My vaccination tracts came in the morning. They were printed by Mr Pitman and I made good use of them in the evening by taking them out to Corshamside and distributing them at a Liberal meeting.

11th A dull day … To Bath by the 3.45 to rehearsal of the Orchestral Society. I went to Mr Harbutt's to tea and had a long talk with him; I bought a *Herald* and found my case of death from vaccination inserted and also a case of a Bath child dying from convulsions after vaccination. Mr Harbutt gave me full particulars …

14th Report of inquest in the Bath Herald and letters on the subject by Mr Askey and Mr Harbutt. Mr H added a footnote to his, mentioning that Dr Kemm and Dr Wood were partners in practice, the one the coroner and the other the vaccinator of the dead baby! Wrote letters to Lord Arthur Somerset and Mr Bannister Fletcher on compulsory vaccination … [The Conservative and Liberal candidates]

16th A beautiful day. Distributed anti-vaccination tracts in Priory Street and Pickwick and Bence's Lane … Dancing class in the evening; Ernest Lanham was there.

17th Had a letter from Daisy Goold.

19th A fine day. Lecture by Mr Awdry on Borneo at the Town Hall in the evening; Colonel Methuen undertook the duties of chairman; there was a large audience. I played a duet with Paul Pym … Mr Matthias's boys sang two glees miserably flat.

21st A dull day … Wrote to Daisy Goold and sent her a piece of music (Schubert's). Lewin went round delivering Mr Bannister Fletcher's addresses with Mr Mayo in the evening.

23rd A dull day … Went to the missionary meeting in the evening. Clare dressed up as one of the Red Indians, a family of six being represented on the platform; the hall was crowded and I made my way into the ante-room where we had some fun with the same toggery.

24th A wet day. Had a letter from Mr Bannister Fletcher on the vaccination question; a fairly satisfactory one. Also one from Mr Beilby telling me that he has received a notice from the vaccination officer to the effect that if his child is not vaccinated within 14 days he will be prosecuted. Went to Castle Combe in Mr Mayo's carriage in the evening to an outdoor Liberal meeting; it was somewhat

'Us Four' younger Spackman brothers:
Wilfrid, Herbert, Ernest, Clare

noisy, the opposing spirits having evidently patronised a public house. Pouring rain coming home.

27th A wet day ... Mary Titt (old nurse) came here in the evening to have a look at us all. She looked very well ...

28th Saturday A good deal of rain in the morning; cleared up by evening. Some excitement waiting for the telegram announcing the result of the East Wilts election, the candidates being Mr Barber and Mr Long; at last about 3 o'clock it came and we found much to our disappointment that Long was in by a majority of 165. We had a grand Liberal meeting in the evening at the Town Hall. Mr William Saunders, M.P., spoke and also Mr Fletcher, Mr Stewart, Mr Hancock, Mr Pictor, Mr Little (Biddestone) and Mr Balch ...

29th A rough wind and rain all day ... Went to Mr Lanham's to tea with Wilfrid ... and talked with Ernest on old love affairs, vaccination and other subjects. We enjoyed some passages of arms between Ernest and his father.

30th A very wet day ... Miss Poock came in the morning and stayed all day ... Had some music in the evening; Miss Poock sang several old songs such as 'Bailiff's Daughter of Islington' and 'Auld Robin Gray'. The last she rendered very nicely.

DECEMBER

3rd (Thursday) Our polling day. I was at Mr Mayo's all day as clerk of the committee room; the polling was very brisk, over 750 out of a possible 800 having voted before the closing of the poll. Mr Bannister Fletcher arrived about 6 o'clock and he was dragged in his carriage all through the town ...

4th Wind and rain all day ... Lewin went over to Chippenham to hear the result of the polling declared: Mr Bannister Fletcher had a majority of 306, a Liberal majority in all of 57.

5th A wet day. Mr Fuller's majority 1694; although it was a very wet evening many people went to Neston to welcome him home.

7th A cold wind ... Mr Story Maskelyne in for the Cricklade division by a majority of over 1700, making in all 5 Liberals out of six to represent Wiltshire.

8th (Tuesday) A hard frost. Mrs Dickson sent down a note to Dad asking him to make out his bill, as owing to reports in the paper concerning her she declined to have further dealings with him. Dad took the accounts I sent to the paper and went to see her, and it was soon put all right. We heard Captain Campbell had refused to deal with Sydney Aust owing to his voting Liberal.

9th Frost. Ma's birthday, 51 years of age. We gave her an album between us, 12s 6d. Lewin and Minnie came to tea, Katie and Lizzie Moody and Aunt Lyd ... Lewin, Clara, Wilfrid, Ernest, Clare and I walked to Rudloe in the evening to see Shakespeare's 'Tempest' and 'Box and Cox' performed by the boys and masters. 'Box and Cox' we enjoyed immensely. It was a pleasant walk there and back.

11th A hard frost ... Went down to the pond with my skates soon after one o'clock and had a jolly afternoon of it. Clara and Minnie came down and Ernest and

Clare took turns; Wilfrid could not come as Dad was in Bristol. There were about 70 down there at one time.

12th Thawing all day ... Bill Bryant fell in the pond, but only up to his middle.

21st Mr Poulsom died suddenly.

22nd A fine day. Wilfrid, Clare and I went down to Fred Cole's in the evening to see his steam engine; it was quite fascinating to watch it going. Mr William Dyke of South Street cut his throat in the afternoon; he died shortly afterwards ... We all went up to Grandma's after tea to see the stripping of the Christmas Tree. It was a pretty sight. Grandma was presented with her much longed-for clock to strike the hours.

23rd A fine day. Busy with my orders ... Wrote to Miss Simmonds and Daisy Goold for Christmas.

24th A fine day. Very busy. Aunt Jane and Uncle Laurie came to stay. I had a very nice card sent from someone in Corsham; I have my suspicions that it was Miss Dore, but am not certain ... Sent cards to Daisy Goold and Miss Millwater.

25th A muggy day ... We had a jolly dinner party in the parlour, just thirteen of us, and amused ourselves with bonbons between courses.

27th (Sunday). A fine day ... Wilfrid and I went to Mr Lanham's to tea. Miss Wall was there and Ernest and she had some capital sparring, amusing us immensely, of course on the usual subjects of sacred and secular music ...

28th A stormy day. Wilfrid, Ernest, Clare and I went to Bath in the morning and had a dip in the tepid baths; afterwards went to Mr Perren's and had our photos taken in a group ... After tea I put on my evening dress ready for the ball at Hartham and we had some capital games in the drawing-room, a new 'Auction' game and the game with letters. Wilfrid went over to Chippenham in Riley's trap to fetch Ernest Lanham to the ball, and we all went up to Hartham together ... the floor was beautiful but the music not too good; a funny old chap played the violin and piano alternately but he was 'out of it' in the sets. We came away about 4.30. I kissed one of the ladies' maids under the mistletoe and also Miss Smith on coming away; we had a lark in Mrs Capper's room after the dance.

NOTES FOR 1885

February 14th Edith Goold: not Daisy's sister but a cousin of Jessie Goold.

March 16th Letter from Daisy Goold: in reply to his of March 11th, describing the walk to Bath.

23rd Uncle John: see May 26th, 1884. Had John Hawkins, the only boy among ten sisters, been spoilt in childhood?

May 15th 'Us five': the four boys and Clara.

July 22nd 'Maiden Tribute' etc. by W. T. Stead, editor of Pall Mall Gazette 1883–8. Written to expose child prostitutions. To prove it he bought a child, for which he was prosecuted and imprisoned.

August 1st Edith Goold: Daisy's sister, an excellent pianist, as her Corsham pupils will still remember, but very shy as a girl. Herbert comments on this in a letter to Daisy.

September 20th Mr Harbutt: of Bathampton, inventor of 'Plasticene' (modelling clay for children).

Daisy and Herbert continue their correspondence, though he often goes for walks with Annie Tinson [from the college at Rudloe where he is teaching?] – until the arrival of Kate Goold, Daisy's younger sister, from Nottingham for a holiday. Manfully Herbert is learning to master the penny-farthing bicycle.

JANUARY

1st (Friday) A dull dreary day. Had a New Year card from Daisy Goold.

2nd A fine day. I am writing my diary by firelight as the gas has failed us owing to scarcity at the gas works.

4th A dull day. Began making an Aeolian Harp ... Went to dancing class in the evening; enjoyed it.

5th Finished making the Aeolian harp but it was not satisfactory.

6th A heavy snowstorm at breakfast time and continued in a lesser degree all the morning. Miss Dickson gave a tea to the mothers attending the sewing meetings and their husbands, and a conjuror from London performed some tricks afterwards; some of them were very clever. Wilfrid, Ernest, Clare and I went up to Miss West's afterwards to spend the evening looking at views through the stereoscope, and playing Speculation etc. Sharp frost

7th A capital slide down the garden; Popham Sainsbury and the Lintons came in and enjoyed themselves on it. Freezing all day. Lewin went to Chippenham about the concert, and heard that Ernest Lanham was very ill with cong stion of the liver.

8th A fine day. Had a capital slide in the garden in the afternoon. Wilfrid and I went up to the Court about 9.30 in the evening to the servants' dance. They had a harp and violin for music, which was very good, but the stone floor was rather hard work in the round dances; I danced about 20 out of 25. Colonel Methuen came down and went through two or three dances. I took Miss Watts home after the dance.

9th Saturday. A beautiful day ... Went down to the pond all the afternoon; the ice was very good ... there were about 200 down there at one time. We tried quadrilles, but it was cold work and we separated after the third figure.

11th A thaw and rain at once settled the question of going down to the pond ... Went to dancing class in the evening. Mrs Baines senior went mad again.

12th Frost. Went down to the pond at 7.15; the ice was very good. Wilfrid, Clara, Clare and Miss Dore were there; we stayed till nearly 9 o'clock. Went down again about 11.30 and stayed till dinner time, but the ice was thawing, not nearly so good as in the morning.

13th A fine day. Ernest, Clare and I went down to Bath by the excursion train ... they went to the Bath pantomime, 'Herne the Hunter'. I took my violin to attend the rehearsal of the Bath Orchestral Society; paid my annual fee ... Called on Mr Harbutt.

17th (Sunday) ... The church choir sat in the chancel, a custom to be continued in the future on Sunday evenings. Jessie Light and Lizzie and Katie Moody to tea.

18th (Monday) A fine day. Mr George, one of the Bath Orchestral Society, came up in the evening to stay with us for the concert and help me with playing second violin. We had a capital practice; Willie Taylor and Mr Brinkworth came over.

19th A fine day. Mr George came with me for the town orders, and I showed him round the premises. We had a good deal of the 'Rose Maiden' through in the day and one or two duets together. His violin is a very good one, much superior to mine ... The concert was a very successful one though the room was not exactly full ... The ladies came out regular mashers, as did we in our cutaways

156

Lewin Spackman

Clara Spackman

... We had a little dancing in the drawing-room afterwards; Willie Taylor played a polka; we dragged George through the quadrilles though he had never danced them; he got on well considering. I slept with him in the spare room.

21st Our hopes of skating dashed to the ground on beholding about an inch of snow in the morning. Such a lovely sheet of ice the previous evening too ...

23rd A snowy morning. Nellie Beavan, Clara, Wilfrid, Ernest, Clare and I went down to the pond before breakfast and had a bit of skating; there was half an inch of snow on the pond but it didn't impede our progress much.

24th (Sunday) A fall of snow in the night and a white world in the morning. Only 9 at early service ... The boys had their new desks in the chancel in the evening. We sang some old tunes out of 'The Union Harmonist'. Our photo came from Mr Perren's in the morning and all were pleased with it.

25th A wet slushy day. Went to dancing class in the evening. Ma came down, and Emily and Aunt Lyd.

26th Wilfrid and Clare attended a meeting at Mr Foster's for the purpose of forming a Society of Change Ringers.

27th A fine day; very dirty under foot. Clara, Emily and us four went up to Miss West's in the evening to her dancing party. There were about 24 there and a very jolly evening we had; we played Speculation and Nap between the dances the floor was smooth and slippery. Went home about 2.30.

28th Albert Thomas ... went to Mr Neate's (with whom he had had a row); they had a noisy interview and Albert came back to the shop and telegraphed for his father to come up; waited all the afternoon in our 'den' and I gave him his music lesson there meanwhile. He met his father by the 4.30. Mr Thomas came to an amicable arrangement with Mr Neate and Albert was to stay on.

29th Had a shorthand reading class in the evening; we started with 'Gulliver's Travels'.

31st (Sunday) ... Mr Newnham preached and couldn't help treading on political ground. He spared no-one but had a hit all round.

FEBRUARY

2nd (Tuesday) (At Bath.) ... Subscription concert at the Assembly Rooms, Mr Packer the oboist having kindly given me a pass. It was the first time I had heard a quartet of strings and I enjoyed it immensely. Herr Ludwig made a capital leader and Whitehouse the cellist was simply superb ...

9th A beautiful day ... Went down to the hall at 8.30 (for the Soirée) and we began with our trio. Mrs Flood sang a song and Mr & Mrs Inkpen from Atworth sang a duet ... Ernest Lanham brought Miss Belcher and Willie Taylor brought Miss Baker and his sister. The ladies were very nicely dressed as a rule, the floor was good, but the music, alas! the violin and cornet failed to turn up and Willie had to play by himself; however we made the best of it. I danced 27 dances and with 23 different partners; I enjoyed a waltz with Miss Baker very much. We came away at 4 o'clock.

13th Blanche Goold called in to see us in the afternoon with Florrie Neate; she is a fine-looking girl.

18th Sun still out of sight ... Clara and Clare's certificates arrived and Albert Thomas's as well.

20th A cold day but a little brighter ... Ernest Lanham came up in the evening and after supper we had a discussion in the kitchen on Roman Catholicism and the Anglican church.

MARCH

4th A cold day. Lewin, Clara and I drove to Box in the evening to the concert. 'John Gilpin' occupied the first part of the programme, and in the miscellaneous part Clara sang 'Light' by Barnby and was encored; I played the overture to Semiramide with Lewin which seemed to please very much; Mr and Mrs Gardner thanked me directly after. Mr Roach sang two songs, his 'Girls at the School' being twice encored ...

5th Clara's birthday. Gave her a song, with violin obbligato, 'Forget and Forgive' ... Ernest Lanham called up in the evening and Emily, he and I went together to see Dew's Minstrels. I enjoyed it thoroughly. Mr Dew's violin solo was very good and so was the harp solo.

8th A fine day ... Ernest Lanham, Wilfrid and I went down to the Fair after shop and looked round for about an hour; I went in the swings with Miss Daniels and had two or three shots at the ranges. Had a talk on heathen mythology in the kitchen afterwards.

11th A fine day, hard frost. Wilfrid, Ernest, Clare and I went down to the pond at 7 o'clock and had some jolly skating up till breakfast time. We extended our sphere of exercise nearly half way down the pond ... After breakfast Albert Thomas and Florrie Neate went down and going too near the water above the railings fell in up to their necks, and after some prolonged exertions on the part of Clare and Lewin they were got out, Florrie Neate being much exhausted. They went to bed as soon as they got home, but soon recovered ...

12th (Friday) A dull day. Ernest, Clare and I went down to the pond before breakfast; Percy Davis was there too and when we had skated for about half an hour he went too near the unsafe part at the side and was immersed. Ernest in trying to pull him out went in too, but he soon got out, and I with the help of a topcoat managed to pull Percy out. The water was only about 3 feet deep, but he made as much fuss as if it had been a dozen feet deep ... Finished reading 'Forty Years of American Life'.

14th (Sunday) A fine day ... Ernest Lanham came up in the afternoon and he went in to Minnie's to tea with Wilfrid and I; we had a talk on vegetarianism and living on 5d or 6d a day. After evening service we went into the town hall to hear some of Mr Eli's (evangelist's) beautiful utterances.

16th Finished 'The House on the Marsh' by Florence Warden, a book I enjoyed very much as I had seen it acted at the Bristol theatre.

21st A fine day ... Special temperance service at church in the afternoon. All the Good Templars came in regalia.

22nd We had our first harmony class in the carpet room in the evening.

23rd A fine day. Willie and Harry Goold, Wilfrid, Courtney Aust and I went up to

27th March 1886

My dear Daisy,
It is a long time since I heard anything of you, excepting that hope-reviving message, which Willie brought with him the other day and which partially compensated me for the absence of any welcome missives from your own dear self. I am afraid Harry is having it all his own way up there. I wish I was an interesting American come home for a holiday and to such pleasant surroundings. And now he has asked me to come back with him and stay for a bit; such a tantalising invitation too, because I can't possibly come now. I have a shorthand class at Rudloe College as well as some violin pupils. And Nottingham is such a long way. Don't I wish it was across the road. What a vain and useless wish! I really believe Harry is sorry I can't come, although he looked so meaningly at me when he asked me. I don't think he gives me the credit of such a charitable belief, however. Perhaps it is best that I cannot accept Aunt Clara's kind invitation: Harry and I might quarrel seriously. Pistols for two and coffee for one (the survivor).

Well, it won't improve matters to go on in this melancholy strain. I must try to forget that *he* is basking in the sunshine of your favour while I am under a cloud.

What a fine boy Eddy is getting! So handsome too; long eyelashes and faultless complexion; as fine a boy as Blanche is a girl. Blanche has shot up too. She just peeped in a day or two ago, so I had a glimpse of her. It was something like looking at a shooting star – gone again in a twink. I hear she plays the piano very brilliantly.

How are you progressing under Mlle. Fromm (is it – I forget?) Do you like her and her teaching? How close Clara is over her letters! Twas like an oasis to the weary traveller in the Desert to see that letter of yours in her hands and then, Oh bitter disappointment, I was denied the favour of a perusal. Not even a part of it; but Harry, oh yes, Harry could look at it. What wonder then that I am depressed in spirit today! I shall go and play 'La Melancolie' on the G string and relieve my pent-up feelings. Would that I had the magician's telescope of the 'Arabian Nights' and could have a peep at you in your Nottingham home. I am afraid, were it so, that business would suffer.

Adieu, dear Daisy, "to memory dear".
Ever your
Herbert

P.S. Love & kisses if you will accept.

[The envelope is addressed in Clara's writing.]

the Court in the afternoon to look at the pictures; I went into His Lordship's bedroom and smoking room for the first time and saw several things I had not noticed on previous visits ... Willie and Harry went to Jessie Light's to tea.

26th Willie Goold went back to Bath ... Harry still staying at Prospect.

29th Finished reading 'Foul Play' by Charles Reade, a splendidly written book.

30th A windy day ... Harry Goold came in from Prospect to wish us goodbye ... We have certain reasons for thinking that he is engaged to Jessie Light, and are patiently awaiting confirmation or contradition of our conjectures ...

31st A fine day, strong wind ... We allowed our imagination to run a little wild with regard to Jessie Light; she is going to America, but not as the wife of Harry Goold, or even his affianced bride.

APRIL

1st A fine day. Made Miss Wiltshire, the cook at Mayo's, one of the servants at the Court and another at Mrs Pym's April Fools ... Went to the concert at the town hall in the evening; Madame Lisle's party. The violin playing of Master John Pitts I enjoyed very much, and the pianoforte playing of his brother Ernest, but the singing I didn't care for; their last duet, 'Excelsior', was awfully out of tune.

9th A stormy day. Cousin Bessie Humphries and Mrs Booth came here in the afternoon and stayed to tea. Harry Goold came in the evening and slept here.

12th Sunday A stormy day ... Had a lark with one of Mr Linton's servants after church.

12th (Monday) A splendid day. I drove Jessie and Gertie Light and Joe Aust down to Bath to meet the 12 train for Liverpool. Poor Jessie was down in the dumps at parting ... I gave her a book to read on the way. Eddie Goold went off in excellent spirits.

13th Mr Page drove me down from Rudloe in his dog-cart; went like the wind.

14th A fine day ... Went to Lodge; they had a coffee supper and some games afterwards and we spent a jolly evening. Wilfrid, Clare and I walked out to Seven Stars with Bill Bryant and others; nice moonlight night.

16th A fine day ... Had a letter from Daisy Goold.

24th A fine day. Went down to the hall in the afternoon and played through Mendelssohn's concerto with Miss Southey and Lewin, and then I played my solo and Miss Southey stayed to hear it. She asked me to go to her house in the evening to play the concerto with her for Mrs Southey to hear, and I did so and we went through several other pieces.

26th (Easter Monday) A lovely day. Dad, Wilfrid, Ernest, Clare and I started on our tour early in the morning. Went up to Calne by the 7.23 train and then walked to Cherhill and Compton Bassett, having looked at the churches and church-yards in each village; Dad accosted many old customers and friends on the way. We had a pleasant walk through the fields to Clyffe Pypard, having to ask the way many times, and there relieved our pockets of some of their contents, i.e. refreshments. We inspected the great monument of marble erected to the memory of Thomas Spackman, costing about £10,000, and went up the tower stairs and took a view of the surrounding scenery. The church is very pretty.

Clyffe Pypard Church: the Spackman Monument

The walk to Hilmarton was uninteresting and we were tired and glad to sit down in the clean and comfortable commercial room of the Beech Tree Coffee Tavern. We had a good wash and refreshing tea, made a note or two in the Visitors' Book and then had a squint at Calne church and town hall. Home by the 6.40 train, making a dash for the town hall for the rehearsal ...

27th We had a very good audience at the concert and it went off well ... I played my solo, Handel's Sonata in A, from memory and didn't forget it. Miss Southey's concerto with orchestral accompaniment was much enjoyed. Jennie Amoore sang two songs; Mr and Mrs Brinkworth helped and we drove them back afterwards.

28th The amateur Bell Ringers gave their first open peal in the evening; I was in at Lewin's when they first rang out and we had some rare fun over it; I posted a paragraph for the 'Herald' on the spot.

29th A storm of rain and snow in the night and much colder. Blanche Pelham's birthday. Had our harmony class in the evening.

MAY

5th (Wednesday) A fine day. Went to Bath by the 5.45 train to attend the rehearsal of the Bath Orchestral Society; went in the Sydney Gardens with Mr George and enjoyed listening to the band for a bit ... Mr Sims made a proposal to the Society to amalgamate with the Philharmonic Society, and it was decided to draw up a proposal to be forwarded to Sir Arthur Sullivan.

7th A beautiful day. Mrs Millard (Toy shop) has gone mad, owing to her business failing. She went across into Mr Bezant's shop in the evening, and although Mr Marks and another man tried to get her out, they had to get the assistance of Mr Daniels before they could get her outside, she screaming the while.

9th (Sunday) A fine day ... Ernest Lanham was over here and we went for a walk with him to the Dry Arch in the afternoon and went down with him to tea. After church Fred Hall joined us and we went through the Hilly Fields and home by the station.

21st A fine day ... Went to the town hall in the evening to hear speeches by members of the Liberal Association on the question of Home Rule for Ireland. Mr George Hancock and Mr Wesby [?] were against passing the resolution expressing confidence in Mr Gladstone, but it was carried.

26th A fine day. First day of the chapel bazaar. I went to the opening by Mr Bannister Fletcher at one o'clock and took notes of his speech. Clare and I played one or two pieces on the harmonium and violin ... Went home with Annie Tinson after the bazaar closed. The day's takings amounted to £40.

27th A very stormy day. Mr Baker opened the bazaar this time ... Albert Thomas and I played some more music and I played a lot of pieces with Annie Tinson. Clare won the biggest raffle, 5 dolls, worth about 30s; Ernest won a nice cushion and so did Ma; Alice won a table cloth. Our family spent over 2 guineas in raffling alone, and won about £3. 6s 0d. The takings this day brought the whole up to £55.

29th A poll of the parish was taken for the purpose of electing a Burial Board. Of the 9 elected Dad came in 5th.

30th (Sunday) A fine day ... Wilfrid and I went over to Chippenham in the afternoon and took tea with Ernest Lanham ... we went for a stroll down by the
canal ... pleasant walk home through the Park ... Annie Tinson's grand-
mother, Mrs Aust, had a fit in chapel and had to be taken home.

JUNE

3rd (Ascension Day, Thursday) A fine day. Went to church in the evening to the
choral evensong; the choral society and choir occupied the chancel. We did
'Lift Up your Heads', 'Worthy Is the Lamb' and the Hallelujah Chorus from
the Messiah besides a Te Deum, Magnificat and Nunc Dimittis. The Amateur
Ringers gave a good peal on the bells both before and after the service. Afterwards walked up Pickwick Road with Annie Tinson.

10th A fine day. Went to the choral festival at Chippenham; started in the brake
from Mr Linton's at one o'clock; got drenched in a storm going there. The
service went off very well and I enjoyed the tea. The concert was very fair; the
dramatic actions (!) of a Miss Stevenson in a song amused us very much. Ernest
Lanham played violin in the band pieces.

13th (Whit Sunday) A fine day. Amateur ringers had a big day. Rang 4 times. ...
After evening service went for a walk with Annie Tinson down Collett's Bottom. Lovely moonlight.

15th A fine day ... Wilts Friendly Society fête day ... In the evening after 8 o'clock I
went up in the field and danced a capital set of lancers with Miss Dore.

16th A fine day ... (cricket) I drove Ethel and Maitie, Ma and Aunt Lyd and Alice
out in the wagonette after shop. Got back 7 o'clock. Annie Tinson was on the
lawn and I went up home and a little further with her.

17th A fine day. Borrowed Mr Moody's tricycle and went to Bromham fête about 4
o'clock; got two boys to help push up Bowden Hill ... Had a dance with one of
the Miss Lewises and introduced myself to two young ladies from Devizes, the
younger girl being very interesting company. I had 4 or 5 dances with her one
after the other and strolled about the grounds; she sang in the chorus when I
went to Devizes two or three years ago to play in the 'Creation'. I was very
sorry to come away. There being no intoxicating drinks allowed in the field,
and sixpence charged for admission, ensures a respectable company at Bromham fêtes. Ernest Lanham and Willie Taylor were up there. Bill Burraston,
Fred Cole and I started for home about 9.30 and reached Corsham at eleven.

22nd A fine day. Tried my hand at bicycling in the evening for an hour on John
Hurn's machine; he held the handle and backbone while I worked it. I managed to keep on all the time but couldn't ride it alone.

23rd A fine day. All got up about 5 o'clock to go to Weymouth by excursion. I went
down to the station to see them off. There was only Dad, Ma and I left when
they were gone. I went over to the dance at Sutton in the afternoon; 16 or 17 of
us started in Page's brake and had a very pleasant drive; arrived there about 4
o'clock and we had dancing right up till 9.45; the two Miss Taylors were there
from Chippenham. Coming home we sang songs and some ladies tried their
hands at cigarettes but soon gave it up. Got home about 12 o'clock. The
Weymouth people had a very enjoyable day.

25th A fine day. Election work beginning again; bills and literature to distribute etc. etc. ...

27th (Sunday) A lovely day ... A lot of us went down to the Weavern again; this time it was much warmer and we went up to the hatches and dived off several times.

28th A fine day. Went up to Rudloe in the evening but the boys had gone to Castle Combe, so I soon rejoined Annie Tinson who was going to wait for me in the field close to Mr Bastin's, and we stayed there lying on the grass for three hours, watching the beautiful sunset over Colerne – in fact looking at everything except each other! Got home about 10.30.

29th A fine day. After shop I had another turn on Hurn's bicycle and both he and Mr Stokes started me; I found that they had left holding the machine and I was riding myself, and after that I managed to go from the Alms Houses to Jimmy Hale's lodge without coming off; and I turned also by the Park gates. I was very well satisfied with my progress.

JULY

1st A matchless day ... After shop tried to bicycle again; tried jumping off first, and as I could do that fairly, ventured on mounting; came off a good many times and over the handles too, but managed to mount twice.

2nd A fine day. Wilfrid, Ernest, Clare and I drove down to Lacock in the trap before breakfast and had a jolly dip; there was a heavy mist at first but it soon cleared off.

4th (Sunday) A lovely day ... Went down to the Weavern in the afternoon and dawdled about an hour in and out of the water ...

5th A fine day ... Conservative meeting at the town hall ... It was rather noisy. Lord Bruce could hardly be heard right in front, and Sir John Gorst was the only speaker who could keep the Radicals quiet; his speech was very moderate.

6th A fine day ... Went out on Hurn's bicycle in the evening and managed to mount much easier. Went round Pickwick on it.

8th Polling day. Wilfrid, Ernest, Clare and I ... went down in Clark's wagonette to Lacock to bathe. Started at 5.30 and had a pleasant dip. We bagged some yellow bills coming home, cheered all through Lacock and Corsham, tying some of the paper to Mr Clark's back and he went through Corsham with it flying.

9th A fine day ... Mr Bannister Fletcher was beaten by a majority of 537. Heard the fatal news about 2.30. Hartham bells were rung and Union Jacks floated from Captain Campbell's and Mr Pictor's.

12th A stormy day. Went to Rudloe in the evening. Annie Tinson came to meet me and we went in the Park and sat down under a tree till dark, then wended our way home. Annie slept at Lewin's.

13th (Tuesday) A fine day. Annie Tinson went back to London ... I had a ride round Pickwick on Hurn's bicycle and down Pound Hill for the first time.

17th Mr Fuller was elected with a majority of 997.

22nd A fine day. Bought young Lumkin's bicycle for 35s.

23rd A stormy day. Went over to Chippenham on the bicycle in the morning to have the tyre on the front wheel fixed and to buy a lamp, also to buy some butter. Saw Ernest Lanham. Went up to Miss West's in the evening and had some more music with Florrie Simmonds.

29th A fine day. Went round Pickwick on the bicycle for a run before breakfast ... Went to Stowell on the bicycle after tea for some honey, but Mr Brinkworth was out.

AUGUST

2nd (Bank holiday Monday) A threatening day, rain falling slightly. Wilfrid, Ernest and Clare went off to Longleat with the Good Templars in brakes. ... Fred Cole and I went on bicycle and tricycle about 10 o'clock for Roundway Park. The roads were very dirty in Sandy Lane, and about a mile this side of Rowde my front wheel slipped in the mud and down I went; Fred was coming along rather close and couldn't pull up his machine entirely, and turned over just as he got to me, buckling his right wheel. After one or two attempts we righted it and proceeded. We had dinner at Cousin Annie's (Franks), and after a walk round the grounds went up to Roundway Park where a fête was being held. We watched the sports and came home to tea at Cousin William Butler's. Went up to the park again after tea and met the Miss Hills who we saw at Bromham fête, and after a set of quadrilles with them I took the youngest for a walk round the park, or rather she took me, as she was more familiar with the surroundings than I. I enjoyed the stroll very much and was sorry when the time came to say goodnight. I was introduced to Mr and Mrs Hill, their parents. After supper at Mr Butler's we called on Cousin Annie to say goodbye, and got home without any accident, but my lamp kept on going out and I had to get off a dozen times to light it and at last gave it up. We passed the party of Good Templars just before we got into Shaw, and arrived home before them. The weather was splendid all day.

6th A fine day. I went up to Kingsdown in the afternoon on my bicycle to witness the review of the soldiers encamped on the down; it was a hard pull up there but splendid scenery. I had never been there before.

11th A fine day. (Cricket match with Lacock.) I went home, had some tea and started on my bicycle for Bradford as the Flower Show was on there; got there about 7.30 and went in the field; about 8.30 I caught sight of Nellie and Lily Beavan, and we saw the fireworks together; the illuminations were good and the fire balloon went up very well. We had a walk round the town afterwards and Bradford looked very pretty in the moonlight with the decorations. Slept at the Beavans'.

14th (Saturday) A fine day. [Actually the weather was mixed this summer, but it was on the fine days that interesting things tended to happen.] Cricket match with Melksham on their ground. Got up my eleven at the last minute and started about one o'clock in the brake hired by Griffin. We won the toss and went in, making 216, of which Clare made 57, I 28, Burrows 34 and Kinneir 22. Melksham went in and made about 40 ... Called on Mrs Burgess afterwards and saw Mrs Wilton (Rosie). Got home about 8 o'clock and told Lewin, who had just arrived from the Isle of Wight, the good news of our victory. I was very glad that all my trouble in getting up a team was not in vain.

17th Started about a quarter to nine on my bicycle for a week's holiday at Street. Had to fall off twice in Bath, once for side-slipping and another time some cows ran right in my path. No damage. The roads were very rough in places and the wind right against me, but I got to Wells at 2 o'clock and enjoyed some lunch at the Coffee Tavern; met with a very nice fellow there studying for the church and we went to the afternoon service at the cathedral together. The anthem was beautifully sung. Started again for Street at 4, reaching it well before 5. Took it easy in the evening with music, and Fred showed me how to imitate the banjo on the piano.

18th A fine day. Fred, Stan and I went down to the brook to bathe in the morning, and also had a lark in Stanley's canoe. In the afternoon we went up to Mr Glover's to mark the lawn for tennis and played, Fred against Stan and me; we won a set each.

20th Stan and I went on the tandem into Taunton. Started about 10 and it was hot work on the way, but we got over the ground well, shooting the hills in fine style. Had some refreshment at the Coffee Tavern in Wells and then went to see Mrs and Miss Simmonds ... had a little dinner and music afterwards. There were two nephews of Florrie's there, nice boys, and one of them, Ben, plays the violin very well. They accompanied us on the tandem several miles after tea, with Florrie on her tricycle.

23rd A fine day. Mrs Porter, Mrs West (Joe's sister), Fred, Stan and I went to Bournemouth by excursion; we paid 6s extra and had a first class carriage all to ourselves. On arrival we had a dip in the sea ... then a row in a small boat and afterwards discussed some lunch in the town. Strolled about the gardens and listened to the band on the pier till evening, when we started for home ...

24th Started for home in the morning ... resting a good many times for the day was so hot ... reached Corsham at 5.20.

26th A fine day ... Kate Goold came here in the evening ...

29th (Sunday) A very hot day ... Nice to hear the organ again. Lewin played "Pratt made two ducks' eggs" and Gounod's 'There is a green hill'. Ernest Lanham came up in the afternoon and I introduced him to Kate and we had a chat on the lawn. I went down with him to tea and walked with him to the Chequers after church. Kate, Clara, Ernest, and Clare came to meet me and we had some fun with the echo by the park gates at Lord Methuen's; it was the plainest I had ever heard.

30th A beautiful day. After shop in the evening Kate and I had a walk down Lacock Road.

31st A fine day. In the evening went for a stroll with Kate.

SEPTEMBER

1st A fine day. Colonel Methuen's birthday. Put up an awning on the lawn for our picnic. Aunt Lyd, Lewin and Minnie and Katie, Uncle and Aunt Laurie took tea, besides all of us, and last but not least Kate Goold. Some played croquet afterwards and Kate read from 'All sorts and conditions of men' to me. We went for a stroll together afterwards.

2nd A wet day ... Went for a walk with Kate in the evening.

3rd A sultry day. Got my old Aeolian harp out, and by taking away the sides I made it answer to the wind in a very pleasant manner, putting it in the sash of the drawing-room window ... Had a stroll with Kate in the evening.

5th (Sunday) A wet morning; fine afterwards. Kate wasn't well so I stayed at home in the morning and kept her company and copied out some music for her. Church parade in the afternoon ... went for a walk with Kate round the park afterwards ... Strolled round Pickwick and Cross Keys with her after evening service.

6th A fine day. Uncle and Aunt Laurie, Kate and Minnie went for a drive to Melksham in the afternoon; Ernest drove. Had some music with Kate and Clara in the evening. Ma joined them in some trios. Finished a very strange book lent me by Mr Linton; 'Dr Jekyll and Mr Hyde'.

7th A fine day. Ernest Lanham came here dinner time to say goodbye before going to London; Kate, he and I had a chat in the drawing-room on actors and actresses, and Ernest waxed eloquent. After shop in the evening Kate and I went for a delightful stroll round Squitters Lane in the moonlight.

8th A dull day ... Kate and I fell out about a paragraph in 'Broken Bonds'. It was an open Session at the Lodge in the evening and Clara and Kate came and sang a duet, 'Our Mountain Home'. I played a piece with Clara (violin and harmonium), and Kate sang 'Close to the Threshold', I playing violin obbligato. The audience was much pleased with our efforts.

9th A stormy day. Wilfrid came home ... bringing Louis, Katie and Vaughan with him. Kate and I went for a stroll up Pickwick Road in the evening.

10th (Friday) A wet morning, finer in afternoon. Kate went to Bath to see her grandfather and Mrs Edwards. I went down to the station to meet her in the evening. Kate came to practice and afterwards Wilfrid and I went for a walk with her in the park. Lovely moonlight.

11th A fine day. Grand musical garden party at Neston Park in the afternoon. ... I went out on my bicycle to hear the London Vocal Union sing some glees and madrigals. Among other pieces they sang 'The Chafers' and 'Strike the Lyre'.

13th A fine day ... Didn't feel very well ... As it was a lovely moonlight night, Kate and I, Wilfrid and Clara went for a stroll in the park.

15th Felt much better. Kate read to me from 'Bleak House' in the afternoon.

16th A fine day. I took Kate down the quarries in the morning; took my bicycle lamp with me and it answered capitally.

17th A fine day. Went for a walk to the Dry Arch with Kate in the afternoon, and we took a seat under a tree and talked. Went to practice in the evening and afterwards went for a stroll with Wilfrid and Kate. Talked to the echo for the last time with Kate.

18th A fine day. Clara and I saw Kate off in the morning; she was very sorry to go and we to lose her.

20th A fine day. Had a letter mid day from Kate Goold. Gertrude Light came to say goodbye as she intended going to America shortly. Jessie Goold called here in the afternoon to see Alice; Mrs Beaulieu from Calstone called and had tea; she brought Miss Spackman with her. Wrote to Kate in the afternoon and copied music for her in the evening. Letters from Harry and Mrs Cole.

22nd Finished copying out Kate's songs and sent them off in the evening. Gave Wilfrid a lesson on my bicycle down Lacock Road.

23rd A fine day ... In the evening had a ride on Tom Cave's bicycle, but couldn't mount it though I tried several times. It was a high 52 and I couldn't get one leg over the saddle; was afraid if I tried the other my trousers would hitch and over I should go.

26th (Sunday) A fine day ... In the afternoon Fred Hall, Wilfrid and I went up to Mr Brett's in Hartham Park, and Fred Brett photographed us three with his brother the watchmaker in the group; we watched him develop the plate afterwards and got home rather late for tea.

27th A stormy day. Went up to Brett's the watchmaker's in the evening and had some music with the harp, Fred Hall joining with the cello; stayed till 12 o'clock; it was the first time I had played with the harp, a very good instrument. Went down to Mr Mayo's in the morning and took down from his dictation a tract on the state of Ireland; went home and wrote it out in longhand which took a great part of the day. Had a long letter from Kate.

28th (Tuesday) A fine day. Clare and I went over to Melksham in the afternoon to give some music at the bazaar in connexion with the Congregational Chapel; we went to Mr Lee's and Edwin showed us round his new warehouse. After tea we went to the bazaar again and played some operatic and other light music at intervals ... I bought a fan for Clara and a little present for Alice.

29th A fine day. Wrote a letter to Kate and sent her a few flowers. Dad, Ma, Uncle and Aunt Laurie and Alice drove to Hinton in the afternoon. Clara, Clare and I went to Box to help with the Harvest Festival ... Clara was encored in both her songs, 'A Little Mountain Lad' and 'Close to the Threshold'. ... Mrs Methuen had a son born early in the morning.

30th A fine day ... Had some practice of dance music at Brett's; had some fun over our 'group' taken by William Brett; it had been touched up afterwards with ink, Fred Hall and Fred Brett being adorned with ferocious moustaches each.

OCTOBER

1st A dull day; rain in the evening ... Had some flowers sent from Kate and a long letter by mid-day post ... Did a little more shorthand for Mr Mayo and he tipped me 5s.

2nd A fine day. Went round Pickwick on my bicycle dinner time and discovered that my inside lamp had been taken and also a spanner. Wrote to Aunt Clara reassuring her as to Kate's health. Wrote a letter to Kate too.

3rd (Sunday) A fine day ... Went out to Yockney Park in the afternoon with Wilfrid and cut the date under Kate's initials on the tree ...

5th A fine day ... Had letters from Kate and Daisy Goold ... both told me that Harry Goold was engaged to Jessie Light – not very surprising news.

7th Wilfrid and I went by excursion train to London; started at 5.30; we had a first-
class carriage to ourselves, that is, with Mr and Mrs Sidney Aust, Miss Daniels,
Addie Aust and a gentleman named Evans; saw Ernest Lanham when we got
out at Paddington and soon espied Kate waiting for us. We had a pleasant chat
together, then Ernest left us and we saw Kate off home from Bishops Road
station. Wilfrid and I then went by bus into the Strand and went to see Dr
Nicholls; we found him a very pleasant man; I bought a book on marriage of
him and we shook hands on leaving ... Then to Aunt Jane's by train; had a jolly
vegetarian dinner there and found Uncle and Aunt both well; called in at Mr
Bell's and he took us part of the way to Kate's; went in and talked to Miss
Kenway. Kate showed us her bedroom, a snug little place. Went to the Exhibition which we reached about 3 o'clock, and had a good look round;
listened to the Coldstream Guards in the Albert Hall from 6 to 7 ... Kate was
looking just as well as ever and we had a jolly day together; the illuminations in
the gardens were very good. We came away about 8.30 and as we had a little
time to spare when at Uxbridge Road we got out and went home with Kate, but
the next train was late and we should not have caught our excursion train
probably, had we not jumped out at Westbourne Park, where our train was due
5 minutes later than at Paddington. It seemed a case of staying in London all
night at one time, but we laughed over it when we found we were all right ...

8th October 1886

Dear Daisy
It was rather remarkable, after this long silence, that you should write
on the same morning that Kate did and for both of you to tell me the
same news, viz. Harry's engagement to Jessie Light. I am not at all
surprised. I thought when they were here that probably they would
marry before they went out. It is rather unwise as far as I can see, but if
they really love each other what matter? they will be happy, or ought to
be, even if they have to struggle for a living. I should certainly like to
see Harry well settled first, though. I wonder what Mr Freeth thinks of
it. I feel rather sorry for her Uncle John, leaving him all alone at Prospect, but it was rather a trying situation for a girl of Jessie's
temperament. She was always fond of company, needed waking up,
you know.
   I am glad Sally's baby is doing so well now. I am too ashamed to
write to her, I have neglected it so long.
   I thought when I saw your letter that it was an answer to the one I
wrote to Aunt Clara, but I see you began it before my letter arrived. I
find that my ideas as to Kate's health are fairly correct; she is looking
as well as ever & was as jolly as possible yesterday. I enjoyed the day
immensely. We arrived in London about 9.30 & there sure enough was
Kate ready to receive us, & we were glad to see her again. After

chatting for about half an hour her train came and she went back to Miss Kenway's & we went on into the city. We went to an aunt's house to dinner & from there to fetch Kate at 10, Darnley Rd. After talking to Miss Kenway for a little while, Kate took us upstairs to her dear little room, as we wished to see it. I wanted to have some idea of the place where she passes her time occasionally. We saw a good deal of the Exhibition, but the crowd was too great for going into details. We also had a comfortable seat at the top of the Albert Hall & listened to the Coldstream Guards for an hour. Perhaps the most enjoyable part was the sitting down together at the little round table and partaking of tea, Kate pouring out of course. At 8.30 we started for home. At Uxbridge Rd Wilfrid and I got out with her and took her home and then returned to go on to Westbourne Park for Corsham. I was sorry to come away. I should like a fortnight in London now. That's only the third day I have been in London & here I am, close on 22; isn't it shocking! It would be jolly fun if I could come to Nottingham at Christmas, but I am afraid I shan't be able to move the Governor, & I am sure he wouldn't let me come before Christmas Day as we are so busy then. I thought perhaps you would have been at the Exhibition yesterday as Kate wrote for you, but I suppose you couldn't get away on such short notice. It was raining a good deal of the day.

I used to be nervous tuning my violin at a concert. I believe most people are, and I have known a lady amateur play with it out of tune because she was too nervous to tune it properly. The audience should wait a fortnight before I would do that.

You can't prevent E strings or any other sort from breaking. Such a desirable end has not yet been gained even in this 19th century. I have seldom found a good gut string; mine generally squeak or do something else disagreeable, so I content myself with Acribella or 'twisted silk' strings which are generally free from the above faults but do not give out such a good tone. Have you ever tried the steel strings now advertized? I don't advise you to go in for them. They have the following disadvantages: (1) they wear the hair of the bow sooner, (2) very unpleasant for pizzicato, (3) difficult to tune as the least movement of the peg sends them up a tone or so. They certainly last longer than any other if tuned carefully, but I never use them myself and don't intend to. I am very fastidious about strings and sometimes try several on before I am satisfied.

I shall be glad to play a piece with you (and many I hope, *privately*) if I *do* come up. Now I must say goodbye and do some work, which by the way I do not feel keen on after yesterday's dissipation.

Ever your affectionate cousin,
Herbert

8th (Friday) A stormy day ... Wrote to Daisy Goold. Went up to Brett's in the evening and tried some of Spohr's 'Last Judgement'.

12th A very wet day. Made a writing table for my bedroom. Went to choral class in the evening and sang bass. It was my first acquaintance with the vocal part of the 'Last Judgement' and I was delighted with it ...

13th A wet morning. Made a fire board for our fireplace in the bedroom, got a cloth for my table and made quite a marked improvement in the room ... Wrote to Kate.

15th A regular hurricane blowing and rain all day. Dad went to Reading to bring home Mrs Johnny Hulbert ... Had a nice long letter from Kate.

16th A quieter day. Wrote to Kate in the morning and in my hurry to send it off, only put one of the sheets in the envelope, so wrote again by the midday post. Mrs Hulbert was buried.

17th (Sunday) A fine day ... Wilfrid and I went up to Mr Brett's at Hartham Park with Fred Hall in the afternoon, and William Brett took the 'String Band', Fred Hall, Fred Brett and myself, and Wilfrid took the cap off the camera while William took his place at the harp. After evening service I went to the Salvation Army barracks to hear a girl sing and play the guitar.

18th A stormy day. Had a big letter from Kate, midday post.

19th A wet day ... Traced out a picture in the Illustrated London News; it was a girl seated in a room reading a love letter and her lover is looking in through the window.

20th A wet day. Lodge in the evening; Mr March and Mr Fido had a squabble on the question of a 6d or 9d tea on the occasion of our taking over the Town Hall (I mean the Good Templars).

21st A fine day. Went down to Bath in the afternoon to hear Charles Hallé and Madame Nerida give a pianoforte and violin recital ... I enjoyed it immensely. Tried to get a cheap edition of 'Bleak House' for Kate but couldn't find one.

23rd A fine day ... John Burraston wanted some ice in the evening and we couldn't get any in the town; I went to Hartham Park to meet Fred, who had gone out on horseback, and he went back with some.

24th (Sunday) My 22nd birthday. Had a long letter from Kate and a dear little violin carved in silver to hang on my watch-chain; I was delighted with it ... Made a little sketch to send to Kate ... Finished reading 'Bleak House', and the pleasure I had in reading it enhanced my good opinion of Dickens considerably; the characters in that work are splendid. Went to see Grandma after evening service.

25th (Monday) A stormy day. Wrote to Kate ... and sent her a copy of 'Bleak House' to read.

26th Ma went in to see John Burraston (who was ill) and he kissed her hand on leaving.

27th A wet day. Went to Lodge in the evening; it was election of officers and I was elected secretary. Miss Wheeler asked me to take part in a dialogue and I consented.

28th A fine day. Dew's Minstrels were here in the evening ... He tried my violin and was pleased with it ... Mr Dew said I must have had a master to teach me, though I assured him I hadn't.

29th A wet day. Had a letter from Kate in the evening; she wrote on thin paper to make it appear less than Wilfrid's in size; but I guessed before I opened it what she had done ... Went down to the British School in the evening to practise two glees for Wednesday ... afterwards went up to Mrs Wheeler's to try through our dialogue; it was very imperfect. Young Davis was very nervous at first; he shook and couldn't speak when first he came in.

NOVEMBER

1st (Monday) A fine day. Had a long letter from Kate mid-day. ... Ma, Emily and Clara went to London by excursion ... Burial Board decided not to have a cemetery.

2nd Wet morning; brightened up a bit the rest of the day. Wrote to Kate. ... Went to Mrs Wheeler's after practice to go through our dialogue; it went much better. Had a letter from Sarah Beilby, and a song entitled 'Once in a while' from Kate.

3rd A very wet day. The Good Templars celebrated the taking of the Town Hall by an opening night; had a tea at the British School and an entertainment and public meeting at the Town Hall afterwards. Dad, Ma, Ernest, Clare, Wilfrid and I went to the tea, and despite the wind and rain the school was full. The meeting went off very well; our dialogue was very successful. I stammered over my first sentence but got on all right afterwards ... Ma, Clara, Ernest and Wilfrid sang the madrigal from 'The Mikado'.

4th A stormy day. Lewin, Wilfrid and I drove to Tytherton in the evening in Merrett's trap to help sing at the Moravian School. The lady principal wrote to Lewin and asked for help; he had been recommended by Mr Brinkworth. They are practising Mendelssohn's 'Athalie' and the girls sang very well ... about 30 were assembled in the schoolroom. The lady principal conducted with much energy and spirit and we found her very pleasant ...

5th A stormy day. Had a letter from Kate; it was written in an unhappy frame of mind owing to an idea she had that Clara was angry with her ... Alice's birthday. Put some Chinese lanterns up in the passage in the evening.

6th (Saturday) Had another letter from Kate in the morning and read it in bed. It was much more cheerful. Wrote an answer by mid-day post. A wet day.

7th Wilfrid up to Mr Brett's and he took me with his camera; also showed me a novel imitation of church bells. Heard after evening service that Mr Newnham's eldest son was drowned in the Indian Ocean ... Finished reading 'Hidden Depths', a tale of cruel wrong, dealing chiefly with that class of girls termed 'unfortunatess'.

8th A fine day ... Had a letter from Kate mid-day post. Got 'Never too late to mend' from the library.

16th A wet day ... Had two letters from Kate, both bulky and one particularly interesting.

18th A fine day ... Tytherton ladies' school concert; we drove Israel in the wagonette; it was a nice drive; the concert went off very well. Lewin and I played the overture to 'Athalie' and also the march ...

21st (Sunday) A dull day ... Lewin received a proof of the hymn he had composed, dedicated 'To My Wife' and printed by Novello.

Sunday evening
21st Nov 1886

My dear cousin Daisy
I wish to send you the very best of wishes for your happiness on this particular birthday, & not only from myself but from *all the family*. Please accept the accompanying Shakespeare from us as a little memento of this day which only comes once in a lifetime to each of us – our 21st birthday. I am no judge of Shakespeares and left the ordering of it entirely in the hands of our local bookseller, & I see it contains the plays but not the poems. Of course the first are by far the most important, but still I wish it had been the complete works. I hope you will like it. Sally told me you hadn't a Shakespeare, so I decided to get one. I was surprised to hear you hadn't one, living in Stratford House, Shakespeare St.

Now Daisy, I wish to inform you that it requires no self control on our part to abstain from intoxicating liquors, because we have never tasted them & dislike even the smell, & if you please, my dear cousin, don't be quite so self-deprecatory. Comparisons are odious they say, but I am sure that I am almost dreading to come to Nottingham because I shall feel such a terrible ignoramus in the midst of so many clever girls, a little pigmy among giants versed in Harmony, German & about ten other languages (N.B. Please talk to me in English if I come), not to mention a general knowledge of things, quite beyond my limited mental vision at Corsham. Better far remain here and let you imagine me a clever fellow than come to Nottingham & expose my incapacity. However, if I should be able to overcome my fears, I will write and let you know when I intend making me 'feel my own littleness' (to borrow your words) by invading Stratford House.

Do please bore [?] me with a *long* letter. It would be such a *startling novelty*, Daisy. Clara generally comes in for that luck.

Do you dread being twenty-one? Are you frightened at being responsible for your actions after the 23rd? & how do you intend to exercise your power? I hope you won't be too wilful.

Daisy, I shan't allow you to resign your bedroom in my favour if I come, & shall dispute the authority even of a young lady who had just attained her majority. I would sleep on the bare ground rather.

I see in the *Bath Herald* a paragraph headed 'A Local Musician' in which your grandfather figures prominently as the composer of an anthem (I think). Have you seen it? I am going to play in 'The Last Judgement' at Bath on the 2nd of Dec. Our Choral Society is practising the same work. It is beautiful music. They are singing it downstairs now. I hope you will have many nice presents & a happy future.

Ever your affectionate cousin
Herbert.

[The envelope is addressed: 'Miss Daisy Goold. 21 years of age, Nov 23/86. *Her own mistress!!!*']

22nd A fine day. Church of England Temperance Society meeting in the evening; the hall was crammed. Ernest Lanham, Fred Hall, Fred Brett, Polly West, Clara and myself took part in the violin quartet with piano accompaniment (Clare). It went pretty well considering. The dialogues were quite a success; Wilfrid's get-up was capital and his intimate friends did not know him; Ernest was very good as the returned colonist.

25th Received a dear little penwiper from Kate, made of little bits of her hat, gloves and dress.

27th A fine day. In the evening I went to the town hall to a conjuring performance by a Mr Sutton; a Mr Jones played the harp beautifully; one of Mendelssohn's Songs without Words and a Welsh air; he played a violin solo too very well. In the dark seance later on, Clare and I ventured to go on the platform as no-one else came forward ... I saw that although Mr Sutton was tied, when the gas was lowered he got clear of the string and did the tricks and then shuffled back again into the strings.

30th Had a very cool letter from Kate, unmistakably studied; replied to it in the evening and reproved her for it.

DECEMBER

1st (Wednesday) Sent off my letter to Kate in the morning and at dinnertime wished I hadn't as she sent by mid-day post a letter just like her old self ... Lewin and I went down to Bath ... he gave a recital on the organ at the New Church, Henry Street; I played Raff's Cavatina with him ... a vegetarian from Liverpool (old gentleman) gave two recitations. There was a sale of work to pay for the expenses of renovating the church; I bought a photograph case and purse.

2nd (At Bath for concert at the Assembly Rooms.) Lewin and I walked to Bathampton bridge afterwards where Clare and Fred Cole met us with the trap; arrived home about one o'clock. There was a letter from Kate waiting for me and I opened it; at the first words I knew we were reconciled. It was a beautiful letter, full of delicacy, and affectionate.

4th A wet morning ... Had a letter and 'Notes on the Holy Land' from Kate. Clara lent me Kate's photo to carry about with me.

6th A wet day. We held a quadrille party at the town hall in the evening, dancing from 8 to 12. Clare and I played a good deal of the time; the two Bretts and Fred Hall joined me in two polkas and a schottische and Lewin played one. There were about 65 there, the ladies and gentlemen being nicely balanced ...

8th A letter from Kate for me ... Ma had her birthday party; Lizzie, Katie, Lewin and Minnie were here to tea, and Aunt Lyd.

11th A wet day. Clara and I went out to Claremont College in the evening to see the girls do 'Julius Caesar'; it was very enjoyable; Dr Crisp and Brother Halsted were there and came home with us. We had refreshments there, and some of the girls came to talk to Clara and me when it was over, in their costumes. Miss Tennant, Miss Banyard and two Miss Sloanes were very good.

13th A wet day ... Received a nice letter from Kate; she wrote it just before going to Nottingham to sing at the concert.

18th Busy in the drapery today ... Letters from Harry; he again asked for me to go out, and also Kate Goold; he said all three could do better if we came out.

19th (Sunday) A fine day ... Had a letter from Kate, and one of her photos sent me by a Miss Dingley (a friend of Kate's) as a Christmas card; it was a very good one.

23rd Frost again; went down to the pond; practised outside edge backwards, crossing legs.

25th Christmas Day. Splendid skating ... Thirteen sat down to dinner. After tea played a new game in the drawing-room, called Parliament.

26th (Sunday) A wet day ... Had a long letter from Kate in the morning. After dinner I prepared for going to Nottingham. Went down to Bath by the 7 train and Wilfrid came with me; we slept at West's. Snow very thick in the evening.

27th Wilfrid came to see me off in the morning. The country looked very pretty going along, the sun shining on the snow. Reached Nottingham about 3.30 (changing at Birmingham). Soon found out the house and Uncle came to the door. Kate and the younger ones were there; I soon had some tea and afterwards we had some music. Willie Goold and Daisy came in about 9 o'clock, and Daisy showed me her violin, a present on her birthday and a very nice instrument. Went to bed about eleven.

28th Went to the free library in the morning, and afterwards called on Sally Beilby to deliver her some letters from home. Willie Goold, Daisy, Kate and I went to the Castle and enjoyed ourselves very much; after dinner Daisy and I had some duets. Willie and I went to Sally's to tea, and afterwards went to a concert with Kate, Daisy and Edith; Daisy's pianoforte teacher, Madame Fromm, played the piano very nicely. The roads were very slippery coming back.

29th Went to the museum, Arboretum and Reading Room in the morning with Bertha and Ernest ... Willie and I went to the pantomime in the evening.

30th Bertha had a ticket given her for the 'Messiah' in the evening, so I went with her and sat in the back seats; Ernest came too. It was an awful cram, but I enjoyed

177

the concert. The choruses went beautifully and the bass-baritone Foote sang 'Why do the nations' in fine style ...

31st Kate, Daisy and I went shopping in the morning and called on Mr Beilby in his office; we went to Mr Thornton's to tea. Willie Goold called there about 9.30 and made a little unpleasantness with Daisy and Kate; at the same time Edgar Thornton attempted to kiss Kate under the mistletoe and Daisy was quite savage about it. It is very good of her to feel so much for Kate, but I think she overdoes it. After going home, Aunt read to us a chapter from 'The Supremacy of Man' while the Old Year went out ... Wrote to Miss Dingle thanking her for sending Kate's photograph.

Kate Goold

NOTES FOR 1886

January 24th Desks in the chancel: the choir had been singing in the Tower.

28th 'Den': the small room behind the grocery shop where accounts were done.

March 22nd Harmony: taught by Lewin at the request of 'us five'. See May 15th 1885. The carpet room linked the grocery shop with Lewin's house.

April 26th Thomas Spackman of Clyffe Pypard prospered as a carpenter in London in the 18th century and became a benefactor to his native village.

May 7th Mr Daniels: policeman.

June 22nd Machine: a 'penny-farthing'.

August 26th Kate: next of age to Daisy, and very attractive!

29th Pratt: a family saying. Once while Lewin was at the organ Clare came in to tell him the latest cricket news, singing it (to avoid interrupting) to the tune of the voluntary Lewin was playing. Henceforth the tune was nicknamed 'Pratt made two ducks' eggs'.

September 10th Grandfather: J. H. Macfarlane, her mother's father.

December 31st Edgar Thornton's choice was Daisy at the time, but neither she nor Kate could bear him!

The year opens, as 1886 ended, continuing a short holiday with the Goolds in Nottingham; but 'Aunt Clara' soon nips the incipient attachment to Kate in the bud! Spring and summer being unusually fine, much spare time is spent in Weavern. 'Ma' suffers what seems to be a slight stroke, affecting her speech.

JANUARY

1st (Saturday) [At Nottingham.] A rimy frost. Kate, Bertha, Ernest and I went down to the canal and skated in the morning. I assisted Kate and Ernest in their first struggles. After dinner I went out again with Willie Goold and we skated in another place, but as Willie's skates were broken I took mine off and let him skate. In the evening we went to Sally's to a little party. I enjoyed myself immensely. We had music, and I and Kate managed to sit together most of the time.

2nd (Sunday) A fine morning, but snow came on in the afternoon ... I went to the Swedenborg church in the morning with Daisy and Aunt. In the afternoon I went for a walk with Kate, a delicious walk all over the cemetery; we got locked in and had to ask the porter to open the gates for us ...

3rd A wet slushy day. Went to Sally's in the morning and stayed to dinner: talked about Corsham people and other things till about 4 o'clock and then went back to Aunt Clara's and practised the violin. Mademoiselle Fromm, Daisy's teacher, came to tea and we had a jolly musical evening. Mlle. F. played a sonata of Beethoven's beautifully and also some duets with Aunt Clara; I played 'La Rêve' with Daisy, and about 11.30 Daisy and Kate and I walked home with Mlle. Had a talk with Aunt Clara about writing to Kate; she told me she wished me not to write to her again.

4th A fine day. Uncle and Ernest took me for a walk in the morning and afterwards I went in the Free Libary and had a look at the Musical Times. Kate showed the magic lantern in the evening.

5th A slushy snow storm in the night. Helped clear away the snow from the front in the morning. Mr Hodges, Daisy's violin teacher, came and played duets with Aunt; his violin was a Ruggerius and he played very nicely ... Mendelssohn's violin concerto among other things. In the evening Daisy, Kate and I went to the tea meeting at the New Church; there was an entertainment afterwards and Kate sang two songs and Daisy and I played. There was a little dancing.

6th A foggy morning. Kate woke me up about 7 o'clock and we had a last chat together. Went to say good-bye to Willie and Mr Beilby. Kate, Daisy and Ernest accompanied me to the station. I was very sorry to say goodbye and they too. Got home to tea and wrote back to Aunt afterwards. Found them all well at home and Minnie a good deal better.

10th (Monday) A hard frost. More than a hundred skaters up from Bath. Sent off the skates I brought from Nottingham by mistake ...

11th A cold day. Went round for orders. Wilfrid and I went down to Mr Clark's to their party in the evening. I played a good deal of the time ... Supper on the grand scale.

12th Wilfrid and I went over to the Chippenham Assistants' Soirée by the 4.30 train; I played violin in the band for which I received 10s; Willie Taylor piano, Mr James from Swindon violin, Mr Broome of Bath flute and piccolo, and a cornet player; the room was very nicely decorated and the floor splendid, just as the County Ball people had it on Tuesday night ...

13th A sharp frost again; very good skating on the pond. I went down about 12 o'clock and stayed till 2.30. Mr Harris the veterinary surgeon was there and we skated together in one corner of the pond, near the boat-house; I practised the double-three figure. In the evening went down to Mr Lanham's and had a little music with Miss Wall. Ernest was there with an attack of congestion of the liver, and Miss Belcher was with him.

14th A little thaw set in. My skates came from Nottingham. Went over to Melksham by the 4.30 train and held my class ... Wrote a letter to Daisy Goold in the Chippenham waiting room and posted it at Melksham.

14th January 1887

Grocery Shop
2.30 p.m.

My dear Daisy,
That wonderful drawing is *supposed to be* a 'Daisy'. You must take the will for the deed. Thank you very much for sending my music and skates; also the 'Morning Lights'; all arrived safe. I have been using Lewin's 'Acmes' up to the present, as those I brought back by mistake were not large enough. Were they yours or Kate's? I had about two hours' skating on our pond yesterday, the best of the season. Lots were up from Bath. One lady had two large dogs harnessed and they dragged her along on the ice. Some of the gentry about here have had sleighs made to drive about the streets in them, but the late thaw has greatly altered the condition of the roads and stopped that. Have you had any skating since I left? How did you get on at the party Wednesday night? I thought of you several times during the evening. Wilfrid and I were over at Chippenham at a dance, but I was playing in the band. There were five of us and I enjoyed the lark. I don't think Wilfrid ever enjoyed a dance so much in his life. The floor was good and the music too. I watched him from the orchestra now and then and his face was beaming with enjoyment. Some ladies from Corsham came over in a fly and gave us a lift back. There were six of us inside, such a crush. The night before that we were at a private dance in Corsham, and the two late nights following made me quite tired and I was glad to get to bed early last night.

Tell Kate Ernest Lanham was at the Chippenham dance with his young lady. I sat next to her at the tea table. She is a peculiar girl. Flatters you one minute and then abuses you and almost insults you the next. She actually drank out of my cup like Kate did occasionally. Perhaps it amuses her and it doesn't hurt me.

I really don't know of any suitable service of song, that is, *good* one. I am disgusted with all I have come across. I hope Aunt's headache was of short duration; I wish she did not have them so often.

Please excuse this sudden change from ink to pencil. I had to go over to Melksham by train and having to change at Chippenham and wait half an hour, I am writing this in the waiting room. With regard to those purses; I did not intend bringing them away. One is for you and the other for Kate if you will accept them. Tell Kate not to waste her valuable kisses on the sheets etc. but keep them till we meet again. It is a shame that we can't write to each other; there is such a lot I want to say to her. Tell me all you can about her when you write, won't you, dear cousin.

How kind of Mr Hodges to give you some music! He may be right about the value of my violin. When I was playing in a band at Trowbridge once, one of the professionals remarked that it was a peculiar-looking instrument. I have a much better one by me now, which a gentleman lent to me (I wish it was *gave*). It is by Edward Betts. I think too, that he places too much confidence in names.

It was very excusable for you to laugh at Kate's mishap, but of course people don't like being laughed at in misfortune. There is one great consolation; although she is heel-less, she is not soul-less; far from it. Fancy you, Daisy, going away soon; why what will they do without you? What a lot of partings there are in this world, to be sure. They will miss you very much. Mind you let me know where you go to. I suppose the children will soon be at school. What a different house yours will be soon. It will never be the same again. I wish it was Dec 27/86 instead of Jan 14/87. No good. I am glad you were not disappointed with me. You must have had a rather low estimate of my character, Daisy, if you found me better than you thought. Well, I hope I shall always command your regard: I value it, I assure you.

Give my love to Edith and Bertha and the younger ones, also particularly to Kate, and kiss her as much as you will for me. Reserve a share for yourself, because you are so generous Daisy, and so good to act as a messenger and sort of medium through which Kate and I may know something of each other. Love to Aunt and please remember me to Sally and Ernest Beilby when you see them. Don't forget Sidney Paul. I shall be glad to hear from you again when your multifarious engagements will allow.

Goodbye dear Daisy.
Your affectionate cousin,
Herbert.

17th A fine morning. Emily, Clara, Wilfrid, Ernest, Clare and I went down to the pond about 6.30 and had a skate; the ice was rather rough ... played cross tag some of the time.

20th A fine day and a little frost. Wilfrid, Ernest, Clare, Clara and I went to Miss West's in the evening to her party ... broke up about 2 o'clock.

25th Choral Society practices commenced at the Town Hall. C. V. Stanford's 'Revenge' and Jensen's 'Feast of Adonis' were the works selected. I sang bass and enjoyed the practice very much.

27th Went to Malmesbury by train in the evening, met Willie Taylor (etc) and went to Tetbury by wagonette and after a good supper commenced the dances; we had a comfortable little orchestra and the room was nicely prepared. Didn't finish till nearly 5 o'clock.

28th Stayed at the hotel till 8 o'clock and then went in the bus to Malmesbury ... Went to bed for a bit when I got home.

31st A fine day. In the evening I went down to the Curfew and rang the third bell while it was muffled; I managed to set it twice.

FEBRUARY

6th (Sunday) A beautiful day ... Ma had an attack of catalepsy and couldn't speak all day. Dr Kemm and Dr Wood were here to see her and gave her some medicine; she could make her wishes known more intelligibly towards evening.

10th (Thursday) A hard frost. Ma a very little better. Lewin, Clare, Clara and I drove down to Box in the evening to the cricket concert. We played an instrumental trio, 'Oberon', and I played a solo and accompanied Clara in 'Doubt and Faith'. Clara was encored in that and also in 'Love is a plaintive song'.

12th A fine day. Wilfrid had a nice letter from Dr Nicholls; good advice with regard to Ma.

14th A cold day ... Tried my bicycle in the dinner hour; found I hadn't lost any power over the machine. In the evening I went to the Salvation Army meeting and heard Miss Keech sing songs with guitar accompaniment. Martin went with me and I went to his house to supper, where Miss Keech joined us. We had some more music; I accompanied her on the violin. The poor girl was frightfully marked with smallpox.

19th A fine day. Busy in the shop at times. Meeting at the Town Hall in the evening to consider about the formation of a Liberal Club. Dad quarrelled with Emily and Clara because they objected to his being so much in Ma's room and exciting her.

21st A dull day. Lewin borrowed a medical book from Frank Baines in which were some interesting remarks on aphasia, Ma's affliction. I copied it out in shorthand.

25th A day that put you in mind of summer ... A large Eskimo dog was offered to Lewin cheap and he bought it. Ma not much better.

27th A beautiful day ... Fred Cole, Ernest, Clare and I went for a long walk round Biddestone, Ford, Giddeahall, returning through Hartham, in the afternoon. Charlie Freeth came over and went to Lewin's to tea. He brought an invitation for us all to go over to Chippenham next Wednesday for some music. Finished reading 'With Harp and Crown' (Besant) which I enjoyed very much; I prefer it to 'The Golden Butterfly' or 'All Sorts and Conditions of Men'.

MARCH

2nd A fine day. Lewin, Minnie, Clara and 'us four' went over to Mr Freeth's, Chippenham, in the wagonette after shop and had a musical evening. Mr and Mrs Brinkworth came in and also a Miss Dreckford (contralto) ... We sang from Messiah, Holy City and Creation. A nice moonlight drive home.

3rd A frost. Ernest and I went to see poor John Burraston in the afternoon and talked to him for more than half an hour; he didn't seem much altered, only a certain look about him which you see on the faces of persons who have suffered a good deal. He chatted quite pleasantly about the news of the day. We brought his harmonium in to Lewin's for him to sell if possible.

4th I saw Ma for the first time for 3 weeks and thought her much improved.

7th Ma much better. She recollected being taken ill on the Saturday night, showing her memory was slowly returning. She knew about how long she had been ill, too.

12th (Saturday) A fine morning but a fall of snow and hail in the evening, turning to frost. Opening of Liberal Club in the afternoon; went up and took notes of Mr Fuller's, Mr Fletcher's and others' speeches, and sent them off to the Mercury afterwards. Went to the public meeting in the evening and Lewin, Clare and I opened the proceedings with 'Overture to the Pirates of Penzance'; Mr Brinkworth gave some amusing songs and a reading, and Mr and Mrs Gough and Miss Gough and Miss Bayley of Chippenham contributed vocal music.

15th A heavy snowstorm all day ... Saw Ma again and found her better; she sewed buttons on my top coat and waistcoat ...

17th A very hard frost ... 22 degrees. Poor John Burraston died about 3 o'clock in the afternoon.

20th (Sunday) John Burraston's funeral in the afternoon ... there were a great many people present and Mr Linton made a touching address at the grave. We also sang 'Just as I am' at the grave, a favourite hymn of John's.

27th A stormy day ... Wrote a letter to Daisy Goold. Ma came down in the drawing-room after dinner and stayed till bed-time.

28th Read 'Her Last Victim' (Family Herald Story-teller).

29th A beautiful day. Went down to Bath by the 5.45 train to attend an anti-vaccination meeting ... it was a good one. Mr Pitman presided; Mr & Mrs Harbutt were there ...

30th A fine day. Wilfrid read his paper on vegetarianism at the Lodge in the evening and we had a capital discussion on it afterwards.

APRIL

2nd A fine day. Public meeting at the Town Hall in the evening to consider the way to celebrate the Jubilee. Many conflicting suggestions were made but nothing much seemed to meet with unanimous approval. At last 5 gentlemen were appointed on a committee to report in a fortnight.

3rd (Sunday) A beautiful day ... Wilfrid's 21st birthday. He received a gold scarf pin from Nottingham, a silver watch from Dad and Ma, slippers from Ma and a promise of cricket pads from all of us ... In the evening Wilfrid, Ernest and I went down to bathe in the Weavern. The water was cold but the dip very enjoyable – the air was so warm.

7th A fine day but cold wind. Went out to Mr Yockney's on my bicycle in the morning and asked him for a subscription towards the testimonial to Mr Pitman; he was very pleasant and gave me 5s.

8th (Good Friday) A fine day ... Went to morning service. After dinner read 'Enoch Arden' by Tennyson, a beautiful poem. Afterwards went down to the Weavern with Ernest to pick some primroses ... Wilfrid and Emily came to meet us and we joined them at the top of the hill. Wrote to Kate Goold in the evening and sent some primroses and violets.

11th (Bank Holiday Monday) A beautiful day. Fred Cole, Frank Riley, Mr Williams and us four went down to Box by the first train and walked from there to Farleigh Monument where we had splendid views; then we walked by the side of the canal along to the viaduct; we went through a very pleasant wood, and had a little lunch which we brought with us, and then climbed up to Combe Down and then a nice easy walk into Bath; met and talked to Mr Kenway for a short time on Bath bridge; then had a dip in the Baths, afterwards going to the theatre to hear 'The Private Secretary' a very laughable piece. After a good tea at West's came home and went to the rehearsal.

12th (Easter Tuesday) A fine day. Our concert in the evening; it was well attended, every one of the tickets being sold. 'The Revenge' and 'Feast of Adonis' went well, and our trio 'Oberon' pleased very much. Miss Southey played a pianoforte concerto and Lewin and I accompanied her.

19th A fine day. Formation of the Primrose League celebration at the Town Hall in the evening; the room was decorated with primroses and flags and there was a fashionable audience. Small and I were the only reporters. Miss Clutterbuck asked me to join but of course I refused ... Lord Bruce and Sir Robert Fowler were the chief speakers.

26th A wet morning but cleared up in the afternoon. Lewin and I went down to Bath to hear 'The Golden Legend' performed at the theatre by the Bath Philharmonic Society ... it was quite a crush but we succeeded in getting a good seat in the gallery ... the music was splendid and the band simply perfect. We slept at the Temperance Hotel.

MAY

3rd (Tuesday) A fine day. First day of the bazaar in the Riding School. After shop ... Clare and I played instrumental selections at the performance of 'The Jacobite' by the Miss Awdrys at the Town Hall; there was a crowded audience; the scenery, acting and costumes were all good. I enjoyed it thoroughly.

4th We closed shop at 3 o'clock and went to the bazaar ... Clare and I played again at the Hall in the evening and the room was even more packed than on Tuesday night, many having to be turned away. (Thursday) The total amount realised by the bazaar and entertainment was £170.

8th (Sunday) A fine day ... We went to the Weavern in the afternoon and had a jolly dip. The water was much warmer. Coming home picked some primroses and anemones.

12th A fine day; uneventful. Whitewashers about the house; puzzle to find your things. Emily and Clara in their glory.

14th A fine day. After tea Fred Cole and I went up to Hartham on the tricycle and bicycle to ask Mr Shewring if we might bathe in the fishpond; he said we might, but if caught we were not to say he gave us permission.

15th (Sunday) A fine day ... Fred Cole, Harry Upsall and us four went to bathe in the fishpond directly after dinner; we took bathing drawers, and I found on entering the water that the elastic failed and they slipped down my legs. I managed to kick them off and then dived for them. Ernest's served him the same way. The bottom of the pond was very muddy, but otherwise it was an improvement on the old place.

16th Mr and Mrs Alfred Cole returned from New Zealand, bringing little Emmie.

20th Lewin bought a new printing press, one to work by treadle; a splendid little machine.

26th A stormy day. Lewin went round to the farmers on Mr Moody's tricycle, asking them to vote for him as Overseer for the parish; he was very successful.

JUNE

4th (Saturday) A fine day. Polling took place at the Town Hall from 3 to 8. Lewin managed to get the assistance of Mr Fuller with his brake to bring men in to poll, and Fred drove old Israel about too. The result was read out by Mr Linton amid cheers from the crowd assembled outside the Town Hall: Lewin 390, Mr Gillie 220, Harry Neate about 20. We talked a long time about the events of the day after shop.

6th A fine day. Ma, Mrs Cole, Alice and Clara went for a drive in the afternoon. Mrs Cole was here to tea and we talked about New Zealand and about going out there.

12th (Sunday) A lovely day ... Went down to the Weavern in the afternoon with the rest and had a jolly dip.

13th A warm day. In the evening there was a C.E.T.S. meeting in the Vicarage garden and we contributed some music; Wilfrid, Ernest and I sang an unaccompanied trio, 'Here's a health unto Her Majesty'. We forgot the second verse and looked at each other and laughed, but they encored it.

14th A glorious day. Went to the Rocks near Colerne on Frank Ryall's bicycle in the afternoon to hear Dr Walter play at the bazaar. I enjoyed the concert very much, especially the violincello solo by a Mr Dorey; a farce entitled 'Freezing a Mother-in-law' was very enjoyable. Pretty scenery all around.

15th A fine day. Read my paper on vaccination at the Lodge in the evening. My resolution condemning the action of the Board of Management of the Good Templar Orphanage in refusing unvaccinated children into their institution was carried without a dissentient. I gave away literature afterwards.

19th A fine day ... In the afternoon went down to the Weavern and Bill Brett photographed us all in two different positions; it was a regular lark.

188

20th Very busy today. The children had their treat; all the schools went up to the Court and had games and tea etc; the procession through the town and avenue was a very long one, headed by the Chippenham brass band. Maitie, Ethel and Katie went up with them and joined in the festivities.

21st (Tuesday) Jubilee Day. Went to a special service at church in the morning, and joined in the procession as a Good Templar afterwards; the great dinner in the tent in the cricket field was a success generally, though the teetotallers were not well looked after, nothing but water (and that not the best) being provided. In the afternoon there were sports; Ernest and Clare entered for some of them and Clare won a prize ... We danced two capital sets after tea.

22nd A fine day ... Lewin, Minnie, Katie and I went down to the Weavern and had tea in Mr Poulsom's orchard; Lewin and I first had a dip in the fishpond and Minnie and Katie watched us half way up the hill. In the evening we went over to the Chippenham Jubilee and I walked about with Nellie Belcher, getting a lift home with the postman.

28th A fine day, very hot as usual. Mr Cole doing the shop front. Martin, Clare, Fred and one or two helpers busy haymaking in the fields by the tanyard.

29th A hot day; nearly 3 weeks without rain. After shop we all went down into the hayfield by the tanyard and had a picnic tea. Mr & Mrs Cole (etc) were there besides all the haymakers. After tea we amused ourselves flinging it about, and then I played the violin for a set of quadrilles. Afterwards we had glee singing and finished with 'God Save the Queen' ...

JULY

4th A hot day. After shop Ernest, Clare, Wilfrid and I went down to Weavern and got in the fishpond; it was moonlight by the time we got out, but the water was very comfortable and we enjoyed the evening dip immensely. Coming home we all went into Mr Sidney Aust's and had lardies and ginger ale. Sep Kinneir was with us.

6th A fine day. Lewin, Minnie, Fred Cole, Harry Upsall, Clara, Emily and Us Four went down to Weavern after shop and had tea in the meadow; the 'males' of the party bathed first and Ernest, while jumping from the tub into the water, the bottom gave way and he was precipitated inside the tub into the water; but he soon extricated himself and beyond scraping his leg a bit no damage was done. After tea we walked some way by the side of the river and the ladies paddled; we had jumping and making ducks and drakes. Fred, Harry, Clare, Ernest and I got in the water again later and the others watched us from the hill. Old Israel had patiently waited $3\frac{1}{2}$ hours for us at Mr Francis's and took us home.

12th Clara took poor old Murfwa to Mr James to be poisoned as she was so ill; the most merciful thing was to hasten her end. We buried her next to Ruff.

13th A fine day. After shop 'us four', Fred Cole, Harry Upsall, and Harry Archer went in to Mr Linton's to play tennis. Clara came afterwards and Colonel Methuen looked in for a short time. Mrs Kemm and Miss Sainsbury were there some of the time. We had supper before leaving about 10 o'clock.

17th (Sunday) In the afternoon went down to bathe in the fishpond; one of the gamekeeper's sons wanted to stop us, but we told him we had permission. Lewin played several pieces on the organ after evening service for Mr Linton to hear; it was his last Sunday before leaving for Germany.

20th A fine day. Went in to Mr Linton's in the evening to play tennis, but first we all had tea down at Ash Villa, sitting round under the 'drooping ash'. Mr and Mrs Cole and Miss Collier, an invalid staying at Grandma's, joined us. Miss Sainsbury entertained us with conversation and refreshment between the games and we enjoyed ourselves muchly.

21st Uneventful. The dark Miss Bullock was married, she 34, he (name of Long), about 18 or 20. A foolish affair altogether; a case of marrying in haste and repenting at leisure ... Received a present of 'Jubilee Waltz' from Mr Lane 'with the author's compliments'.

25th Had tea on the lawn; I was nearly all day working on a screen from the sun.

27th Lewin and Minnie, Clara, Lizzie Moody and I went down to Claremont in the afternoon to hear the young ladies sing a cantata called 'Red Riding Hood'; it took place in a marquee erected on the lawn. Alice Boscombe made a very good Wolf and Katie Moody did her part well. We had a capital tea after the performance, and I poured out from the urn ...

28th We all went down to the Weavern in the morning and were photographed by Bill Brett; Robert Wild came with us and we had a fine lark. We were taken by

The Bathing Pool at Weavern

the hatches ... Saw a copy of our photograph in the evening and it was very satisfactory except that Robert came out with an awful grin. Gave Ernest 'The Vicar of Wakefield' (in shorthand) for a present.

29th A fine day. The men employed by Mr Cole are getting on nicely with the front (of the shop); all the pillars made to imitate granite and the cornice above the window very artistically grained. I like watching them do it.

31st (Sunday) After church in the evening went down to the Weavern and bathed by moonlight; the water was not cold.

AUGUST

1st (Bank holiday Monday; fête and sports. A lovely day.)

3rd Wilfrid, Clare and I went over to Chippenham by the 4.40 train to a party at Stuart Cook's; Ada Ayliffe came too and there was a large number of ladies and gentlemen assembled when we arrived. We had a very pleasant evening; some of us went down to the river and watched some diving etc. before the dancing commenced; Cook had engaged Rebbeck's lawn at the Templars Hotel and Willie Taylor played the piano. There were several nice girls there and I danced nearly every one. We three slept at Cook's in one bed.

4th (Thursday) Got up about 6 o'clock and went down to the Chippenham swimming place and had a dip; I dived from the board twice. Went back to Corsham by the 9.45 train ... Emily went to Uncle William's for a holiday. Maitie, Katie and Ethel Kenway came here for their midsummer holiday; they took lodgings at Mrs Pillinger's with Miss Stevens to take care of them.

7th A fine day ... Went down to the fishpond in the afternoon with the usual Sunday party; Harry Upsall occasioned amusement 'committing suicide'. Ernest Lanham and Miss Belcher came in after evening service and we had a little music.

8th Sun as fierce as ever; water getting short nearly everywhere. Outdoor entertainment at 'The Grove' in the evening; Katie Kenway played a violin solo and also a duet with Clara. She plays very nicely and Maitie makes a good accompanist.

12th A fine day. Ernest Lanham was up in the evening and I walked out to Claremont with him and we had a talk on love, marriage etc.

13th Fred Barnes dying with lockjaw caused by falling from a tree in the cricket field.

16th Saw poor Fred Barnes ... he knew me at once and showed me which thumb was supposed to be the cause (of the lockjaw), but I could see not even a scratch. I kissed him before leaving.

22nd Got up at 5 o'clock, had breakfast and we all started in two wagonettes about 6.30 for Bradford; reached it easily by 8 o'clock. The train was so crowded we couldn't get together. On reaching Weymouth took a dip in the sea and then went for a row in small boats and had some rowing exercise. We had dinner together at a restaurant and afterwards went to Portland in the steamer and visited the convicts and the pebble beach, returning about 5 o'clock. Had a little tea and then to the railway station. We all got into one compartment coming home and had singing, cards and a sham fight with paper. Fred Hall played the tin whistle too.

23rd A fine day. The shops closed at 2 o'clock, being Bowood Flower Show. Played tennis at Mr Linton's after tea.

24th A fine day as per usual. Tennis again after tea. We had a children's party here on the eve of the departure of the three Misses Kenway; we had dancing in the kitchen at 8 o'clock and I played the violin.

27th Letters from Harry and Amy. In Harry's letter to Lewin he writes about the advantages of daily practice on some favourite instrument and (evidently having Clara in mind) speaks against too much church-going.

31st (Wednesday) After dinner went over to the Chippenham Flower Show by train; listened to the Royal Marines Band till 6 o'clock. They played Mr Lane's (Calne) waltz and I saw the composer himself, highly elated of course. Went to Mr Belcher's to tea ... had some music and saw the fireworks from Frank's window ... Went to Mrs Taylor's ball and enjoyed myself thoroughly. Had several waltzes with a girl whose step suited me. Willie Taylor played hymn tunes to the dancing.

SEPTEMBER

7th Played tennis at Mr Linton's and after Wilfrid, Ernest and Clare had gone to ringing, Miss Dell played with Ernest Lanham against Harry Archer and me; it was very dark towards the last and Ernest Lanham cheated by keeping a ball in his hand and when it was served to him he sent his own ball back. We didn't find him out; he told us.

8th Went down to Ernest Lanham's in the evening and had a conversation with Miss Wall on phrenology, she taking the defence of a phrenologist named

Goold Silver Wedding Group: Edith, Ernest, Bertha,
Daisy, Joseph, Clara, Kate,
Rene, Stanley, Vivian, Amy.

Cohen whom we heard in Bristol. Ernest and I were sceptical.

13th Edith Goold came here on her way to Cornwall.

14th A dull day ... Lodge entertainment in the evening. Wilfrid, Ernest, Clare and I sang 'The Letter' unaccompanied, and we were encored; we introduced a novelty by singing part of a waltz we played. Clara sang Gounod's Serenade. Mr Austin presided (Lacock) and eulogised our family as very musical etc.

15th A dull day. Edith went on to her destination in the morning and Clara went with her to Bath. She brought back a splendid photograph of a family group at Nottingham; one and all came out well. We were all in raptures over it.

19th A fine day. Paid my first visit to Tytherton to teach at the Moravian School. I went to Chippenham by train and walked to the school.

28th A fine day. Wrote to 17 persons, chiefly old pupils and musical friends, for testimonials as to violin playing and teaching, for future use.

29th Michaelmas Day. Clara sang at the harvest festival concert at Box in the evening. Lewin and Ernest went over to the Biddestone harvest festival to help sing. Clare and I were engaged for dance music at Mrs Henry's class at the Town Hall, but as only Willie Taylor, Mr Birch and his two sisters turned up, after waiting a little and laughing heartily over the failure, we brought the Miss Birches in here and had some music and bagatelle. Dad and Ma, Uncle and Aunt Laurie went by excursion train to Swansea and had a capital day.

OCTOBER

4th A dull day. Mrs William Hancock complained because Ernest had put 'Esquire' on her goods, thinking he had meant it as a joke, while as a fact it was quite unintentional.

8th Ernest Lanham looked us up in the evening; he said he had been understudying at the theatre in London.

9th (Sunday) A fine day ... Mr Kenway came in the afternoon and stayed till the 7 train. He showed us a photograph of the lady he is engaged to, a sister of his brother's wife.

10th A cold day and very wet in the evening. Drove to Tytherton dinner time; took my testimonials to Spinks' to get them printed ... Got on very well with the teaching; they wanted to know if I could teach the harmonium; of course I replied in the negative, though I wished I had been able. Nearly broke my neck falling into a ditch coming out of the house, it was so very dark. Got home safe about nine o'clock and went in to Dr ——'s mesmerism entertainment.

11th Went to the meeting at the Town Hall in the morning convened to consider the question of a drainage scheme. There was only Barnes reporting besides me. Bertie Spackman made a very good speech in opposition to the proposed scheme ... Ernest and Clare were mesmerised (?) at Dr Sutin's entertainment in the evening and were instrumental in making many converts to the superstition, Ernest particularly; Miss Awdry was so alarmed at his state that she went to Lewin and asked whether he hadn't better come off the platform.

19th Lovely weather again. In the evening gave my paper on vaccination at the Liberal Club. There was a good attendance and we had a good discussion on the question ... They passed a vote of thanks to me at the close.

23rd A lovely day ... In the afternoon went for a walk right through Hartham Park from the Golden Gates with Wilfrid and Fred Cole; the autumn tints were beautiful on the trees.

24th Had a little fruit knife sent by post as a birthday present from Ma (on holiday in London) and a letter. Also a telegram from Street, wishing me many happy returns of the day. There was a Church of England Temperance Society meeting at the Town Hall and I helped in two instrumental pieces. A very good dialogue was given, entitled 'The Unexpected Convert', and there was much excitement when Robbins, the convert, comes up on the platform from the body of the room to argue with Ernest, who makes a speech.

26th Had a little birthday party in the evening. Invited Mrs and Miss Simmonds and Miss West down to tea, and we had a jolly musical evening. Went through 'Feast of Adonis', 'The Revenge' and 'Ancient Mariner'; we four sang 'The Letter' which they enjoyed very much, and I played several duets with Miss Simmonds. Heard that Katie Kenway was very ill with pleurisy.

31st Sir John Dickson's birthday. We closed shop at 2 o'clock and all went up to Hartham, Mrs Lanham and Miss Belcher accompanying us ... There were roundabouts, coconuts, nigger minstrels, sports and other amusements provided, and a free tea was given in the large tent. A monster bonfire was lighted on the slope of the hill, and a good display of fireworks, finishing with a facsimile of Sir John's head in fire ... Nice moonlight night.

NOVEMBER

7th (Monday) A stormy day. Drove over to Tytherton in the morning; let old Israel down twice just beyond Chippenham and scratched his knees a bit; it was on level ground and I wasn't driving fast.

8th A fine day ... Sent 30 testimonials round Chippenham in the evening by post.

12th Ma came home by the 3.30 train; she was looking very well, but her speech has not perceptibly improved.

19th After shop Wilfrid, Ernest, Clare, Fred Cole, Clara and I practised changes with Mr Foster's handbells up to twelve o'clock; I quite enjoyed it, being such a novelty, but my fingers got very sore.

21st A fine day. Finished reading 'John Inglesant', a most peculiar book and I didn't care for it altogether; a good deal about the Jesuits at the time of Charles I, the Roman Catholics and their politics; a touch of musical interest in the book.

23rd Went down to Bath in the afternoon, called in at Mr Pitman's and had a look round the premises, seeing the machinery etc. Bought a copy of the engraved edition of 'Book of Common Prayer' ...

26th Some hand-bells which I wrote for from Devizes came by mid-day train and we tried them after shop. Fred Cole came up and we went through 120 changes.

30th A fine day. Great Liberal meeting in the evening; Mr John Fuller's first appearance before his electors. A torchlight procession was formed at the top of Zion Hill and, headed by the brass band, made its way with Mr John and Mrs

Fuller, in the brake, up through the town, the streets being crowded with people. As they passed the Liberal Club, which was decorated with Chinese lanterns, some coloured fires were lighted. Mr Fuller made a capital speech, introducing to my surprise the question of compulsory vaccination. I reported under difficulties, on the box of the brake with a man to hold a candle up above my book. The square was crowded and it was a most enthusiastic meeting.

DECEMBER

1st Ernest, Fred Cole, Polly West and I drove out to Corshamside in the evening to the Good Templar entertainment. Polly and I played a duet ... There was a good audience but the boys and girls made a fearful row some of the time. Ernest took part in 'The Unexpected Convert' and 'The Colonist's Return'.

7th Clara went to Bath with Lily James. Juvenile entertainment at the Town Hall in the evening. Among other items in the programme was 'A teetotal Alphabet', 26 children wearing a letter (each) and reciting all their lines in turn. Dad and Ma went.

8th (Thursday) A very wet day. The Good Templars were due at Bradford in the evening to give an entertainment at the Town Hall. Clara, Emily, Clare and Fred Cole went in the wagonette in the afternoon; they took Podge the kitten with them. Wilfrid, Ernest and I came in the evening with the others in the closed brake. We arrived a little late. The room was quite full and Nellie and Ben Beavan were there. We gave two performances with the handbells, lent by Mr Foster; Clara sang a song; I played a solo; Wilfrid, Ernest, Clare and Clara gave two unaccompanied vocal quartets. The audience seemed pleased. Went to Mr Beavan's to supper afterwards, and had a very rough drive home.

11th Ernest and Wilfrid went over to Chippenham in the afternoon and had tea at Mr Freeth's; they went to the Roman Catholic chapel in the evening and helped sing in the choir ... Finished reading 'Julian Home' by Canon Farrar, a very nice book.

15th Ernest, Lewin, Clare and I went up to Mr Joyner's in the evening to practise some glees with the boys, and I renewed my boyish recollections by looking over the old schoolroom. After the practice we had a look at the boys' drawings, some of which were very good indeed; then Mr Joyner amused us by reading some specimens of his pupils' compositions relating to the life of Oliver Goldsmith. We also inspected some autographs of celebrities which he had collected.

25th Christmas Day. A rather dull day ... Received several cards, one from Joe Ward, another anonymous one from Corsham in a lady's handwriting ...

27th Emily, Clara, Wilfrid, Ernest, Clare and I drove to Bradford in the afternoon and went to Mr Beavan's to tea and supper. We had music and dancing in the evening and the ringers had a pull on the bells at the parish church. We started back soon after eleven; it was a frosty moonlight night. Mr Kenway was married to Miss Headley.

28th A rather dull day. Harry, Arthur, Ben, Nellie and Lily Beavan and Mrs Willie Beavan came over in the afternoon and I went down to the pond with them and had some skating; the ice was good but there was some water on the top. As Arthur was coming off he went over a hole and went in to his middle. I found a change for him for the rest of the evening. We had music etc.

29th A hard frost; went down to the pond with Clare before breakfast and had an hour and a half of good skating ... There were nearly 300 on the ice in the afternoon. I wheeled Minnie, Clara, Emily and Katie Moody in the small chair some of the time.

31st A fine day ... but I didn't go down to the pond as Dad was unwell and we were busy. Fiddled the Old Year out at twelve o'clock. The old ringers rang the church bells.

NOTES FOR 1887

January 3rd Sarah Beilby is now 'Sally'. 'Writing to Kate': 'Aunt Clara' had in mind a better match for Kate!

14th Daisy kept all Herbert's letters, most of which have survived, including this one, still with its Melksham postmark.

31st Curfew: rung nightly (till after the 1914 war).

March 12th Major Brinkworth was still giving recitals in the early 1900s – the whole of Tennyson's 'Enoch Arden' at Chippenham Secondary School and of Dickens's 'Christmas Carol' in Corsham Parish Room, from memory. See November 23rd, 1880.

April 2nd 'A fine day' – and for most of this April.

April 8th 'Wrote to Kate Goold' – the excuse her birthday on April 8th!

May 14th Fishpond: beyond Weavern farm.

16th 'Little Emmie': born after about 20 years of marriage!

June 28th The fields by the tanyard (formerly part of the Goold Pound Pill property), provided fodder, rest and exercise for the horse.

July 6th Mr Francis's farm: in Hartham Park above Collett's Bottom.

12th Ruff: see Aug. 22nd 1880.

25th Screen: the weather was continuing fine.

August 29th Jessie had left Prospect to keep house for an uncle at Easton Piercy.

September 13th Edith was at a boarding school run by an old pupil of her mother's in Cornwall. She used to break her journey at Corsham.

15th 'Family group': probably taken to celebrate the approaching Silver Wedding, 14th January 1889.

October 11th Bertram Spackman, of Calne: son of H. Dunsdon Spackman.

November 30th Zion Hill chapel is at the top of Station Hill.

December 15th Mr Joyner had succeeded Charles Hulls as head master of the School.

(age 23–24)

In contrast to 1887, this seems to have been a very unpleasant
year for weather, with a long snowy winter – hardly any
skating – and a wet stormy summer – hardly any bathing. But
nothing seemed to interfere with other leisure activities; and
they got around, by train, brake, wagonette, bicycle or on
foot, to parties, rehearsals, concerts, missionary and political
meetings, entertainments (for various good causes), bazaars,
church and chapel services, family visits and so forth, in all
weathers and at all hours of day and night. Herbert went to
everything – except when dates clashed as they often did –
either to take part or as reporter.

JANUARY

3rd (Tuesday) A hard frost. Went down to the pond for an hour and a half before tea. The ice was in capital condition, but few were down there, not suspecting it was skatable. Choral practice in the evening, the first after Christmas. Caleb Davis came.

4th Miss West's dance. Clara and we four went; started about 8 o'clock and got home about 2.30. Had a lark with the girls under the mistletoe.

5th Miss Lewis's dance. We four were driving out in the trap after shop when the shaft broke and we had to dismount and walk the rest of the way. Enjoyed ourselves very much at the dance; Miss New played some of the time and Clare the rest. Got home about 4 o'clock. Mr Kenway and Maitie paid us a flying visit in the afternoon.

13th Mrs Dickson's ball; Lewin, Wilfrid and I, Fred Cole and Mr Cole went up in our wagonette at 9 o'clock, and Clara and Mrs Cole were to come directly after us in Griffin's, but he was late and they missed the theatricals. The ballroom was splendidly done up. I danced 21 out of 24 and had Miss Carrie Dickson and Mrs Peters and Edith Awdry as partners. Fred Cole, Wilfrid and I walked home together; it was very dark and we almost had to feel our way ... Didn't get home till 6 o'clock.

18th 'Elijah' at Chippenham. Porter's brake came over to fetch us; Minnie and Katie, Ernest, Clare, Wilfrid and Dad came. There were a frightful lot of muddles in the performance. Miss Awdry sang soprano and Mr Nash the bass. Got home about 11.30.

20th Biddestone concert. Clare and I went over in the trap in the evening and after tea picnic-fashion amongst the school children the entertainment commenced. We played two pieces; the children sang very well from tonic sol-fa and they acted capitally. Very foggy night.

23rd Wilfrid's dance. It was quite a success. There were about 130 there, many coming from Melksham, Box, Bath, Chippenham, Draycot, Sutton, Biddestone etc. I played with Willie Taylor, but danced 4 times, 3 of them being Leap Year dances; Mrs Clark asked me for the waltz which I enjoyed.

25th Wootton Bassett concert. Lewin, Wilfrid, Minnie and Katie, Clara, Ernest, Clare and I went up by the 4.40 train; two conveyances were at Wootton Bassett to meet us and we drove to Cousin Bessie's. Herr Slaboski the violinist was there and he was a great joke; his violin solos were all fireworks. The audience encored our 'Pirates of Penzance' overture ...

28th (Saturday) Clare and I went to Street by the 2.20 train, reached Glastonbury at 5.24 and got in the bus; Mr Porter and Stan met us. After tea we had some music and then went to the hall for a rehearsal of the band pieces for the concert; I enjoyed it very much. Watched the eclipse of the moon (total).

FEBRUARY

1st (Wednesday) Entertainment at Pickwick. Captain Jones and the two Miss Awdrys acted in two extracts from Dickens' 'Martin Chuzzlewit' which were very amusing. Captain Jones played a violoncello solo and Mrs Jones sang two songs in excellent style. Three Miss Awdrys sang 'Three Little Maids from School' very well together.

2nd Had some skating on the pond during dinner time. Lacock entertainment. We drove our wagonette down and took Mr Bolton, Fred Cole and Mr Jones. We did some hand-bell ringing, and our everlasting 'The Letter' which was encored. Ernest and Clare took part in a dialogue entitled 'All Is for the Best', which amused the audience. Had some refreshment afterwards and then walked home. It was snowing all the way.

4th Had a paper from Joe Ward with an account of the concert at Street; cracked Clare and me up beautifully. Dad's birthday, 64 years of age.

9th Great excitement in the house over the forthcoming Spelling Bee; everyone looking up dictionaries ...

10th Corshamside entertainment. Walked out there in the evening to get a report of it. One of the Miss Wallingtons played a banjo accompaniment to her songs very well, and two Miss Clutterbucks acted part of 'Martin Chuzzlewit'. Captain and Mrs Jones also took part.

14th [Having spent the night at the Belchers in Chippenham after playing for a dance.] Awful snowstorm in the night; didn't attempt to get home in the morning so had some music with Nellie, and Mr Belcher showed me over the malt house. Started to get home by the 2 train, but owing to the snow the trains were all late and I didn't arrive home till tea-time.

22nd Went to Lodge in the evening and Sergeant Hawthorn from India, a member of the Grand Lodge, paid us a visit and made a speech.

MARCH

5th Clara's birthday. Coming-of-age of 'Bittens'. Wilfrid, Ernest, Clare and I gave her a bookshelf made by Mr Bromley, and I put it up for her. She had many nice presents and letters from Nottingham, Liverpool, London etc. Poor John, the jackdaw, died in the morning.

6th My vaccination meeting ... It was well attended. Mr John Fuller took the chair. Mr Harbutt had prepared two diagrams which did good service on the platform.

7th (Wednesday) Harry and Edith Cook, Lewin, Minnie and Katie to tea; Clara's birthday party. We played Nap and the spelling game till supper time.

8th Bought 2 vols. of bound music (trios, symphonies, etc.) which at one time belonged to Miss Poynder.

12th Clare went down to Bath and had 12 teeth out, preparatory to getting a new set of false ones. He didn't take any gas.

15th Mr Schottler came up from Bath with my new violin in the morning. I paid him £12 for it then, leaving £4. 5s to pay. I took him down to the Town Hall and through the park and saw him off at the station by the 12 train. I like the violin very much on a first acquaintance, and the splendid case.

22nd Ernest Lanham was here to tea, come down for a rest and left London for good.

APRIL

2nd (Easter Monday) Frank Ryall, Fred Cole, Frank Dyer and us four started off for Bath after breakfast via Colerne and Batheaston and had a jolly walk on the downs. Had some lunch at the Pioneer Coffee Tavern, and in the afternoon went to the 'Cloches de Corneville' at the theatre. Schottler was playing first violin. It was very enjoyable. Had tea at West's and back by the 7 train.

7th Packed up the album for Kate Goold's birthday present and sent it off; also wrote her a letter.

13th A fine day. Clare and I played at the dance held in Colerne school-room. I had to tune the piano first; it was in a frightful state. It was a very jolly dance and no intoxicating drinks were allowed. We walked there and back and reached home a little before 5 (a.m.).

18th Good Templars' anniversary. Public meeting in the evening and Brother Churchill was made a presentation of a handsome regalia and portmanteau. I played 'Trovatore' as a violin solo and also obbligato to 'When Lovers Say Goodnight'. Mr Brinkworth read a humorous piece of poetry and also sang a song, and Ernest and Clare took part in a capital dialogue. The room was full.

29th (Sunday) Minnie went to Bristol to fetch Willie's son.

30th Had a telegram from Joe Spackman asking for help at the concert at Eastbury as they had been disappointed at the last moment by Newbury friends. ... Had a letter from Schottler asking me to play for him at the theatre on Thursday. Minnie came back from Bristol, with Harold.

MAY

1st Grandma's birthday (79). Wilfrid, Ernest, Clare and I went up to see her before breakfast and sang 'Many Happy Returns of the Day' outside her room. Clara and I went to Eastbury to help at the concert; Joe met us at Shrivenham and we had a windy drive to Aunt Clare's. I was enthusiastically received in my two solos and repeated part of one of them. Sang a duet with Clara and played obbligato to one of her songs. A Miss Burbage, a friend of Aunt's, played the piano very nicely.

2nd (Wednesday) Had a capital game of tennis after breakfast with Joe and Mary. Had a wretched drive in terrible wind and rain to Hungerford in the trap. Aunt gave us a half-sovereign each on leaving. We all went to Grandma's to tea in the evening and afterwards went to Mrs Baines' to a quadrille party which was very enjoyable.

3rd Went down to Bath in the afternoon to attend a rehearsal of 'Pirates of Penzance' at the theatre, taking Mr Schottler's place ... The performance went very well; I could watch some of it. This was my first appearance in a theatre orchestra.

4th Finished reading 'Knight Errant' by Edna Lyall, one of the best books I have ever read.

8th A most peculiar letter came by post today from someone in Nottingham addressed to Madame Bianca Goldozin, c/o Mr Spackman. We could make nothing of it.

9th The mystery about the letter was explained by Daisy Goold writing to Clara

Weavern Farm

and confessing it was a lark she and Miss Fromm, the pianist, had with a gentleman of Miss Fromm's acquaintance; we were delighted to find that he had answered it so wittily.

11th Painting the greenhouse a good part of the day. Clara heard from Nellie Beavan in the evening to say that poor Ben had died in his sleep Thursday night from syncope.

13th (Sunday) A delicious day ... In the afternoon Wilfrid, Ernest, Fred Cole and Frank Ryall went down to the Weavern with me and we got in the fishpond and had a capital swim. The water was a little chilly for the first time.

17th A wet day. Made an imitation oar for Clara's 'Grace Darling' at the waxworks show.

18th Dr Kemm died early in the morning; he had only been ill from Tuesday.

23rd Beautiful weather. We shut shop at 12 o'clock and attended Dr Kemm's funeral ... After dinner Clara, Emily, Kate Wild and Katie Moody, Fred Cole, Ernest, Wilfrid and I went down to the Weavern and had tea at Mrs Poulsom's after a bathe. Coming back we had a set of lancers at Collett's Bottom.

24th Once more in harness ... I took Kate Wild to Number 7 shaft in the afternoon and we went down and had a look at the stone industry beneath. Mr Yockney was very attentive and provided us with lamps, asking us to rest at his offices and even to take tea at his house. Emily came with us.

27th (Sunday) A fine day. Went for a walk round Westrop and Dry Arch in the afternoon with Miss Barrington and Miss Wheeler, assistants at Crook's, and after church in the evening went over the Batters with Miss Wheeler.

JUNE

3rd (Sunday) A beautiful day. Went out for a walk with Miss Wheeler in the afternoon, down Collett's Bottom, and dawdled about till nearly 6 o'clock, only getting home just in time for church. Went out again with her in the evening.

4th Went for a walk with Miss Wheeler over the Hilly Fields in the evening.

5th Went for a walk with Miss Wheeler to the Dry Arch in the evening.

7th Went for a walk to Hartham Church and back with Miss Wheeler in the evening.

10th (Sunday) A splendid day ... In the afternoon went down to Bath by the 2.10 train with Miss Wheeler and went through the Victoria Park and had a look inside the Abbey. Went to tea together at West's and then had a nice stroll up to Beechen Cliff and came back in time to catch the 7 train. We got out at Box and walked home over the hill.

11th Went for a walk to the Dry Arch with Miss Wheeler after shop.

12th In the afternoon Clare and I drove up to Colerne to play at their dance ... It was very showery and the dance had to take place in the barn instead of on the grass. Didn't break up till 12 o'clock. A lot of drunkenness on.

14th Went for a walk in the park with Miss Barrington in the evening.

17th Had a letter from Miss Wheeler, and also from Miss Burbage offering two tickets for the Handel festival.

24th (Sunday) Made up my mind to go to London for a little holiday if the Governor was agreeable. When I got home popped the question and it was all right.

25th Drove over to Chippenham in the afternoon to catch the excursion train to London for a fortnight's holiday with Aunt Jane.

27th Had an order for the House of Commons sent by Mr Fuller, and went down there in the morning, looking in at Uncle's shop first, and also into Schott's shop and bought 4 pieces of music. Heard Gladstone and Sir Michael Hicks Beach speak on the Channel Tunnel Bill, and saw Bradlaugh, Sir Wilfrid Lawson, Lord Randolph Churchill and others. Went to Madame Tussaud's in the evening and enjoyed looking at the waxworks.

29th In the morning Miss Burbage and I met Lewin and we went to the Crystal Palace; got good seats for the Festival and the performance of 'Israel in Egypt' by the tremendous body of voices was excellent. Lewin went back to Corsham afterwards; I stayed and had a look round the Palace, going on the toboggan and the switchback railway.

JULY

3rd (Tuesday) Went to South Kensington Museum with the two Miss Bells, Ernest Bell and Aunt Laurie, and then on to the concert at Prince's Hall by myself. Heard Thomas the harpist play and other interesting items. Had tea at a restaurant and then went to Moore & Burgess's Minstrels which I enjoyed immensely ... very clever performance on sleigh bells and dulcimer.

4th Went to tea at Mrs Coxall's and afterwards to the Prince of Wales Theatre to hear 'Dorothy'. The band was capital and the acting too.

5th Ernest Bell and I went to the Crystal Palace in the afternoon. Saw Leonie Dare make her wonderful balloon ascent, and visited the picture gallery. Splendid fireworks at 9, one piece to imitate the Spanish Armada. Some very good juggling also took place, and last of all 'Midsummer Night's Dream' ballet which was a really beautiful spectacle.

7th Back to Corsham by the 12.13, a quick and comfortable journey ... Lewin, Clare and I went to Lord Methuen's in the evening to play some music while a party of gentlemen were having dinner. We enjoyed the novelty of the situation – behind a screen.

28th Very wet day; Chippenham cricket match postponed. Mr Wolper, Blanche and Edith Goold (from Bath) and Edith Goold from Nottingham came here in the evening; Blanche played one or two pieces on the piano.

AUGUST

2nd Ernest Goold came here to stay for a bit.

6th Bank Holiday. Emily, Clara, Ernest, Clare, Wilfrid, Edith and Ernest Goold and I went to Edington in the brake with the members of the C.E.T.S. Reached it 9.30. Ernest took his microscope with him and caused some amusement. We had boating, swinging, a look at the church and a ramble over the downs. I was about with Florrie Holmes most of the day.

7th A fine day. Went to Mr Alfred Cole's to supper in the evening; Wilfrid, Clare, Emily, Clara, Edith and Ernest Goold were there. Had a letter from Kate

(Nottingham) asking for the loan of her photo for copying. Heard of Frank Wheeler's death in New Zealand, June 21st.

9th Choir outing to Avebury. Started about 10 o'clock – we shut up shop, Dad coming with us. We stopped at Cherhill and had lunch in a field, then to the Monument and White Horse. Drove on to Silbury Hill, which we went up, and then into Avebury. Went in Mr Kemm's grounds and played cricket there after tea. Service at the church in the evening.

19th (Sunday) Got up at 4.30 and drove Ernest to Seend to catch the train for Newbury; it was very cold and foggy, but better coming back. In the afternoon Charlie Freeth and his sister Annie came over and went for a walk to Collett's Bottom with us ...

23rd In the afternoon took Edith and Ernest Goold, May King and Lily James to the quarries; had 3 lanterns and made a good exploration.

29th Bazaar at Elm Grove. The waxworks exhibition was the great attraction. It was a trying ordeal to keep an immovable countenance through it all. We came out in our fantastic garb on the lawn, and then went in to tea in the ladies' company.

SEPTEMBER

2nd (Sunday) Had a great deal of music during the day as it was wet and Cousin James was with us. Wilfrid and I and Cousin James went out in the park in the afternoon, but it was raining all the time. Lewin played 'Adoramus' after evening service.

4th Went to Dr Crisp's to see about a report of his wedding, and he tipped me half a sovereign.

5th Polly Goold (Mrs Wolper) came at 4.30. She was looking very well.

12th Lily and Nellie Beavan and a Miss Pearce came over from Bradford in the afternoon and stayed to tea ... Polly Goold tried Mr Moody's tricycle. Supper at Minnie's and music afterwards.

OCTOBER

3rd Harold Moody went away from us, leaving us all very sore-hearted. Willie Moody fetched him. Spelling Bee at the Town Hall in the evening; large attendance. I was one of the referees. Clara won 4th prize; the bank clerk (Barnes) won first, a gentleman named Shovelton (Chippenham) second and Miss Rosie Churchill 3rd.

5th A cold day ... James Balch and Albert Feaviour came in the shop in the afternoon, having returned from New Zealand, and we had a long chat together; they were not much altered except for their beards.

7th (Sunday) A fine day. Clare had a letter from Mr Gladstone of Lacock, offering him the post of organist at Bowden Hill church for £17. 10s a year; after consultation with the Governor he decided to accept it.

11th Performance of 'Daughter of Moab' at the Baptist Chapel in the evening went off very well; the chairman, Mr Webb of Melksham, in his speech spoke in very complimentary terms of the violin playing.

14th A beautiful day. Went for a walk to Hudswell and back through Yockney's Park before morning service with Wilfrid. In the afternoon we went to the Weavern and back round Rudloe; a sore toe partly spoiled my enjoyment.

17th Spelling Bee at the Town Hall with the following results: Miss Fry, 1st prize; Wilfrid 2nd, and Clare 3rd; Miss Chapman 4th. There was a short entertainment afterwards concluding with a dialogue ... Minnie went to Bristol and brought back Harold next day.

22nd A Liberal meeting at the Town Hall in the evening. Mr Fuller, M.P., explained the new Local Government Act, making a capital speech ... Mr Mayo was unanimously elected county councillor. Reported the meeting and transcribed up to 1.30.

24th My birthday (24th). Had a little frame for Minnie's and Rover's photograph given me by Ma; a tie from Alice; umbrella from Dad. Went to the concert at Bath in the evening and heard Madame Stirling, Henry Guy ... Barrington Foote, Miss Geraldine Morgan (violin), Monck ('cellist) and Pachmann (pianist). Walked home afterwards; Wilfrid (& co) met me at Box.

NOVEMBER

8th (Thursday) Went to a Conservative meeting at the Town Hall. Mr Donati was the speaker, and after he had finished, Mr Morris, a Hartham man, came on the platform and spoke as a Radical Socialist, which was rather fun; the majority present were Liberals and cheered him to the echo. The meeting terminated with cheers for Gladstone. Wrote it out afterwards.

21st Went over to Chippenham in the evening to attend the concert and hear Mrs Langston play the violin; I admired her bowing and full tone, but her intonation was not good throughout. A Miss Haggard, whose name was very misleading as she was a pretty girl, sang and also Miss Awdry.

27th [Concert at Calne.] ... I slept at the Coffee Tavern on a spring mattress which was a new sensation to me.

DECEMBER

3rd Went to the Band of Hope entertainment in the evening; the Rev. Foster of Gloucester gave an interesting magic lantern show and some local celebrities were exhibited, among them being Mr Linton, Mr Lyne, Lewin and Clare, Clara and Katie Moody, George Robins, Wood the fish man and many others.

6th Went down to Bath with Clare to play two pieces at Mr Harbutt's exhibition ... a little boy played the harp wonderfully well. Had a look at the pictures, then went to Mr Harbutt's to tea ... I stayed to see 'Yeomen of the Guard' and enjoyed it immensely. Slept at West's.

12th Choral Society Concert in the evening. There was a capital attendance; the orchestra sat surrounded by pot plants and ferns and I felt very comfortable. Polly West got on very well for her first appearance. Clara sang the solos in the 13th Psalm, and both that and 'Joan of Arc' went well. Had the usual family-circle confab over the events afterwards.

13th Went to Sherston with the Good Templars in the evening; a rather cold drive, but we enjoyed ourselves; I played two solos with harmonium (!) accompaniment, and Clare, Ernest and I sang 'Dame Durdon' and 'A Little Farm Well Tilled'. Refreshments afterwards; moonlight drive home.

15th (Sat.) Two columns in the 'Bath Herald' of my news.

23rd (Sunday) Katie Moody was christened after evening service.

24th Had a card from Edith Goold. Went in to Minnie's to tea with the rest and had a jolly evening party, singing and dancing etc., and a new game, 'History of England'.

25th Christmas Day ... We sang a Te Deum by Sullivan and an anthem by Barnby. In the afternoon the choir sang a Christmas Service of Song entitled 'Christmas tide'; Ernest made an awful muddle of his bass recitative, but the rest went all right. Went to Mrs Baines's party in the evening and enjoyed ourselves.

29th In the evening went to West Kington and Castle Combe with Mr Fuller in the brake and reported the meeting ... a very cold night. Clare was appointed secretary of the Provident Club in connexion with the Bath Stone firm.

31st A frost. Went over to Chippenham in the evening to a little party at Mr Freeth's ... The dust we made on the carpet made me cough, but otherwise the evening was very enjoyable. Claude Gane played a waltz for half an hour and I danced it with Fanny Freeth, and the poor girl was upset afterwards, though she said she wasn't tired ... Clare received his appointment as organist of the Bowden Hill church at £20 per annum.

NOTES FOR 1888

February 1st Captain Jones: Captain (later Major) Aylmer-Jones was the father of Felix Aylmer-Jones who became famous on stage and screen as Sir Felix Aylmer; he was born in Corsham in 1889. Among other parts he played Polonius to Gielgud's Hamlet in the 1930s. See also 30th October 1889.

March 5th 'Bittens' – Clara's pet name – bestowed by Wilfrid?

15th 'My new violin': Herbert's own note on this, written in 1939, reads: 'Bought my third and last violin ... It has been with me all round the world and a valued companion. I have tried violins made in Cremona valued from £100 to £1000, but on neither of them have I felt so much at home. I am sorry it came from Germany – but never mind!'

April 29th Harold Moody, Willie Moody's son, was adopted by Lewin and Minnie, but kept his name.

May 1st 'Aunt Clare': widow of Clare Flower Spackman.

8th Bianca Goldozin: the letter has survived!

June 4th Hilly Fields: footpath from Pickwick to Neston.

17th Exit Miss Wheeler!

August 7th Kate's photo: to be copied for John Coy, her fiancé!

19th Annie Freeth: Later teacher of Standards 1 and 2 at the Methuen School.

29th Waxworks: Herbert was 'The Ancient Mariner'.

Herbert's new violin – his last – sees good service in concerts and dances, and in teaching. He buys a 'safety' bicycle at last, shared by the family (see October 22nd). Kate Goold's marriage to John Coy is noted. At the end of the year Corsham gets its own water supply.

JANUARY

1st (Tuesday) Clare and I went down to Bristol in the afternoon to attend a party at Mr James's. I took my violin ... and had a very appreciative audience; one lady saying I could earn £20 a week in London! We played Nap and had songs, keeping it up till after 1 o'clock.

2nd A hard frost. Clare and I plunged in Mr James's bath in the morning. ... [Back to Corsham.] Mr Lyne gave Clare a dress jacket and waistcoat, making the third stroke of luck within the last two or three days for Clare. Mr Cole's piano came and was taken to their house without Mrs Cole's knowledge so as to be a surprise for her.

3rd Hard frost. Clara, Wilfrid, Ernest, Clare and I, and Lewin and Minnie went to Miss West's dance in the evening. We had great fun by having sets entirely of ladies and then only gentlemen; I got into the new waltz capitally with Miss Holmes. Kissed a lot of the girls under the mistletoe on leaving.

5th Frost again. Went down on the pond about 12.30 and stayed till 2. There were about 200 down there, a good many being strangers. Douglas Pictor fell in up to his neck near the railings, and Smith, pupil teacher at the British School, went in up to his middle; the pond was cleared about 4 o'clock.

14th A dull day. In the evening went in Mr Fuller's brake to Seagry, Sutton and Christian Malford ... At Christian Malford the people were very enthusiastic and the meeting was held on the green. At Sutton there was considerable opposition, started by the vicar of Draycot ... he was very insolent and un-mannerly.

16th A dull day. Clara, Wilfrid, Ernest, Clare and I went to Mrs Baines's in the evening to a dancing party; I took the violin and played some of the time ... I danced 5 waltzes with Miss Holmes, one with Clara and one with Ada Ayliffe who said she had never enjoyed one so much. We stayed till about 3 o'clock.

18th Mr Filter, the Primrose League candidate for the county council, was to have held a meeting at the British School, but the keys not having been obtained the meeting was abandoned.

21st C.E.T.S. meeting at the Town Hall in the evening; the bell ringers played 'The Merry Peasant' and 'The Harmonious Blacksmith' on the hand-bells. Ernest sang the Blacksmith's Song in character, with anvil and all on the platform. Very full room.

27th (Sunday) A beautiful day ... In the afternoon went over to Chippenham with Miss Holmes and heard Willie Taylor play 'The Lost Chord' on St Paul's organ; walked about Chippenham a bit, then took it quietly home ...

FEBRUARY

5th (Tuesday) Confirmation at the church in the afternoon; 92 candidates. Katie Moody and Emily were 'done'.

7th A fine day. Went out to Mr Fuller's in the evening with Major Brinkworth, Wilfrid, Ernest and Clare to help with the music at the supper given to the workmen on the estate. Before supper we went into the library and talked with Mr and Mrs Fuller, Mr John Fuller and Miss Fuller. After the supper Mr Fuller made a speech and then for the rest of the evening there was dancing

(Clare and I played), and Mr Brinkworth gave songs and comic readings. Mr Inkpen also sang several songs. Kept it up till about 12 and then the fly took us home. Very enjoyable affair.

11th A cold day. Helped Frank Baines prepare the room for the ball. (Cricket dance.) We did it with French chalk and found it answered very well ... It went off very nicely; the bats, wickets and balls lent by Mr Ayliffe, together with the evergreens and flags, gave the room a cheerful appearance. There were about 130 present and a set had to be formed on the platform to make room for them all. Clare and I and Workman from Swindon were the band and we got through it very well. Finished at 4 o'clock. I had 3 waltzes, 2 with Miss Holmes and one with Clara.

12th Miss Awdry's wedding ... Lewin had a guinea for playing. We four, Wilfrid, Ernest, Clare and I, had a sovereign each from Mr and Mrs Fuller for helping at their supper on Thursday last.

16th Aunt Sarah and Louis came for a short stay. Enjoyed hearing them sing after supper. Such a treat to hear a boy's voice producing notes with such ease and perfect intonation.

18th A dull day ... Clara, Wilfrid, Ernest, Clare and I went to Mr Fuller's to the tenants' ball and enjoyed ourselves immensely ... There were 25 dances down on the programme but Clare and I played 5 extras, and the band (Willie Taylor's) played several more, so that there were nearly 40 dances in all; I danced 13 or 14 with Miss Holmes – she waltzes so nicely. There were nearly 200 people there, of course not all dancers. There was a splendid spread for supper and refreshments were to be had all the evening. I regret to say several partook of more than was good for them. There were cheers for Mr and Mrs Fuller at the close, 3.45.

19th In the afternoon Mr Brown and Mr Osborne came in to see Dad about letting the school room for the Primrose League meeting, and Mr Brown blamed Dad for the 'missing key' on the last occasion; so the Guvnor fired up and at last showed Mr Brown the door, [he] using some not very Parliamentary language as he ignominiously retired.

21st To Lacock in the wagonette ... to help with the entertainment for funds towards the new piano for our Lodge; I played Handel's 'Largo' ... Louis sang 'Who's that a-calling?' and was encored, and responded with 'The Finger Post'

24th (Sunday) A fine day ... In the afternoon went over to Chippenham with Miss Holmes and walked up to Hardenhuish church; stayed to the service and then went back to Mrs Culvert's to tea. Went to the parish church in the evening and then walked back; went in to Mrs Baines's and had a little supper.

26th Finished reading 'A Terrible Temptation' by Charles Reade which I enjoyed very much.

MARCH

7th Very wet day. March Fair; miserable business; about half a dozen head of cattle.

8th Very heavy rain all day; went to Melksham in the afternoon; the water was very high at night and Fred, who came to meet me, had to drive through it up to the horse's knees. It was very rough driving home, sleet blowing straight into us.

12th Received a letter from Miss Holmes in the morning accusing me of being false to her and other accusations for which there wasn't the slightest foundation; I didn't answer it. She was in the shop in the evening with Mrs Baines, but I didn't speak to her.

13th A fine day. In the evening went to Lodge and heard a paper read by Miss Aust on 'Ought fermented Wine to be Used at the Lord's Table?' There was a discussion on it afterwards and a resolution was passed, discountenancing the use of fermented wine.

15th Dressed the drapery window for the first time, Wilfrid and I; we got quite interested in it.

19th Stormy day. Started for Melksham at 5.30. Had a rehearsal of our trio 'Andante' from Mendelssohn's D Minor trio, and found Mr Rowland Hill a very nice player and a pleasant fellow; he played for a solo Schubert's 'Ave Maria'. There was a good audience and they loudly applauded our quartet 'Mélodie Religieuse' ... Afterwards we all went into the schoolroom to supper; enjoyed the evening very much as the people were all so sociable.

20th A stormy day. Anniversary of the Good Templar Lodge in the evening, and inauguration of the new piano. Lewin supplied it to the Lodge for £22 10s which Ernest had collected all but about 30s. ... I played 'Carnival at Venice' and variations, and attempted to play it from memory but failed and had to refer to the music; everyone seemed pleased with it, but I was thoroughly disgusted with the performance. Clare opened the piano with a solo and Clara sang 'The Quaker's Daughter'. Our violin quartet went very well.

28th Heard of John Bright's death.

28th (Thursday) Heard from Mr Harbutt mid-day post who informed me to my great surprise that I had been unanimously elected a vice-president of the Bath Anti-Vaccination Society, and asking me to stand; I wrote back thanking the members for the honour they had done me, and particularly Mr Harbutt, who I felt sure I was indebted to more than anyone else, and accepted.

30th Deeply interested in a book entitled 'Without a Home' by E. P. Rowe.

APRIL

8th Went up to Mr Joyner's in the morning for shorthand lesson; tried a different dodge by making the boys correct each other's exercises instead of their own and gave them marks according to their mistakes. George Freeth came in the afternoon. Miss Bolwell and party from Bath gave a temperance drama at the Town Hall in the evening entitled 'The Fruits of the Wine Cup'. Some of the acting was very good, others very poor ...

10th A fine day. Had a turn-out of my music and commenced making a catalogue. Went out to Mr Owen's in the evening and came back on his safety-bicycle which I brought on probation; he wants £5 for it.

12th Went to Melksham in the afternoon on Mr Owen's 'safety' and put it up at Mr Burgess's where I had tea. After giving lessons it was raining, and I was undecided about going home, but thinking they would be nervous about me I started, and by the time I reached home I was wet through. Of course I dismounted a good many times, for all the hills. Had my supper in my nightgown in Ma's room.

13th Decided not to invest in the bicycle unless I could get it for £4, as it needed additions to it; but Mr Owen was in in the evening and said he had a lamp and splasher, and would split the difference; so I bought it for £4. 10s.

21st (Easter Sunday) Lewin played the Hallelujah Chorus in the evening. Wore a new suit of clothes. Received an Easter book from Miss Holmes.

23rd Stormy day. Second performance of the Shadow Pictures at the Town Hall in the evening, it being very successful on Monday. I played violin obbligato to Clara's song. Rosie Wilton (Burgess) came over from Melksham and sang two songs.

27th A fine day … Ernest Lanham and Miss Belcher up in the evening. Had a crop in the morning at Little's and afterwards shaved off whiskers.

Corsham Cricket Ground

MAY

1st Had our first game of cricket in the field in the evening. Albert Feaviour was there, bowling in his old style. Afterwards went up to see Grandma on her 80th birthday. She was in good spirits and had received a good many letters and presents and also a telegram from Uncle John.

2nd Heard that Mr Linton was going to leave Corsham, on very good authority, Mr Linton having himself told Mr Neate so.

11th (Saturday) Lewin's office nicely papered and painted; put down some floor-cloth for him … Albert Thomas came here and slept in the spare room with me. We had a walk after supper and he told me of his affairs with Florrie Neate.

18th Finished reading 'Amelia' by Fielding; had heard much about the immorality of his works but failed to see any signs in 'Amelia'.

22nd Poor Piggy Wiggy died; I gave him some medicine about 11.30, went again about 2.30 and found him dead in the stable; Martin buried him in the tanyard.

25th A dull day. Match with Lansdown. They made 69 and we only 29. Then came some very sensational cricket; Clare pegged in his left-handers and took 6 wickets for no runs, and they were all out for 12; Corsham then made 53, the required number of runs, for the loss of 7 wickets, and it was very exciting at the finish. Sir John Dickson Poynder made 33 not out and hit the ball twice on to the Methuen School.

28th Went round for orders in the morning and Mr Coates caught me making a short cut into Hastings Road from Paul Street; I promised not to go that way again.

29th Went to Lodge in the evening. Mr Barnes gave a paper on vegetarianism, and after the discussion some pudding, brown bread, fruit, coffee etc. was handed round at 3d per head; it was a very enjoyable evening.

JUNE

16th (Sunday) A fine day. We thought it quite time we had a fine Sunday. Went to Weavern in the afternoon and got in.

23rd Went for a long walk with Dad in the afternoon round Monks, Elm Grove and Chapel Knapp, to Ladsbrook and home through the hay field where we rested a short time. Had some strawberries and cream in at Minnie's in the evening; delicious.

27th Went to Melksham on bicycle in the evening and had a bathe with Albert Burgess at a capital place behind Taylor's mill; afterwards went to Miss Parker's (lessons); before coming away had some sherbet and bread and cheese ... Mr Linton's sale; a great many people there; I went over the house for the first time; it was like a maze.

30th Mr Linton's last Sunday amongst us ... In the evening he preached his farewell sermon and there was a very large congregation ... many of us in the choir found it difficult to sing the last hymn.

JULY

2nd (Tuesday) In the evening Mr Osborne, Mr Hatherell, Lewin and I went down to Mrs Kemm's to present Mr Linton on behalf of the choir with a nice volume of Blunt's Dictionary of Sects, Schools of Thought etc. Mr Osborne presented it and Mr Hatherell read an address which had been written out by Clare; Mr Linton was much affected and said the choir had helped to brighten many a service. Mr Belcher and Reynolds presented him the same evening with a cheque for £233 subscribed by the inhabitants of the town and an illuminated address. Mr Linton came in to say goodbye in the afternoon.

4th Went to Chapel to a missionary meeting in the evening and took Alice; a black clergyman gave an address and showed a wonderful command of our language.

15th (St Swithin.) A beautiful day ... Sarah Goold came here; she drove over from Kington St Michael with Jessie Goold and Jessie stayed to dinner.

24th Ernest came of age. We gave him a silver watch to go with the chain Uncle

Laurie made for him. He received a good many other presents. At Lodge in the evening, the members of the Lodge made him a present of a very nice album with musical box attached. George Robins made the presentation and I shall never forget the amusing way in which he did it; he had evidently got up [a speech] for the occasion, using words he neither knew the meaning of nor the pronunciation, and as luck would have it the musical box at first would not go, and then, when it did, kept on interrupting the speech. The Lodge was in a roar. Lewin and we four gave a programme of Sullivan's music ... Ernest invited the officers of the Lodge to supper here afterwards and they didn't depart till one o'clock.

25th To Calne and Melksham ... where I heard a lot about Mr Harris and his sudden death. (Bicycle accident.) His mother was Roman Catholic and candles were burnt at his death-bed and a hammer and pence placed in his hands, the one to knock at the gate of Heaven and the other to pay the toll.

29th Had a telegram in the morning to say that Aunt Clara, Kate and Mr Coy were coming down from Nottingham by excursion and would call here. I met them by the 2.20 train; Bertie Goold came too. We found Mr Coy a very pleasant man; he is an amateur photographer and brought some photos of the house in Shakespeare Street. Also a fine copy of Kate's. Aunt and Bertie had to go back by the 5.15 and I went down with them. Lewin played on the organ after shop for Kate and Mr Coy to hear; I blew.

30th Saw Kate off in the morning; Wilfrid and Clare came down to the station with me and Mr Coy was in the train. Went out to Mrs Millin's in the afternoon to her open-air concert ... Mr Lyne, who took the chair, spoke very kindly about me as the violin teacher. I was introduced to the mothers of several pupils who questioned me as to their daughters' learning. The dancing of the pupils was good, and I enjoyed the tea.

AUGUST

1st (Thursday) Clare's birthday ... Dad had a cheque for £250 sent to pay Mr Linton's account; we were very jubilant about it.

4th (Sunday) Dad, Ma, Wilfrid, Ernest and I went to Hillcot for the day; started about 4.30 and drove to Devizes in our wagonette, and went to Woodbury by train, reaching Hillcot at 7.30 ... In the afternoon we went for a drive to Pewsey, Wilfrid going for a walk with Kate; old Israel was at Devizes to meet us and we reached home at about 11. The weather was beautiful.

5th (Bank Holiday) C.E.T.S. outing to Clifton; Ernest, Clare and I went. Started at 8.40 and on reaching Clifton went to the Zoo ... after dinner went to see the county match between Gloucester and Sussex ... we saw W. G. make 84 and the match was otherwise interesting ... Got to Bath about 11; a nice girl next to me in the train chatted all the way. Mrs Little, aged 50, of Linley's ... lost the train looking for her son, Mr Temple Evans, so I walked home with her from Bath; she was so tired that I brought her into the kitchen and gave her some lemonade. She found her son all right when she got home.

13th Saw the Belle of Chippenham, Miss Giles, at the White Lion Hotel; very light hair, powdered face etc.

19th [At Seaforth, Liverpool, on a visit to the Rowells.] A dull day. Went to the waste ground in Church Road in the morning and played cricket with Louis and Walter Briggs. In the afternoon Katie, Louie, Walter and I went to Liverpool by train; went to the Museum, Picture Gallery and then to the Cathedral where we heard a nice musical service. After tea went to Bootle Baths ... I enjoyed the dip very much.

22nd A stormy day. Auntie and I went into town ... met Uncle ... and I went with him for a two-hours' cruise in the bay; the landing stage was a novel sight to me and the sea trip was awful fun, as the sea was rough and the water came right up on the upper deck, drenching the people ... On coming back we went to Randall's Exhibition and saw a model of Mrs Maybrick. The other waxwork figures were good, particularly the 'Angel's Gift'.

23rd Had a letter from Maitie Kenway fixing today to come and see them. In the morning I had a musical treat; Mr Shaw, a fine violinist, Mr Thomson, another good player, Mr Dowling, a flute player, Mr Baker, his son Willie and daughter Annie were all here about 11 o'clock. Mr Shaw played one or two solos beautifully ... After dinner I went with Katie to West Kirby to see the Kenways. We got there about 5 o'clock and found them very much grown. I was delighted with the place ... Mrs Kenway I found very pleasant.

26th In the afternoon went to New Brighton and the two Miss Bakers came too ... we were in time for the concert and also saw a very clever flying-trapeze artist's performance ... We had on roller skates and chased each other; tried the switchback railway and finished with dancing to the full band ... Katie and I had 4 waltzes, 2 Schottisches, a polka and lancers. The effect of the lamps around the river coming home was very pretty.

29th (Thursday) Got up at 6 o'clock and after breakfast bid adieu to Uncle, who was in bed. Auntie, Rover, Katie and Louis accompanied me to the station (we cabbed it); I found the two ladies I came up with and got in the same carriage ... In spite of unfavourable weather which prevailed a good deal of the time, I enjoyed my holiday very much. We had to change at Stockport and there three other gentlemen joined us, one of them being very intelligent; he had travelled on the Continent and related some of his experiences. The scenery all through Derbyshire was exceedingly pretty ... Found them all well at home.

SEPTEMBER

1st (Sunday) Lewin, Wilfrid, Sepp Kinneir, Ernest and I went down to the Weavern in the afternoon and bathed; the water was rather cold. Went up to see Grandma for a bit after tea.

19th Wrote out a short letter to Miss Simmonds who was shortly to be married, bringing in nearly 30 musical phrases.

21st Kate Goold was married to Mr Coy.

26th The new vicar, Rev. J. D. Dunlop, came in the evening.

OCTOBER

3rd Dad, Lewin, Clare and I went to Salisbury to hear a political speech by Sir William Harcourt. Mr Fuller drove us in his coach and four and also the brake; I sat just behind Mr Fuller on the coach and we had a splendid drive through Melksham to Trowbridge, and there we booked excursion train to Salisbury. The market house was crowded, about 4 or 5 thousand people there. I reported Sir William Harcourt for nearly an hour. Mr Fuller was well received. Mr Lucas was great fun going. We were sleepy coming back; reached home about one.

6th (Sunday) A stormy day. Harvest Thanksgiving. The church (nicely decorated) was simply crammed in the evening and many could not get admission. ... The choir sang Barnby's anthem, 'Sing to the Lord of Harvest', with duet for trebles and afterwards for tenors and basses.

10th In the morning went on the lake with Mr Bartlett and Wilfrid; took turns at rowing; we chased the swans. Stayed till nearly 8.30.

12th Went to the meeting at Castle Combe in the evening in Mr Fuller's brake ... sat on the box going home; nice moonlight night. Mr Reynolds was drunk in at White's and treating everyone who came in; Ernest went in for a bottle of ginger beer and watched the people for some time; we all thought he had a pretty good nerve.

13th (Sunday) Went over to Castle Combe on Johnny Boscombe's bicycle ... went to Mr Knowle's and they pressed me to stop; had tea and afterwards some music; then they showed me all their fancy work which I thought done extremely well. The eldest Miss Knowle (Mary) gave me her photograph ... Reached home 9.30 without accident.

16th Lewin gave his paper on Caxton at the Lodge open session; large attendance. Mr Neate was buried; Dad was one of the mourners so I took his place as undertaker and had to wear a high hat. A great many tradesmen followed him.

22nd In the evening there was an illuminated procession of cyclists down the High Street. Tom Jakes had a large wooden frame attached to his 'ordinary', on which were hung Chinese lanterns, and his machine was the best. Clare had a Japanese umbrella fixed to our safety, and with small lanterns and coloured balls hanging it looked very pretty. The band headed the procession in the brake, and there were a large number of people about the streets. Mr Lyne and Major Jones were the judges.

23rd Went to Calne (lesson day) and straight from there to Bristol to hear Sarasate the Spanish violinist ... there was a very large audience and the programme couldn't have been better for me, as three pieces he played I had studied. I could hardly breathe while he was playing. Not a note out of tune and all done with so much ease ... I slept at Mrs James; saw a photograph of Gilbert's young lady, Miss Hughes, a very pretty girl. Finished reading 'A Child of Night' by Buchanan.

24th Met Polly West at Bristol Station and we saw Sarasate there; he got in our train and we had a look at him when we got out at Corsham; I wanted to thank him for the treat of last night ... My 25th birthday. Bought 'The Musical Profession', a useful book for future guidance. Had a pair of slippers, a pair of scissors, a piece of music from Lewin and plenty of good wishes.

29th Fred Brett and Miss Bird were married; also at the same time Alfred Bird and Miss Brown.

30th In the evening Major Jones gave his dramatic performance at the Town Hall, commencing with a comedy entitled 'Second Thoughts', and then the comedy 'David Garrick' ... It was splendid and Major and Mrs Jones were all that could be desired; the Yockneys and Awdrys also acted well. Lewin and Clare played music, and refreshments were handed round. It didn't conclude till 11.30.

31st Went to the second performance of 'David Garrick' ... all swells this time; I didn't think it went off quite so well – the performers appearing not quite so much at home. There were refreshments provided on the grand scale, but they entirely forgot the band, and we came away in a not very good humour.

NOVEMBER

1st (Friday) Harold's birthday; 4 years old.

4th In the evening Clara, Wilfrid, Ernest, Clare, Willie Dinham and I drove over to Chippenham in the wagonette to help with the music at the Young Men's Christian Association meeting. Just before we got to the railway bridge we saw a splendid meteor shoot across the sky, half as large as the moon. The little room where the entertainment was held was crammed, and a very bad place for sound. I was encored for 'Carnival at Venice' ... Mr Turpin made an excellent chairman.

6th To Calne ... and on to Melksham afterwards in order to play at the Bazaar at the Free Hall, in connexion with the Congregational Chapel I gave two lessons first and then went in to play a trio (Gypsy Rondo) with Mr Maggs and Mr Rowland Hill, and also to play 'Carnival at Venice'; they encored me for the latter and I told them I was coming on again later. After giving Miss Parker a lesson I went back to play 'Trovatore'. They encored me; I bowed, but it was no use, they insisted, and I played a bit of my first solo again. I received much praise privately, so as to be almost embarrassing; I told Mrs Stratton that if she heard Sarasate she wouldn't want to hear me again.

13th Lewin, Clare, Ernest Lanham and I went over to the Chrysanthemum Show at Melksham in the afternoon to help with the music ... Ernest sang several songs. There was such a cram in the Drill Hall that the people became very noisy and we came off before the programme was finished. Ernest Lanham made us laugh till our sides ached coming home.

14th Our Choral Society concert in the evening; we did 'May Queen' and Mendelssohn's 'Lorelei', and between these two works a Mrs Phillips and her daughter played harp and violin solos beautifully ... There was a good attendance. I walked out with Florrie and Louie Daniel and Mrs Dunsdon afterwards.

DECEMBER

2nd (Monday) In the evening we 4 went up to Mr Hughes, steward to Lord Methuen, to an evening party. Mr Bartlett was there, George Robins, Alice

Dinham, and we had an enjoyable evening.

3rd A hard frost ... Mr Green, master at the school, thrashed Tom Ryall for disobedience, and was sent away by Mr Joyner for doing it.

5th A hard frost. Went down to the pond before breakfast with Clare. Sepp Kinneir was down there and we had a capital skate on a splendid sheet of ice. Went down again after dinner but it was thawing a bit. Skated about with Kate Dyer, Ada Ayliffe and Katie Moody. Robinson and the boys were down there.

7th Fall of snow, several inches. Not very busy in the shop in consequence.

9th (Monday) Went to Mr Joyner's in the morning and took my examination with the first and second class; neither of them were as good as I could have wished, and the second class papers were very bad; they seemed to have entirely forgotten the 'N hook' ...

10th Lewin and I went to Calne mid day to attend a rehearsal for the concert. An altercation ensued between Ten Brink, the leader, and Mr Pullin as to the beat and the time of one of the choruses; they got rather warm and at last Pullin told Brink he was not engaged to teach him. ... There was a pretty good room at the concert; I played viola. The first part was miscellaneous and the second part Van Bree's 'Saint Cecilia' ...

14th Corsham Waterworks were formally opened. The directors went to Lockswells from whence the source arose, and visited all the works between that and Corsham; on arriving at the Methuen Arms they experimented with the water, sending it over the house, and again visited the Vicarage and Town Hall ...

17th Clara and I went to Claremont in the evening for the prize distribution, and entertainment. I played an Elegy by Bazzini for a solo. Mr Dunlop was very witty in giving the prizes. The scene from 'The Merchant of Venice' was very well done. Afterwards there was dancing and Clara and I joined in ... Frightful mud walking home.

25th Christmas Day. Albert Thomas and his sister Ada were both married at Bristol ... Service of Song in the afternoon (Christmastide). Ernest didn't wander in his recitative this time ... At 8 o'clock Clara, Wilfrid, Ernest, Clare, Miss West, Polly West and I went to the Hartham dance; it was held in the laundry, and the company staying in the house came down and joined in. I took Mrs Burton and Miss Bella Dickson for a Swiss Country and afterwards had a polka with Miss Katharine Dickson which I enjoyed very much. I made good use of the mistletoe in the passages, and larked with the servant who used to be at Mr Linton's. We drove home about 2.30 ...

26th After tea Clara, Wilfrid, Ernest and I went up to Grandma's and sang carols, and afterwards went to the Christmas entertainment at the Town Hall. The programme was very good; 'Alanadale' went very well. The Toy Symphony was great fun; three of my pupils were playing violin in it. The Policemen's Chorus from 'Pirates of Penzance ' was good. The room was packed.

27th Social gathering of the Good Templars at the Town Hall; came away ... at 9 to go to the Court Ball. Clare and I played, and Clara, Wilfrid and Ernest went too ... we didn't finish till close upon 5 o'clock. We had several compliments paid us on the music.

NOTES FOR 1889

February 16th Louis Ventura: Aunt Sarah Hawkins's son by her first marriage. Katie (see 19th August) was her daughter by her second marriage to Jack Rowell.

July 15th Sarah Goold: now Sarah Beilby, visiting her cousin Jessie.

29th Kate was now engaged to John Coy (of a well-to-do Leicestershire family) in the Indian Civil Service. 'Bertie', the youngest of the nine Goolds, later adopted his second name of Vivian. Born 1877, he was christened Herbert at Daisy's special request!

August 4th Kate, a Spackman relative.

23rd Mrs Kenway: Mr Kenway had re-married and moved to West Kirby.

September 19th Florrie Simmonds replied, asking when he was going in for an 'augmented second'.

21st This day has a drawing of a flying female fairy, waving a wand and clad only in a girdle.

October 30th Major Jones: see 1st February, 1888.

'Never heard of such a summer'; so little Weavern!
To everyone's disappointment Harry has changed his mind
about coming home in May, and instead urges Lewin and
Herbert to come to New Zealand. In June 'Ma' and Clara
visit Nottingham, and probably talk of this. Daisy sends him
a song, 'Thou'rt Passing Hence' (Sullivan) which revives their
correspondence! He visits her in London. In December she
visits Corsham and they become engaged.

JANUARY

4th (Saturday) Reckoned up my year's accounts and found I had netted £84 1s 0d after paying insurance and not reckoning interest and shop salary; an advance of £14 on last year.

5th Drove Clare to Bowden Hill in the morning; very windy ... Heard from Joe Ward that Mrs Moore was dead; we were much surprised and pained at the news.

6th Received New Zealand mail with the wonderful news that Harry intended coming home in May with Amy and the children, chiefly for his health, and with the suggestion that Clare should go out to take his place in the meantime. We talked a lot about it during the day.

7th A stormy day. I went to Dauntsey in the afternoon to play viola in the parish church at the performance of 'Christ and his Soldiers' ... I had two titled ladies next to me, one playing violin, and the other violoncello ... Supper at the Rectory ... then I was driven into the village and slept with Mr Swinton the schoolmaster. We chatted till about 12 o'clock.

8th Mr Swinton and I had fun in visiting the almshouse ladies whom he was supposed to look after ... I bid adieu about 9 o'clock ... Wrote out an elaborate account for the Gazette ... To Miss West's party where we went through a capital programme of 24 dances, one of them a gentlemen's set of lancers and also a handkerchief dance. Came home about 3.30.

15th Clare and I went to Crudwell beyond Malmesbury to play at the Rectory dance for Willie Taylor ... There were only about 14 dances on the programme but we played 4 or 5 extras and kept it up till 1 o'clock ... We slept in the servants' hall and they brought blankets and pillows for us.

16th We had fun in the morning over our peculiar position and the wretched fare provided for us. Got home by the 10 train ... Martin's birthday, 67.

17th ... Mr Dunsdon of Linley's was thrown from his trap and cut about the face.

28th ... Used the waterwork tap in the morning for the bath for the first time.

31st To Melksham ... and while giving Mrs Stratton her lesson a telegram came for me from home to say that Willie Taylor wanted me for the dance at Kington Langley, so excused myself and had tea with Mrs Stratton and then off home; took about 10 minutes to change and then to Chippenham by the 7 train. The dance was in the schoolroom; Willie and I drove there in the pony trap, and coming back the animal went like the very devil; I thought we should be upset.

FEBRUARY

6th (Thursday) ... 'Christ and his Soldiers' at Malmesbury Abbey. Went very well.

10th ... To Bath by the 5.15 train to attend a fancy dress dance at the Assembly Rooms. Went to Frank Ryall's lodgings ... he donned his yeomanry dress and I my tennis flannels and we went off to the Rooms ... I danced 23 out of 24. The dresses were very good; 3 men had dominoes, one was representing Mephistopheles, another Buffalo Bill; jockeys, sailors, Highlanders, porters, Japanese, Italians and all sorts were there. Came home about 5. I had to refuse one partner some claret.

11th (Tuesday) ... The great talk of the town was the Vicar's behaviour at the

C.E.T.S. meeting the previous evening, with regard to the Presidency. He abused Mr Lyne right and left, blaming him because he was not elected President; Mr and Mrs Foster, Miss Storey and others left the room and the programme of music was abandoned. The matter was left thus: can the Vicar claim his right as vicar of the parish to constitute himself President if the members refuse to have him?

17th Bath orchestral concert in the evening ... Herr Ten Brink led the band and I played just behind him. He played 'Scene de Ballet' for a solo ... Afterwards Clara and we four went to Mr Brett's dance, Pickwick Road; Clare and Clara played some of the time and Fred Brett violin. We stayed till 3 o'clock. I had a game with Annie, servant at Hartham, who used to be at Mr Linton's.

25th ...Bills of our concert were out, and my name very big as leader of the band.

MARCH

5th Clara's birthday ... and choral concert. 'Messiah' was a great success, the choruses going splendidly ... but attendance not good, especially in the front seats. The choral society will probably lose £2 to £3.

24th Went down to Bath with Eddie Goold by the 2 train; went to the Pump Room concert and enjoyed it immensely; it was the first I had been to for more than a year. Afterwards called on Mrs Goold at the Baths and then went with Eddie to his aunt's to tea. Blanche and Edith were at home. At 7 I went to the anti-vaccination meeting ... and was again elected vice-president ... indignation was expressed that the Board of Guardians did not suspend prosecutions till after the result of the Royal Commission was made known. Went back with Eddie to sleep; we went in Mabel Goold's bedroom and watched her sound asleep; she looked so pretty.

31st Heard that the Post Office had fallen to young Bryant, who used to be at Mr Neate's.

APRIL

1st (Tuesday) They tried to make me an April Fool at breakfast by covering the egg-cup with a cosy; I scented it, however.

3rd Wilfrid's birthday. He received a splendid present of 4 volumes of 'Plutarch's Lives' from London; benefactor unknown.

4th (Good Friday) ... In the afternoon I went for a solitary walk down to the Weavern and picked some primroses ... Church practice in the evening. It was my first experience of Mr Dunlop [vicar] as choir master and I didn't relish it.

7th (Easter Monday) Outing to Bromham (16 including some friends). In the evening went to the C.E.T.S. entertainment; I played Overture to 'Zauberflöte' with Clara and Clare; Revd. Lyne sang 'The Lost Chord', his last appearance at a public entertainment in Corsham.

8th (Tuesday) 'Rose Maiden' at Calne (rehearsal and concert). There was a crowded room and the concert went off successfully. I had a solo part for the viola in Mr Morgan's tenor solo 'The Sleep of Even'.

14th A fine day. Dad and I drove to Devizes at 12 o'clock in Beard's trap (for rehearsal and concert) ... Called on Mr Simpson at the Gazette office who again complimented me on my musical reports. Dad, during the rehearsal, inspected the churchyards in Devizes. Nice drive home.

15th Brass band concert in the evening at the Town Hall; Mr Clutterbuck presided. I played Danckler's 'Romance and Bolero' and was recalled; I bowed, but that did not satisfy and I played Raff's 'Cavatina' ... the band showed much improvement and there was a full attendance.

17th Dad received good news from Uncle William (financial).

19th Primrose League meeting at the Town Hall in the evening; I attended to report; there was a very full room; Mr Clutterbuck asked to supper ... Lord Bruce and Sir Robert Fowler were there and yelled at each other across the supper table, telling anecdotes of their experiences in the House. After supper, over which Miss Clutterbuck presided, the gentlemen retired to smoke and coffee, Barnes and I with them, and stayed till one o'clock; then I walked home with West ...

22nd In the afternoon Fred was taking round the goods and one of Mr Osborne's children upset his trucks with about 5s-worth of eggs in the boxes; he brought the remains home and we had to separate the goods again. I sent off a lot of candles to Hartham by mistake, and Ernest had to walk out and fetch them; it seemed an afternoon of accidents.

23rd Went to Calne as usual. Heard Handel Cossham was dead as I was leaving Chippenham, but hardly believed it; found it was all too true when I saw the Bath Herald. He had a fit suddenly in the House of Commons and was taken to a neighbouring hotel where he died in half an hour.

24th Miss Fuller's wedding day ... The ceremony was witnessed by a very large and influential congregation; the three little pages looked very nice; Clare played the Wedding March. I was writing a report of it from 3.30 to nine o'clock for the Gazette.

28th A fine day. Went up to Mr Joyner's in the evening and gave Horne (assistant master) his first lesson on the violin. Afterwards went for a walk with him and Griffin. (Bank clerk.) Nice moonlight night. Letters from Harry. He again referred to the advantages we should all enjoy if Lewin and I came out, saying we should make 6 or 7 hundred a year, together. He said he couldn't come home without someone to fill his place properly in his absence. We were disappointed after looking forward to his coming.

29th ... Commenced reading 'Three Men in a Boat', a very amusing book lent me by the Rev. Lyne.

MAY

1st (Thursday) Grandma's birthday; 81. Ma, Dad, Uncle and Aunt Laurie went up to tea, and all of us paid her a visit during the day. Went down to the lake in the morning before breakfast with Wilfrid and Mr Bartlett; we got on the island and picked flowers; it was a lovely morning. Had a good practice at rowing.

3rd Our first cricket match with Widcombe Institute; we won by about 80 runs first innings. I made 6. Sir John Dickson Poynder, Albert Aust and Eli Smith were the chief scorers. I kept wicket and stumped one out. Dinner time I drove over to Chippenham with the old 'safety' and bought a new one from Warrilow; he allowed £3 on the old machine and I had to pay £5 on the new.

14th ... Griffin and I went on our bicycles to Bath in the evening, starting at 6.20 and arrived in Bath 7.20; went to the theatre to hear 'The Gondoliers' which I enjoyed immensely. Had a little refreshment at the 'Pioneer' and started back 10.30, reaching home about 11.50.

16th Frank West dropped down dead close to the Chippenham Union about midday. He was in the grocery shop apparently quite well in the morning, and Lewin spoke to him in Chippenham shortly before he died ... Went to Melksham; tea at Edwin Lee's. He spoke to me about his little pilferings when at our shop. He wanted to give restitution, but I wouldn't take it.

18th (Sunday) A lovely day. Went to chapel in the morning and heard the Rev. Aldis, a vegetarian preacher of 82 years, former tutor of John Bright ... After tea Griffin and I went on our bicycles to Castle Combe, called at Mr Knowles and Katie was at home; she locked us in, but Griffin jumped through the window. However we waited till the others came back from chapel, and then went for a walk on the hills and had a splendid view.

20th Received a photograph from Daisy Goold, the best I have seen of her; I wrote and thanked her for it in the evening.

21st ... Played cricket after tea; Wilfrid and I picked up sides and my side made 110; I made 46; went in first and was out last. Bessie Humphries came here to tea.

24th Great Liberal demonstration at the Town Hall in the evening; speakers Mr Fuller, Mr John Fuller and Mr Fife (East Wilts), Alderman King, Sir Charles Hobhouse, Mr Mayo, Mr Eaton Young, etc. Splendidly decorated Town Hall. Miss Hobouse sang two songs very nicely. I reported.

Cricket match with Lansdowne; Corsham made 228, Sep Kinneir not out 83 and Arthur Kinneir 48. Lansdowne made 121. 4th victory for Corsham.

25th (Whit Sunday) ... In the afternoon Fred Cole, Griffin and I went to the Weavern intending to bathe in the old place, but Mr Poulsom was there and objected; however we went on through the orchard and had a dip there. The water was warm, but there wasn't much room to swim.

27th (Tuesday) [At Chippenham to play at the Bazaar.] Afterwards went up on the canal and had a canoe ride, which I enjoyed very much ...

28th To Calne to give lessons ... In the evening Clare and I rode down to Lacock on bicycles; Walter Dinham lent Clare his, and I strapped my fiddle to my back, as we were engaged for the dance at the Oddfellows Hall. There were about 50 there and though the charge for admittance was low they were very orderly. We came away at 3, reaching home in the daylight at 3.30.

29th C.E.T.S. entertainment in the evening. Fred Brett, Edward Hoyle, Fred Hulbert and I played Scotson Clarke's Gavotte for 4 violins ... Mr Lyne had several presentations at the close of the entertainment: an £84 cheque from the parishioners; photographs of himself and wife from the C.E.T.S. beautifully done on porcelain; a photographic album from the Bible Class. Mr Lyne made a very good speech. Mr Brinkworth, Mr Gunn, and Mr Roach gave songs and readings.

30th ... Mr Lyne was presented with a clock, in the evening, outside the church porch; it was given by the choir and Mr Osborne made the presentation.

JUNE

7th Cricket match at Bath ... I stayed there all night with Fred Cole and we went to 'Maritana'. The soprano, tenor and alto were good, but the chorus – as far as personal appearance went – were as scraggy a lot as I've seen on the stage. Fred and I sat close to the orchestra and had a good view of the violins.

8th (Sunday). Fred and I stayed in all morning as it was wet; we amused ourselves by reading and looking through the telescope at some girls in the opposite lodgings; they made signs back to us. Went to the Abbey in the afternoon but didn't like the service.

11th Gave my paper on 'The Violin' at Lodge in the evening – read it from my shorthand notes. They appeared to enjoy it very well. I took down the 'Musicians' Album' and several violin fittings to show them. Stormy day.

15th (Sunday) A beautiful day ... In the afternoon went in the Park with Fred Cole and read 'Zenone'; we lay on the haycock. The park seemed quite gay with all the people about ... Mr Fry's cows got in our mowing grass about 9.30 and Dad and I went and drove them out. We put them in the Pound, 20 of them.

18th Went to Calne, and stayed in Chippenham in the evening and went to see 'Caste' performed by Miss Morton's company; it was very enjoyable and made me laugh almost as much as 'The Private Secretary'.

19th ... Ma and Clara went to Nottingham ... Capital report of my paper on 'The Violin' in the Gazette.

20th (Friday) A fine day. Went over to Melksham on my machine in the afternoon and who should I see walking the street but Stanley Porter. I almost thought it was his ghost. It seems he has taken a situation at Spencer's Iron Foundry to learn the engineering ... Went on to Chippenham and heard 'East Lynne' performed ... it was very good. The double-bass player ended up with a solo.

21st Cricket match with the Bohemians at Bristol; Lewin and Clare went. We were delighted and astonished to receive a telegram as follows: "Bohemians 138 Corsham 164 for 6 wickets, Sep Kinneir not out 103'. Of course we had full particulars when the team came back; it was a very near shave, getting the runs before time ... Lewin made the winning hit, a cut for 5.

24th Mr Flint's horse fell in the well in the back premises and they had great difficulty in getting it out; it was in the water more than 2 hours.

25th ... All our people, Mr and Mrs Kinneir and Sep, Mr Griffin, Mrs Cole and Mr Bartlett (Court) had tea in the hayfield; I came back from Calne by the 5.45 and went straight to the field. Before leaving some of us got up top of the rick and turned somersaults over the beams.

JULY

8th (Tuesday) Ma and Clara came home from Nottingham ... Clara brought me a letter and a song, 'Thou'rt Passing Hence' (Sullivan) from Daisy Goold.

9th ... Wedding festivities at Hartham. (Miss Dickson had been married in London

224

the previous Saturday.) All the tradesmen and their wives, farmers and wives, and labourers on the estate were invited and numbered about 500. They had a meat tea provided and afterwards there was dancing in the tent to the Corsham brass band; ventriloquism and comic songs were provided, and though the weather was wretched, things went off well.

11th All the morning and afternoon I was up at Uncle Laurie's house, helping in with the household furniture.

14th Aunt and Uncle Laurie slept in their new house for the first time ... Received the sad news of Mr Linton's death at Bonn; Mrs Linton telegraphed to Mr Mayo.

16th ... In the evening went down to the Weavern where the Lodge held a picnic session; we intended to have tea in the open air, but the rain coming on, we took refuge in Mrs Poulsom's. There were about 50 present ...

17th Went to the funeral service for Mr Linton in the morning; sang part of Sir John Goss's Order for the Burial of the Dead; Lewin played the Dead March and a muffled peal was rung. Very heavy rain.

18th ... Frightful wet evening. Never heard of such a summer.

20th (Sunday) Mr Awdry preached a very nice funeral sermon on Mr Linton and I took it down. In the afternoon I drove Dad, Ma, Uncle and Aunt Laurie, and Aunt Lyd down to Box and back through Atworth and Shaw; it was a splendid afternoon for a drive, no dust, not too hot, and fine.

23rd ... To Melksham; went to Stan's lodgings and got back Daisy's photo which they had stolen from my mantelpiece ... Uncle Joseph from Nottingham came here to stay for a short time.

From a letter to Daisy, 24th July:

An awful thing happened to me since I wrote last. I lost your photo for 10 days!! Some regular scamps (practical-joking friends of mine) came to see us on Sunday week, and seeing your photo on our bedroom mantelpiece, guessed that yours was the one I should miss the most, and with that malevolent perverseness of human nature determined to inflict upon me the most severe mental torture they could devise, and so pocketed – ah sacrilege – your lovely photo ... So your poor cousin Herbert ... missed that 'pair of sparkling eyes' beaming on him the next morning ...

On Wednesday I went over to Melksham on my bicycle and went to my friend's lodgings. Fortune was in my favour! He was out! I gained access to his room, I fled with nervous haste to the mantelpiece; there you were, enthroned in a frame! ... I seized it, rushed out and meeting my friend in the street flourished it defiantly in his face. He denied having taken it and said he knew nothing about it till the next morning, when his friend had left, he noticed it ... Enough, however; I had regained my lost treasure and was happy ...

Uncle Joseph is getting about seeing his old friends with commendable energy. It is jolly to have him down here. I wanted to hug him when he came, but was afrain of hurting him. Didn't we just pitch into that cream, brown bread and Gorgonzola ... No-one has told him about my intended visit to London. Not that I think he would mind, but we won't burden his conscience with the secret. Will you be up there on the 16th of August? ... And do you think it will be possible, Daisy, for me to come to your place ... and bring my violin, and then we can play and sing together? ... I have read your "Chronicles' and am delighted with them ... I must go now, so goodbye, dearest of my cousins. May I? xxxxx
Yours affectionately,
Herbert

24th Fine ... Uncle Joseph went about visiting old friends. Mr Pictor died in Bristol asylum.
26th Fine day ... Sent Daisy Goold a letter and some chocolates.

From a letter to Daisy, 26th July:

Daisy, you are a darling. The song you have sent me is a splendid one and I like it the more every time I sing it. I think I shall really try and overcome my 'natural timidity' and sing it at our Lodge meeting some day ... I am so glad you are going to have a holiday. I am sure if any girl deserves one, you do ... There is nothing I should enjoy more than being shown about by you, but I am afraid I should bore you, dear Daisy, because I know I should be lingering on the doorstep of your lodgings all the time waiting for you ... If I came I should very likely take lodgings at Mrs Coxall's Welbeck St. ... The prospect is too delightful, only I am afraid something will prevent it coming off. Please accept chocolates; I know you like them.

AUGUST

1st Clare's 21st birthday. Gave him 'The Musical Profession', the same book I sent to Harry. Other presents were a splendid pair of cricket shoes, music studies for the piano, a song, etc.
3rd (Sunday) Had some music with Uncle Joseph and Clara after dinner. Saw Grandma and promised to put a looking-glass in her window so that she could see the procession on Monday.
8th In the afternoon Mr and Mrs Butler of Calstone and their two daughters Julia and Clara (who are in drapery shops in London) drove here and stayed to tea; after tea Mrs and the young ladies invested in dresses, etc., and we had a lark

comparing prices, methods and experiences.

Letter to Daisy, 11th August:

Dearest Daisy,
The best part of your letter is the hope it gives me that you will be able
to stay the fortnight ... It will be better for me to stay at Mrs Coxall's
(23, Little Welbeck St) ... A fourpenny tram ride will bring me to you
very soon, and you may be sure I shall use it well ... As for it being one
room, you known my dear Daisy, or ought to, that any room or house
will be all the more sacred and lovable for being used by you.
Inconveniences indeed! It will simply be Elysium. I shall be with you
any morning you like to appoint as early as you will admit me, and
won't we make a noise with our two instruments? Please bring some
duets that we could sing together ...

14th Went down to Mr Lanham's in the evening and played duets with Miss Wall;
heard that I was to be best man at Ernest's wedding on October 8th.

16th (Visit to London) Fred drove me to Chippenham in the morning to catch the 9
train. George Coxal met me at Paddington ... and we went on to Welbeck
Street. After dinner went up to Daisy's lodgings and stayed with her having
some music till Willie Goold came and then we had tea. After tea had a splendid walk on Hampstead Heath; such a pretty place with its little lakes, roundabouts and walks. Willie was very amusing and Daisy very interesting so I enjoyed myself immensely.

17th (Sunday) ... In the afternoon went to Willie's lodgings in Liverpool Road and
after a while Willie and Daisy came too and we had some music. Was immensely amused at the musical box with a cat playing the fiddle and three
kittens dancing to him. Daisy and I went to St Paul's Cathedral in the evening.

18th In the morning I called for Daisy and we went down to Kennington Oval to
watch the match, Surrey v. Lancashire. First of all we had a sixpenny place, but
after lunch we went in the shilling enclosure which was much more comfortable
... There were 6,661 persons present. Daisy and I had tea together at Ludgate
Circus and then we parted ... In the evening I went to the Criterion with Mrs
Coxall who had two tickets for the dress circle; it was a very amusing comedy
entitled 'Welcome, Little Stranger', all about two babies with very fond fathers.

19th (Tuesday) Very wet day ... Went to Daisy's to dinner and tea and had a very
enjoyable afternoon together. In the evening we went to Willie's lodgings and
had some music. Mr Hutchings invited nearly all his neighbours in and they
quite filled the room. They seemed pleased with our music. Daisy accompanied
me and we sang together once. They had a musical chair and several musical
boxes.

20th Daisy and I hired a piano for her lodgings. It was an Indian one and minus an octave in the bass and treble, but nicely in tune. I went up to her after breakfast but she was gone to Mr Parker's for her singing lesson, so I went back to Brompton Oratory and heard part of Cardinal Manning's sermon on Cardinal Newman. What little music I did hear was beautiful. I admired the building very much. In the afternoon had music with Daisy and after tea ... went in a hansom to Covent Garden Promenade Concert, classical night. Carrodus was leading. Edward Howell played the 'cello divinely. Mr Ben Davies sang ... the orchestra played Beethoven's 5th Symphony ... A very enjoyable evening.

21st Went to Kew in the steamboat with Mrs Coxall and had a view of the Gardens; the Palm Tree House with its centre staircase amidst the trees I specially admired. It came on to rain, but we went on by tram to Richmond and from thence ferried across to Isleworth and had tea with a friend of Mrs Coxall's ... came back by train and walked from Waterloo to Charing Cross, bussing the rest of the way.

22nd Daisy and I did some shopping together, visiting Cramer's, Augener's, Whiteley's (which I had never seen before), and then we had a capital vegetarian dinner in Newgate Street (omelette and tomato pancake and Gorgonzola cheese). Then in the evening we went to see 'Judah' at the Shaftesbury Theatre and went in the upper circle, 4s seats. It was a capital piece and was a take-off on spiritualism, faith healers and other people who fatten on the credulity of the British public.

23rd ... In the afternoon went to the baths with George and had a swim; very good place ... In the evening went up to Daisy's and had a capital moonlight stroll over Hampstead Heath. Walked home (4 miles).

25th Went to meet Clare and Sep Kinneir at Paddington in the morning and drove with them to Lord's, then went to meet Daisy at Swiss Cottage and brought her to the match. M.C.C. made 440 something and Clare caught and bowled Vernon for 11, but didn't get another wicket. Wiltshire only made 66 and were out just before drawing time. Clare unfortunately hit round to a straight ball and was bowled for 0, and Sep only made 4 ... Daisy and I found it rather cold watching. We had some chocolate and buns together at luncheon time. After the match Clarke (of Chippenham), Sep and Clare came with us and had tea; we laughed heartily over the indifferent fare. We went on to the Strand and heard 'Our Flat', a very amusing play. The three cricketers slept at Paddington. Saw Daisy off and then walked home. A wet night.

26th (Tuesday) [Daisy at Maidenhead for the day. Herbert went to Forest Gate and visited Mrs Lockwood, formerly Florrie Simmonds.]

27th After breakfast marched off to Mansfield Road, enjoyed a dinner of mushrooms with Daisy and had music. In the evening we went to the Holborn Restaurant and had a jolly good dinner together, 3s 6d each and about 7 courses and very nicely served; an orchestra played music all the time and it was a great novelty. Daisy couldn't eat all of hers, so I would relieve her of part of her plate sometimes. About 8.30 we went to the Promenade Concert; a Miss Sherwin sang splendidly; I never heard a more bird-like performance from a human throat before. Willie Goold was there. Daisy and I had an ice between us with a straw each.

28th Went up to Mansfield Road after breakfast and had a last turn at duets with Daisy. Went off to Hadley Woods, a most charming place, and enjoyed a stroll round there; sometimes we rested under trees, sometimes on seats, and I read a little of 'The Tinted Venus' to Daisy. We had tea in the public house, during which there was a storm of rain. Reached home about 10.30.

29th Had a walk with Daisy to Abbey Road, St John's Wood, in the morning, and after dinner went with her to Waterloo Station to carry luggage and see her off to Southampton. Was very sorry to say goodbye after having such pleasant times together ...

30th After breakfast packed up and then went down Oxford Street and visited Carey's music shop, Novello's, Ashdown's, Beer's ... Francis & Day where I bought some dance music; had dinner at the Alpha Vegetarian Restaurant but it was very unsatisfactory. Out of the three vegetarian places I tried while in London only one was satisfactory. In the afternoon ... George Coxall saw me off at Paddington; reached Chippenham 8.30 and Fred met me with Israel. Found all well at home.

Letter to Daisy, 31st August:

Dearest Daisy,
My first question will be, did you arrive at Southampton all right and did your friend meet you? ... I feel like a widower, all forsaken and forlorn. I have given them a complete history of our doings in town. Of our shopping together; how I laughed at your remark about the tea-cosy; ... how you were always thinking smuts were on your face; how I was always looking at the compass; how stubborn you were about my paying for you; of the landlady and her interest in us; of your partiality for large hats and sweetmeat shops; of your horror of discussing our relationship ... Dear Daisy, it has been a memorable and a splendid fortnight for me and how I shall settle down again into ordinary life, I don't know ... I feel very grateful to you darling Daisy, for being so kind to me, for giving up so many things for me, for putting up with my many shortcomings, for accompanying me so nicely on the piano and many other things, and for what? Absolutely nothing ...

With much love from your bereaved cousin
Herbert

SEPTEMBER

3rd Ernest read a paper on the public houses of Corsham at Lodge; it was very good ... Wrote to Daisy ... Had some music with Cousin James.

> Dearest Daisy
> I was so delighted to get a letter from you so soon, and such a nice long one ... So you have seen Emily Cole and her little idol 'Emmy'. She is a heavy girl for her age. I wheel her along in one of those fashionable carts sometimes, but should not care to carry her far ... It seems cruel that I cannot come and see you just once a week, say ... How much quicker the week would pass! ... I feel I have missed a great deal in not knowing of your doings in past years. We have been living our lives quite apart till lately. Sweet Daisy, promise me you will let me know something of your future so that I can be with you in spirit sometimes ... I want to go to every place you are at, isn't it absurd?

6th Cricket match at Swindon. I went instead of Allard. I was delighted with the pavilion; felt quite like a county man stalking about there ... I caught 2 at the wicket and Clare bowled well, taking 5 wickets for 30 runs ... Afterwards ... went to the Coffee Tavern and we had 4 cups of tea, 3 eggs and 9 pieces of bread and butter between 3 of us for 9d!!!

8th Had a letter from Daisy Goold. Enamelled our two plunge baths and greatly improved their appearance.

> Letter, September 9th:
>
> Daisy, you *must* come down at Christmas because it will be almost impossible for me to come to Nottingham, as I never know two days beforehand but what I may be wanted for a concert or a ball ... Confession is good for the soul, and so I will say that the reason I sometimes congratulated myself that we were not real cousins was the knowledge that people consider that first cousins should not form that closest tie of all, marriage. And, though I am not a marrying man (I don't think I care about marriage), if by some terrible decree I was obliged to marry tomorrow ... I should ask my sweet Daisy. I like a bachelor's freedom but I know no-one who I could more willingly resign it to ... I oughtn't to say all this but it is better to be honest and out with it ...

10th Went to Lodge; it was 'Who shall be chief templar?', any Brother asking the Chief a question, and unless he answered it correctly he had to give up his regalia to his questioner, who in turn was asked another question, and so on.

15th (Monday) Letter from Daisy ... Lewin's 32nd birthday.

17th Choir outing to Chepstow and Tintern. We started by the 8.35 train and reached Chepstow about 11 o'clock. Visited the Castle, where we had much fun helping the ladies to climb the ruins, also played with the soft ball until it went over the cliffs ... Had a capital dinner at the Beaufort Arms and then on to Tintern by the train; clambered the walls of the Abbey and enjoyed the scenery. Emily was taken sick up top and didn't recover till after tea ... Left at 6.30. Clare and Kate Moody, Alice Dinham and I kept together going home and had fun in the carriages, especially in the tunnels ... Reached home at 11.30 after a very enjoyable day. We closed shop and all but Alice and Ernest came with us.

Letter, 19th September:

Another precious little parcel with a note or two of music neatly written on the envelope came about dinner time on Monday ... I did not reply at once for two reasons; first it was our choir outing yesterday and I thought I would wait and tell you about it, and secondly if I write back at once it seems such an unearthly time since I have anything to do with you, right from Tuesday till the following Monday. We had such a capital day at Chepstow and Tintern ... Such splendid scenery, such nooks and crannies to investigate, rowing in boats on the Wye, playing cards in the train, larking in the tunnels, etc ...

22nd (Monday) Clare and I went over to Biddestone in the evening to help with the Lodge entertainment. Fred Brett, Hulbert, Boyle and I played the violin quartet; Ernest, Clare and I sang the 'Trickling Trio'; Clare and I sang 'Friendship'. We put old Israel up at the pub, and when we went to get him to go home he was apparently drunk, rolling about from one side of the road to the other; I suspected he had been given alcohol to drink and so would not pay the man, who blustered; Israel was unfit to be put into the harness, so we dragged the wagonette home and Fred led Israel. I went to fetch Mr James, who with his assistant came and gave the animal some medicine; they maintained it was paralysis, but we were all of a different opinion.

23rd The talk of the place is that our horse had been made drunk ...

24th Clare and I went to Melksham on bicycles ... there was a Bicycle Meeting at 7 o'clock, about 150 present; a torch-light procession with coloured fires, etc. was held and Clare and I joined it; we paraded the streets and then finished up with a smoking concert at the King's Arms ...

Letter, September 26th:

You clever girl! I only wish I could write poetry like you. I never tried,

---

but I think if I had any talent that way it would have developed before now. The same with music. Though I am so fond of playing and listening to music, the idea of an original melody never strikes me ... If you will send me a song or two I will see what I can do in the way of a violin obbligato, but I cannot promise you success ... A great many writers of songs fill in an obbligato because it is the fashion, without any consideration as to the necessity or suitability of the song for the purpose ... You darling, you know I would *love* to have the photo you speak of ... I must pay off my debt by copying out songs ... Clara and I had some music last night and between the pieces I read one or two sentences from your letter, and when she saw the quantity she remarked, 'You two spoons' ... I hope you will burn my letters ... because they only take up room and might get you into trouble ... I think I liked Hadley Woods the best day, because we were all by ourselves with no bustling people and cabs and omnibuses and endless noises. It was such a peaceful quiet happy day ...

29th Wilfrid and I went up to the Court at 10 o'clock and helped them dance, it being the gardener's baby's birthday ... Had a letter from Daisy. Sent her a song I had copied for her.

Letter from Daisy, c. 28th September:

... The photo I am sending is the cabinet of which I spoke to you in London ... I am also sending you a little song I have just composed (words and music) ... Now I will answer your questions first as it will give me an excuse for looking at your letter again (the idea of my destroying them; why, I read them all over times and times while I am waiting for your next) ... I quite agree with you about an obbligato that is simply in unison with the voice being worse than nothing ... I don't mind how long your letters are. The last was rather thin, and it never arrived till Friday morning! ... Do you know that it is just a month ago today that we were at Hadley Woods. I wish we could have that day over again ...

After bemoaning to Mother the other day about not being properly appreciated by people, I finished up by saying, 'Well, it's a great consolation to know that you are first in the world to somebody'. And Mother said 'yes, but it is one thing to be first to somebody for a few months, or even years, and then be given over for some fresh novelty and find yourself very much second, and another thing to be first for life, so that no change either in yourself or in circumstances can alter your position' ...

Daisy Goold in Alsatian costume

233

30th ... Had a beautiful photo of Daisy sent me; she was taken in peasant's costume. In the evening there was a lecturer on the National Church at the town hall, of course very one-sided, but he was fairer to the Nonconformists than I expected ... Afterwards the Rev. Newnham got up in a white heat and asked the lecturer whether he expected us to believe all he had said, and then left the room immediately ...

Letter, 30th September:

... Oh! I was entranced this morning when Dad threw on my semi-somnolent head your photo, and I knew it was come. I was sure it would be splendid but it even surpassed my expectation. Confound that Mr Lambert, I say, that he has the privilege of being near such an angel and acting with her ... Don't think me presumptuous, I know I am not good enough for you ... but you see, I have always remembered our sort of infant betrothal and felt as if you had a right to me and I to you. And though Kate did come and steal me away from you for a time, I know she felt guilty about you, and I am sure I did. The dear girl's conscience was tender about Wilfrid too, who had somehow paired off with Kate ... Tuesday morning after receiving your photo I was like one dazed, so you can guess I wasn't in a fit state to call on about 30 people for orders ... My usual absent-mindedness was alarmingly developed ... I always was susceptible to female beauty. It is rather absurd but I can't help myself. Even in the shop serving, I get nervous occasionally when my customer is a pretty girl. But when I get to know them, beauty alone would never satisfy me ...

OCTOBER

1st (Wednesday) Alice and Ma went to Mr Brinkworth's, Stowell, to tea ... Wrote to Daisy.

5th ... Read some of Kate's letters over, and found several references to Daisy in them ...

6th Ernest Lanham was up in the evening talking about the wedding. He bought some gloves for me in Bath, and I met the 7 train with our presents (my bag, and rug from the rest of the family) for him to take to Chippenham.

8th Ernest Lanham's wedding. I acted as best man. We went up to Chippenham – Mr and Mrs Lanham, Mrs Dudley, Ernest and I – by the 10.40 train and drove straight to the church ... I settled the fees, etc. after the ceremony and then went back to the wedding breakfast. Had to respond for the bridesmaids and then to the toast of 'best man'. In the afternoon we hired Porter's coach and had a splendid drive up Derry Hill, through Bowood Park and down Bowden Hill, getting back to Timber Street about 5.30. Of course I saw the bride and bridegroom off by the 3 train, 1st-class carriage to London. They received 70 presents. Lewin, Clara and Emily went over to the ceremony.

11th Mr Sayers, an old gentleman who gave Ma away on her wedding day, came here and slept.

12th Clare's photos came, the best he has had taken.

15th Mr Sayers went away; he hadn't been to Corsham for 33 years ... Wrote to Daisy.

... Clara and I went to a concert at Calne last night (programme enclosed). We drove all the way there, 10 miles, in a fly, and coming back we talked such a lot about you ... I love to talk about you and have someone to confide in, and Clara is just the one, but she teases me, of course. She puts all sorts of wild notions in my head; for instance, that the song you have written, the words, are intended for *me*. I daren't hug that lovely delusion ... Daisy, it is rather too much to expect a young fellow coming into contact with you as much as I did last August and yet never picturing to himself how lovely a lifelong companionship such as that would be ... I know you do not care about marriage ... and Aunt Clara, I expect, has more ambitious views for you (especially after Kate's marriage) than a union with one so obscure and insignificant as myself ... Now I will try not to say anything about it again, but I have had many happy little dreams about it ...

16th Went to Trowbridge in the afternoon to attend the concert of the Avon Vale Society in the capacity of musical critic for the Gazette; had a front seat ticket; very fashionable audience. Splendid concert, hardly a flaw from beginning to end. Haydn's symphony by the band was grand; the chorus in Mendelssohn's 95th Psalm was splendid ...

22nd Wrote to Daisy in the evening; it was the last letter I posted in the old Post Office. George Goold came up from Bath to say goodbye before going to Portland, U.S.

... In about 7 weeks – I shall count them one by one – I hope you will be here and then won't we have some lovely talks and music and strolls. Would you like to learn to skate? Perhaps we shall have our chance on our lake. I fell in up to my neck once and was nearly drowned; I'll show you the place when you come.

23rd Wrote to Aunt Clara, a birthday letter ... it was the first letter I posted in the new Post Office.

24th My 26th birthday. Had a pretty little present from Daisy, a handkerchief with the initial 'H' worked in the corner and daisies twined about it. Also was enclosed a little stamp purse.

27th Tennis Club dance ... went very well. I had a waltz with 'Bittens'. Had a letter from Daisy.

28th ... C.E.T.S. meeting. The Vicar carried out his opposition to the society by preventing Mr Edwards, diocesan secretary, from attending as advertised. Mr Newnham however was able to get a gentleman from Bath to bring some views illustrating a journey from Bath to the Niagara Falls, and Mr Churchill gave a temperance address on Cruikshank's Pictorial History of the Bottle.

29th Wrote to Daisy.

First of all I must thank you very much indeed for that beautiful little book, 'The Angel in the House' ... Oh what a lovely kind letter you sent me on my birthday! ... Didn't it take you an awful long time to work that pretty 'H' on the handkerchief? ... I am glad you didn't wash it. There was a perfume about it which reminded me of you, and I had it at the dance on Monday night and smelt it at intervals and had little wideawake dreams between the dances and imagined you with your head on the pillow, fast asleep. I only danced once and that was with Clara, a waltz ... Do you waltz, Daisy? It is my favourite dance and I know very few ladies who do it better than Clara ...

I should like to have heard that lecture by George MacDonald ... I have only seen pictures of him and he puts me in mind of Uncle Jospeh ... Aunt Clara said you didn't tell her about London; you preferred to manage you own affairs ... She gave me an uncomfortable feeling that you were at loggerheads ... Oh I hope, dear Daisy, I am wrong ... You see, we here, as a family, live very happily together, or I should never have stayed at home as long as I have. And it is difficult for me to conceive of any other relations between the members of a family than that of co-operation ...

From Daisy, late October 1890:

Caro Mio, This week has been busier than ever and until today I have not had a single moment to write to you – but thank heaven I am never too busy to think of you, and I often imagine you with me on all sorts of occasions and act it all through in my mind. For instance I went to a party the other night at Dr Stewart's. I was asked to sing and I pretended that you were there and played violin obbligato to my song ... The other day when I went into a draper's shop I just pretended for

NOVEMBER

2nd (Sunday) Made extracts from Burns's poems.

10th Went to the Spelling Bee in the evening at the Methuen School. Mr Churchill was the interlocutor and Mr Mayo and Lewin the referees. There were only 10 competitors, 7 ladies and 3 boys ... After a tussle between Clara and Mrs Crisp, the latter failed in 'desiccated' and Clara won first prize.

> To Daisy, 12th November:
>
> I am so glad you liked the poetry. I am beginning to have quite an unaccountable liking for poetry and have copied one or two more pieces ... I never used to care much for it.

12th ... Our musical contingent went up to Chippenham by the 7 train. Mrs Wookergy was not a success in the solo 'O rest in the Lord'. Clara took the honours; she sang 'Jerusalem, thou that killest' as a solo. After it was over we were entertained to supper, and then to fill up the time before the conveyance arrived Mr Brinkworth began proposing toasts, among which he included 'The Profession', coupling Mrs Wookergy's name with mine, and I had to respond. I never felt a more arrant hypocrite in my life than when I praised Mrs W. for her solo. It was a wet drive home, but Wilfrid kept us amused with 'Will o' the Wisp' à la Mr Osborne.

18th Went to Mrs Alfred Cole's about tea time and she asked me to stop; we talked about Daisy's coming visit.

> To Daisy, 19th November:
>
> Mia bella Daisy, I never write your pretty little name without thinking of the meaning in the language of flowers, 'Innocence', and I don't think you could have been christened more appropriately, darling. Have you ever read Burns' sonnet 'To the mountain daisy', and Wordsworth's poem to the same flower? ... I have had a bad cold pitch right in my eyes and have had to lie down with them covered up. How I wished you could have been with me and read to me! Have you invested in any new hats? I shall quite expect to see a miniature umbrella on the top of your head when I meet you at Bath ...

21st Wrote a birthday letter in the evening to Daisy ... Account in the Wiltshire Times of the Vicar objecting to Lewin's conducting at the Tabernacle, Chippenham.

22nd Sent Daisy a book on the violin and a silk handkerchief for her birthday.

23rd (Sunday) Daisy's birthday. Very windy weather. Copied out 'An Evening Song' (Gounod) for Daisy.

28th Went to Calne; country covered with snow; slippery travelling.

DECEMBER

1st Had a nice long letter from Daisy.

To Daisy, 3rd December:

Both Clara and I are amused to think of 'clever Daisy' learning such a humdrum sort of thing as shorthand, and yet dear, you would find it very useful in many ways. I will teach you every day if you wish, and perhaps you will not mind showing me a little harmony, which I am very ignorant of. This would remind me of Byron in his 'Don Juan':

' 'Tis pleasant to be schooled in a strange tongue
By female lips and eyes – that is, I mean,
When both the teacher and the taught are young,
As was the case, at least, where I have been.
They smile so when one's right, and when one's wrong
They smile still more, and then there intervene
Pressure of hands, perhaps even a chaste kiss.
I learnt the little that I know by this.'

I am inclined to agree with you in your theory about our 'other halves', but yet I don't think the feeling should be encouraged because it would induce a sort of fatalism ... I would rather leave marriage to natural selection (Darwin).

6th Went down to Bath by the 12.45 train to Sarasate's concert, at the Assembly Rooms. Got a very good seat for 3s 6d. I took Mendelssohn's concerto and followed him; he took the Finale at an awful rate. There was a tremendous audience. Sarasate and his accompanist were on the platform as I was going back and I spoke to the accompanist and talked about Sarasate. He played on a Strad.

9th Ma's birthday. I resolved to sell my 'cello and give her a screen for the drawing-room.

To Daisy, 10th December:

... I don't think you will feel at all strange when you come, because through my reading bits of your letters to the others, you will be more familiar to them. And then there is your poetry, 'The Chronicles', which has made your name famous in the house. Have you ever read 'Won by Waiting' by Edna Lyall? I like the heroine very much ... Clara thinks you had better bring an evening dress, because we shall have at least one concert and perhaps a dance ... Don't forget your Alsatian costume. Oh, I wish I were in Mr Lambert's place next Friday ...

Daisy, sometimes a sentence comes in your letters which makes me think you are really unhappy at home, and I can't bear to think of it. It makes me long to come for you and take you away from it all ... You are something like me in one respect. I don't see much of the money I earn. It goes to swell the household receipts; or as Wilfrid would say in his comforting(?) way, 'It all goes into the pit'...

Will you go and see Grandma when you are here? I showed her your photo the other day and she said she would be sure to like you ... Your photo is a constant companion and comfort to me, dear. I take it in all conceivable places. It is getting quite worn just about the lower part of the face ...

Herbert Spackman

11th Had a book called 'My Beautiful Lady' sent by Daisy. Finished reading 'In the Golden Days' by Edna Lyall; enjoyed it almost as much as 'Won by Waiting' and 'Knight Errant' ... In the evening played a new game called Halma.

14th (Sunday) Called at Mrs Kinneir's ... saw Miss Kinneir No. 2, christened Millicent Ethel.

15th Went down to skate in the afternoon; played football some of the time and it was great fun. Wore Wilfrid's 'Acmes', a present from Lewin.

17th Went down on the ice again in the afternoon; hundreds from Bath. Had cramp in the leg afterwards ... Wrote to Daisy.

I am always glad when the time for writing to you comes round ... Daisy dear, you will be nice to me, just while you are here, won't you? ... I am dreading to look at the almanack after January and can't bear to think of anything that takes place after you are gone ... Only ten days more, darling ... We have had some capital skating this week, and I wished so much you could be here ... You must bring a lot of songs. I shall want you to sing all your compositions to me ... One more letter to you and then, ah then for a few weeks we shall not want paper or pen.

Your longing
Herbert.

18th ... All the applicants for Pitman's certificate failed. It somewhat discouraged me as I had worked hard for the boys at the school.

19th Very heavy fall of snow in the night.

20th Snow still falling ... Uncle and Aunt Rowell and the children were expected, but sent a telegram saying the weather would prevent them.

22nd Uncle and Aunt Rowell, Katie and Louis came from Liverpool. Louis slept at Lewin's and Katie at Aunt Jane's, Uncle and Aunt here. Daniels the policeman was drunk in the evening and laid down in the snow; Ernest tried to get him up, fearing he would freeze to death, and with Dad's help they at last managed it.

24th Daniels came in and thanked Dad and Ernest for helping him the other night.

To Daisy

I was afraid this horrid weather would affect your throat, dear ... but I do hope you won't be prevented from coming. It will spoil my Christmas if you are not here, and I have been looking forward to it so much, so don't *don't* disappoint me, darling, if you can possibly help it, will you? ... Railway travelling is simply beastly in this weather. I wish

I could be with you to see to warm rugs, foot-warmers, refreshments
and all the little attentions I should be delighted to perform. I shall feel
kindly to the train if it brings you safely ... P.S. I have just taken some
nice carpet down to Mrs Cole's – I believe it is for your bedroom ...
What delighted me was her invitation to come down whenever I liked
... If you will bring your skates I think I might teach you, dear; you'd
be very quick. Please accept the little card and chocolates. I chose the
calendar for you to keep in your room, and of course the forget-me-
nots tell their own tale ...

25th Christmas Day. Went down to the pond in the afternoon; it was pretty good in
the paths, but very rough everywhere else. In the evening Wilfrid, Ernest, Clare
and I went to the Hartham dance; Clare played. I danced with Miss Dickson
and Mrs Coates and they chatted about music and other matters very agreeably.
26th ... Sang carols to Grandma for an hour in the afternoon, and then went to tea
at Aunt Jane's with Aunt Sarah. Went to an entertainment in the evening at the
Town Hall and enjoyed being a listener; the representation of the Old Year and
the New was capital. Little Badminton dressed up as the New Year looked
simply charming.
27th Went down to Bath by the 12.45 train to meet Daisy at the Midland Station ...
We went in the bus to the G.W.R. and left the luggage and then went to see Mr
Macfarlane; he was giving a lesson, so Daisy and I went down in his den and
stayed by the fire till he came ... Had a very happy evening at Mr Cole's.
28th To church in the morning; called for Daisy and she sat in the choir. In the
afternoon she went to Grandma's and helped sing carols, and she cried at the
thought of poor Grandma being bedridden. Went to church in the evening and
Daisy again sat in the choir; after service Lewin played several pieces for her to
hear, and we sat in the church listening.
29th Went down to Mr Cole's in the evening and stayed with Daisy.
30th (Tuesday) In the evening went to the Choral Society practice; Colonel Methuen
came, but not with his violin; he sat in the chair close to me and followed my
part; he examined my violin and admired it. Daisy came and sang soprano, as
Clara was at Biddestone singing at an entertainment. I went into Mr Cole's
afterwards and had supper.
31st In the morning went down to Mrs Cole's and wrote report for the Herald.
Daisy did some shorthand by my side, and when the opportunity came I asked
her to be my wife; she didn't actually refuse, but asked for time to think about
it. I wasn't surprised as I had great misgivings as to my success. In honour of
Mr and Mrs Cole's wedding day, Dad and Ma, Aunt Jane, Aunt Sarah and
Mrs James Cole went down to tea, and I went afterwards and had some music
and singing with Daisy; before the Old Year died I went in the other room with
Daisy and we talked for some time into the New Year, and I found the dear girl

relenting a bit, though nothing definite was settled. We all wished each other a happy new year before we parted. Fred Cole said goodbye before going to the Cape. Daisy gave every one of the family – Louis, Mr and Mrs Cole, Aunt Rowell and Emmie – presents, and I helped her choose and mark them. She gave me a pretty book entitled 'Love Letters of a Violinist'.

NOTES FOR 1890

April 3rd The unknown benefactor was 'Sep' (Septimus) Kinneir.

June 15th The Pound: hence Pound Pill (corrupted to 'Pump Hill'). 'Pill' meant stream, used by the tanyard. Part still runs through the Batters.

July 11th Uncle Laurie's house: in Pickwick Road, near Alexandra Terrace.

23rd Uncle Joseph: Daisy's father.

Letter, July 24th 'Chronicles': this and its sequel were two long and witty sets of verses written by Daisy about her own family. She also wrote some charming songs, words and music. (See Appendix).

August 16th Daisy was staying in London, perhaps studying for her L.R.A.M.

Letter, September 30th The 'photo' is of Daisy in her Alsatian 'peasant' costume which she wore when acting in the operetta with Mr Lambert, of whom Herbert was furiously jealous!

'Infant betrothal': when Clara Goold's Daisy arrived a year after Eliza Hawkins's Herbert, their mothers seem to have agreed, in fun, that they might one day do for each other. (See poem at end).

Letter, October 15th 'The song you have written'. This has survived: the first verse goes:

'The ivy loves the sturdy oak,
The flowers love the sun,
The river flows to meet the sea,
Until their lives are one.
And I with you, sweetheart, to love,
Would change my lot with none.'

October 22nd George Goold: half-cousin.

24th These presents were kept all his life, and have survived.

Letter, October 29th 'Aunt Clara'. Daisy's letters perhaps give a rather one-sided view of her mother, who had had a very difficult time with a large family and little money except what she earned herself by teaching music. So she was naturally anxious that her own children should not marry without adequate means.

Letter, December 10th 'Into the pit': for many years, most of the family's earnings had to help pay off the debts incurred by the failure of Uncle Uriah Goold's tannery business. The wonder is that this never caused any friction or bitterness between the two families.

December 27th This very special day is framed in red! J. H. Macfarlane, Daisy's mother's father, taught organ, piano, singing, etc. and kept a music shop in Bridge Street, Bath. Daisy was staying with the Coles for their Silver Wedding on January 1st, 1891.

31st Was Herbert the only man ever to propose in the middle of a shorthand lesson?

18 91

JANUARY – APRIL

Daisy stays in Corsham till January 24th. Music engagements continue despite bad weather. A letter from Harry in New Zealand early in March finally decides Herbert (his father and Daisy consenting) to emigrate, and the ensuing weeks are filled with preparations and farewells. Daisy arrives for her last visit before he sails on May 1st.

JANUARY

1st (Thursday) Called in at Mrs Cole's in the morning and stayed with Daisy a short time and then took her down to the pond which we walked across; there were a good many skaters ... To Mrs Cole's again to spend the evening.

2nd A mucky day ... Daisy came with me to my shorthand class in the evening at the Methuen School, and then came in to supper here afterwards. I had a little music with her at Mr Cole's.

3rd Had an hour's shorthand lesson with Daisy in the morning. In the evening wrote to Uncle Joseph asking his and Aunt Clara's consent to our marriage; I submitted it to Clara before sending, and made a slight alteration at her suggestion. It was a trying letter to write. Reckoned up my yearly account; saved about £90 besides £38 for half salary and interest.

4th ...In the afternoon Daisy came here and we had some music. I played some of her songs on the violin and she gave me a lession in expression. She sat in the choir in the evening; Lewin played as the organ voluntary, 'Thou'rt Passing Hence'. I took Daisy home at 10.30.

5th Went down to Pound Pill with Daisy and Emmie in the morning. It was a nice bright morning. Went down to Mrs Cole's in the evening; Daisy put on her Alsatian costume and I gave her a long shorthand lesson by the fire; we tried over a new song, 'Beauty's Eyes', with violin obbligato, which I enjoyed very much; Clara came down to supper and slept with Daisy. Aunt Sarah, Louis and Katie went back to Liverpool.

6th Went for orders in the morning. Had a letter from Uncle Joseph mid-day post, saying it was for Daisy and I to decide for ourselves what should be our relationship, but his advice was to wait for more money and experience. Had a talk with Daisy about it in the evening ... Stayed at Mrs Cole's till 12 o'clock.

7th Hard frost again and bright sunshine. Went down to Bath with Daisy for the day. Did a little shopping and then went to Mr Lambert's and had my photo taken ... had some dinner at Mr Shippey's and then went to the pantomime, 'Babes in the Wood'. I enjoyed the children's dancing very much. We went to Mr Macfarlane's to tea and then left for the train; had the carriage to ourselves going home. Daisy had toothache. Went to Mrs. Cole's in the evening. She had a little party and Wilfrid, Ernest and Clare, Sep Kinneir and Clara were there besides ourselves.

9th Daisy went to Bath for the day ... Met her in the evening and then we strolled about the park till 8 o'clock ...

12th Brought Daisy up from Mrs Cole's to stay with us. C.E.T.S. Social Gathering in the evening ... Went and had a talk with Uncle Laurie as to the value of rings ...

13th ... Had a chat with Daisy in the kitchen in the evening after choral practice, and I hurt her feelings very much because I suspected her of having the intention of breaking off the engagement. I apologised afterwards.

14th (Wednesday) Daisy and I went to Chippenham by the 7 train to attend the Assistants' Soirée. Enjoyed the dances very much and had a great many of them with Daisy ... Came away about 2 o'clock and we slept at Mr Freeth's.

15th Mrs Freeth made us both very comfortable for the night and had breakfast ready about 9.30. Daisy slept with Fanny Freeth. We walked back from Chippenham as it was a beautiful morning ...

16th Went to Calne to give lessons in the morning. Daisy and I went to Dew's Minstrels in the evening; went in the Coffee Tavern afterwards.

17th Went down on the ice with Daisy in the morning and she got on very well. Went to Mrs Cole's to tea.

19th Went down on the ice with Daisy in the morning ... In the evening Daisy and I went to Bath to hear Grossmith at the Assembly Rooms; both enjoyed it very much. Afterwards went for a short walk and then to West's to sleep after a supper of sausages and coffee.

20th In the morning went into Daisy's room and woke her up; after breakfast at Sheppey's she went to see Mrs Goold, and while there I went to see Simms about playing at our concert ... We had dinner at Sheppey's and had the words 'I love Daisy' engraved on the inside of her ring. Returned to Corsham by the 2.20. In the evening Clare and I drove to Bowden Hill to play at a dance at Mr Gladstone's and took Edwin West with us; awfully wet drive and I got my shirt front saturated. Clare had a splendid piano to play on and the music went well. The supper was good. Finished at 4 o'clock and got home about 5.45.

21st [Morning on the ice with Daisy and a friend] Spent the evening with Daisy and she read stories from Hans Andersen; she put on her Alsatian costume.

22nd Daisy not very well with a stiff neck; I took up her breakfast for her. Our concert in the evening; Daisy sang her solo beautifully. Lady Hobhouse was there and spoke to me afterwards, asking me about our family and on which side the music was inherited. Had a long talk about the concert round the supper table afterwards. Daisy and I sat up till 1 o'clock.

23rd ... Shorthand class in the evening; afterwards we went up to Aunt Jane's to supper.

24th Went off by the 10 train with Daisy after affectionate goodbyes. We went to Mr Macfarlane's and had a little lunch; I told him of my engagement to Daisy and he gave me some advice but said nothing against it. The train left the Midland Station at 12.10. Put Daisy into a carriage by herself and stayed with her to the last. Felt the parting from her very much.

26th Had a letter from Daisy in the morning saying she arrived at Nottingham all right and Bertie met her.

From Herbert to 'Uncle Joseph' [Daisy's father]
[Postmarked, January 26th, 1891]

Dear Uncle,
I suppose you have been expecting a letter from me ere now but the fact is I was waiting for an opportunity to have a talk with Lewin on the matter, and he has helped me in calculating expenses, etc. His opinion is quite favourable with regard to the possibility of my

marrying, even at the present time. But I mean to increase my earnings to £150 before I ask Daisy to come to me. I am learning tuning and shall make a good deal by that as there is a good district around here, plenty of good country houses, etc.

I also intend to work up for the Licentiateship R.A. which I think will be a help to me in teaching and concert playing. Since I have taken up the viola as well, I have had several engagements for oratorios and concerts, as it is not so easy to get viola players as violinists.

Dear Uncle, I love Daisy far too much to take her from a good home unless I could comfortably provide for her. My love for Daisy is not merely selfish. I am ready to make any sacrifice for her and would study her wishes in every way. She will never be pressed, nor will she be prevented by me from exercising her musical ability. I shall leave that entirely to her, and so far from being 'buried in oblivion' here, there will be plenty of scope for her musical talents in this and the neighbouring towns. I understand and appreciate Daisy and our tastes are very similar, while there is much that we can learn from each other. In one sense, no man is really worthy of a good woman, but it shall be the aim of my life, God helping me, to make myself more and more worthy of dear Daisy every day.

For the present, as far as I can see, as long as the business continues my place is at Corsham, helping father, as he becomes less able every year to take active part in it. The business is a good family one and as long as we keep it up, I believe will remain so. This is then the answer I must give to you about 'looking at the world'. I think if one has the determination to work hard, a little ambition and push must bear fruit, and even little Corsham, which you despise so much, may afford us a happy and comfortable home.

Letter to Daisy, January 26th:

My own sweet Daisy,
After I had watched your train out of sight I couldn't help having a little cry to myself – don't think me a baby – as I felt so miserable all alone and knowing how long it would be before I saw you again. I took refuge from the pouring rain in the Corridor, and looked absently in the windows without much impression of their contents. Afterwards I had a cup of tea in Sheppey's at the same little corner, and then caught my train ... I never wished so much in my life before that I had some title, or was famous, because ... it seems there is so very little cause for congratulation on your side. But there, you darling, you

> don't seem to mind a bit, and if you don't, I care little what the whole
> world thinks ...

27th (Tuesday) ... The screen came from Mr Hulbert's for Ma; she was delighted
with it. It was my birthday present to her; I gave my 'cello for it.

28th Major Jones's theatricals at the Town Hall in the evening. Full room. The first
play was 'Sunset', in which Mrs Jones, as the heroine, sacrifices her engagement to her lover because she discovers an attachment between him and her
half-sister (Miss Awdry). The second play was 'Still Waters Run Deep' and was
not concluded till 12 o'clock. Major Jones was the hero, John Mildmay. Lewin,
Clare and I played items of music at intervals ...

FEBRUARY

> To Daisy, February 7th:
>
> ... If only I had a little more money! I would ask you to marry me at
> once, but there are so many things I should have to deny you ... I
> really believe, darling, that if we married and lived in Corsham, our
> expenses would not exceed £90 a year; but I am afraid that would not
> include a servant ... Lewin wants you to come down about the 2nd
> week in April (paying your expenses of course) and take the soprano
> solos in the Choral Society concert. Do let it be 'yes', sweet Daisy. It
> would be such a delightful break in the long separation ... If your
> home does really get unbearable, we will try and precipitate matters a
> little bit ... only of course we must have a house to come to ...
>
> I went to see Grandma the other day and she said she believed we
> were 'made for each other' and she hoped she should live to see us
> married.

15th (Sunday) ... In the afternoon went for a walk with my three aunts Emily, Lydia
and Jane. Had tea at Grandma's and read to her out of the book sent me by
Daisy.

23rd Finished reading 'Blessed be Drudgery', a charming little book, one of the sort
I should like to buy 50 of and give away.

MARCH

2nd Letters from Harry, strongly urging me to go out, saying that I should earn
more there in two months than I should in a year in England. Dad seemed more
favourably inclined to the idea than I ever knew him, and I determined to have
a talk with him on the matter after consulting Daisy.

4th Wrote to Daisy consulting her about New Zealand.

This letter must be a separate one from Saturday's because I want to ask you a very important question, and on your answer will depend to a very great extent my future life ... A letter came for Dad from Harry and ... I will give you his words ... 'There is not the slightest doubt that Herbert would make £300 to £400 a year and save three quarters of it ... There is no violin player any good between Auckland and Wellington ... I am sure that Herbert would get 70 or 80 pupils and that means from 6 to 9 guineas each year ... One of the objects I had in getting away from Corsham was that there might be a probable chance of making a future home for any of us that might need one, and I am sure that I did the right thing. I anticipate that the business will not be enough to support 4 or 5 different homes when the boys have a desire for one of their own.'

... My one absorbing thought has been, how to make sufficient money so that I shall not be ashamed to ask you, darling, to share the future with me ... But I want your full consent and approval, as I feel I could not go away without your good wishes and your sanction ... Harry's position was even worse than mine when he went. Not a single friend or face he knew out there. And leaving his betrothed behind him, for whom he had to wait 2 years. However, all has ended well so far, and if Clare, as is most probable, came out in 12 months or so, he could bring you out to me, if you still loved me well enough, darling. I would remain true to you, Daisy my own, and write to you every mail, once a month. And New Zealand is nothing like so far as it used to be, speaking in one sense. Between 5 and 6 weeks' journey now, when it used to be as many months. It would be a lovely climate for you, darling; hardly any winter worth speaking of, and I don't think you would feel lonely out there with Amy and the children (I am sure you would like her) ...

Letter, March 8th:

I should have added in my last important letter that Father, who when I mentioned going to N.Z. 3 or 4 years ago, strongly opposed it, said (when Harry's letter was being discussed and Ma remarked, 'Oh but we can't let Herbert go!'): 'Well, he must please himself about that'. I believe that his private opinion is, that there is not much prospect of my making headway in this small place – not enough scope, but doesn't like to say so, lest it shall seem like sending me off. And one of Dad's strongest feelings – I was going to say failings – has always been to keep all his children at home ...

5th Clara's 24th birthday. I gave her Goring Thomas's album of songs. Sep Kinneir gave her Edna Lyall's 'Hardy Norsemen' ...

7th Fred Aust left after long service; he had taken a situation in Bath.

9th [At Street] Awful snowstorm commenced in the afternoon and prevented many going to the concert. Clare and Clara didn't come till the 5.30 train from Highbridge ... I was encored three times and Clara twice; Eva Neate was encored twice too.

10th The weather still too bad for travelling; roads and railways blocked. Had to give up trying to get home. Mrs Joyner got off about 3.30 but didn't get home; she was snowed up in the train, and being the only lady, was carried over the snow to a farmhouse where she stayed the night, and didn't reach home till the following night ...

11th Bright morning. Some more trios with Mr Ward after breakfast. Started for home about 10.30 ... had to wait at Glastonbury till 1.15 and then booked to Bridgwater, changed there for the G.W.R. and waited from 2 to 3, and then went to Bristol; another wait of three quarters of an hour and then home – just in time to catch the 6.32 at Bath. Only had buns at Bristol since the morning, so made a good tea.

Received a letter from Daisy giving her consent to going to New Zealand. She was very nice about it in spite of her disappointment.

12th ... Had a chat with Dad in the evening about New Zealand and he seemed to favour the idea of going and also saw no reason for delay, but didn't think it necessary to go to a college of music before leaving England; decided that I would try and leave early in May.

Letter to Daisy, March 13th:

I hardly know how to begin, but first of all, I love you more and more, if possible, for being so nice about N.Z. ... Not one word of fretfulness, upbraiding or ill temper ... but just your own sweet self, loving, reasonable and so good. I can picture you to myself, after recovering from the first shock, taking out pencils and notebook in your little methodical way and jotting down the pros and cons ... All I want in N.Z. is a decent income which will provide for both of us, and a little over for contingencies ... Of course I shall send home your passage money ... as Harry did for Amy ... You are quite right, dearest, in saying it will be hard for me, because putting aside my separation from you, my home has always been a little earthly Paradise to me and Corsham has entwined itself into my affections in many ways. As far as I know I shall start early in May ... Harry seems to think no time should be lost, and of course June is their winter and the musical season. Yes dearest, of course you could have your dear Dad out. Who knows but what there my be quite a little colony from the old country out there in time! ...

16th Telegraphed to Harry to say I would come out to him in the *Tongariro* on April 30; it cost £2 12s 6d – five words at 10s 6d each; expected Harry to get it by 9 o'clock in the evening.

> Letter, March 17th:
>
> The die is cast and I have telegraphed to Harry ... I hesitated a bit with the money in my hand before I went to the Post Office, knowing that once done there was no retracting ... In the book you sent Clara, these lines come opposite our birthdays: Nov. 23rd: 'Good actions crown themselves with lasting bays. Who well deserves, needs not another's praise.' Oct. 24th: 'The world was all before them, where to choose Their place of rest'.

19th Received a letter from Daisy full of questions about New Zealand. In the evening ... down to Mrs Neate's to Ada Ayliffe's 21st birthday party; I was much amused seeing Mrs Neate and Mrs Ayliffe dance in Sir Roger. Broke up about 4 o'clock.

21st Wrote to Daisy answering her 31 questions.

22nd (Palm Sunday) In the evening Clara asked me with tears in her eyes to attend Easter morning communion; it was very hard to refuse her but I could not bring myself to consent. I asked her not to upset herself about it.

23rd Busied myself seeing about my boxes for the *Tongariro* in the morning; decided on one of Bryant and May's match boxes for the large one. Went down to Bristol by the 2.20 and got measured for some suits at Clark's; ... I selected one light, one dark, one dress suit and a cover-coat ... Wrote to Aunt Clara telling her of my intended voyage and also selected Berth 51 and upper deck and sent off the passage money.

25th Went to Lodge ... played Brindisi Waltz for the solo and the second one played 'L'Adieu' and told the audience I had chosen it because it was the last time I should play on the temperance platform at Corsham for some years. Mr Thomas Harris (Chairman) spoke a few words saying how sorry they would be to lose me, and that they had by their applause (it was encored) shown not only their appreciation of the piece but their good wishes for my welfare in the future ...

APRIL

1st (Wednesday) Went to Chippenham by the 4.40 and gave George Freeth and Mr Parkway their last lessons. Clara and I went to the fancy dress ball at the town hall in the evening; I played violin with Pike and Milsom. Clara went as 'Mary Mary Quite Contrary'. I had a splendid waltz with her and another with a lady from Gloucester. We slept at Mr Freeth's.

3rd Wilfrid's birthday; gave him a sovereign. In the afternoon Clare and I went to Wootton Bassett station and were met by the innkeeper named Gale with a conveyance; he drove us to Clyffe Pypard and on the journey we had fun with him, pretending not to know anything about the country, but the old chap was rather fly. We stopped at his inn reading, till 7.30 and then had some supper; at 8.30 we went up to the school-room to play at the dance; there were 27 down and we played an extra; it was after 4 when we finished. Tom Uncles and his sister were there, and Horton, an old schoolfellow of ours. Slept at the inn.

7th (Tuesday) ... Polly West gave me a very valuable set of gold studs and I wrote and thanked her for them.

Letter to Daisy, April 5th:

Some friends of ours asked Mother *before me* if she was satisfied with my choice. It was not necessary for me to hear Mother's assurance that she was entirely so, because I knew it, darling, and I am very glad; it is so much pleasanter for all. And it is comforting for me to know that there is only *one* dissentient in your family. Perhaps in time dissent will turn to approval, but I have not heard from her yet.

11th Went off to Burghclere by the 10.43 ... the conveyance met me and drove to Cousin Polly's (Mrs Booth's) where I saw her husband, Ethel and Ernest Booth and a younger daughter; stopped there half an hour and then on to Uncle's; soon became at home with Mrs Marsh and Uncle came in later. He took me to the Reading Room ... and about the village. Sad fatal accident to a boy of 13 happened in the afternoon; he was harrowing and the horses ran away. He got entangled in the machine and was killed almost instantaneously.

13th Mrs Marsh drove in to Burghclere with me in the morning and we called at Mr Booth's on the way. Uncle gave me £5 for a present and paid my expenses up; Mrs Marsh gave me a silk handkerchief. Reached Corsham 2.20. In the evening Mr Joyner's entertainment at the Town Hall; I played 'Scene de Ballet' and was recalled and encored ... Clare played as piano solo 'Where the Bee Sucks'. The boys acted 'Ici on parle Français' very nicely.

14th Went round for orders for the last time. In the evening Lewin, Wilfrid, Ernest, Caleb Davis and Albert Aust drove with me to Trowbridge to Mr Millington's concert ... went off well ... said goodbye to the Bath fellows as it was the last time I should play with them. Had fun about the concert going home.

15th Went to Miss West's in the evening to a little party ... Wrote to Daisy and Bertha ... Aunt Jane gave me a travelling glass for a present.

Letter, April 15th:

Uncle Laurie has given me a beautiful set of studs and links of
carbuncles set in gold … What do you think that kind old Uncle
William gave me? £5!!! He said he gave all his nephews £5 when they
got married, and as he was not likely to see me married he would give it
to me then. He also paid my expenses up to see him (15s) and asked me
not to forget him but to write sometimes. I showed him your photo
and he praised you, darling, and so did Mrs Marsh, his housekeeper.
   … I have a photo of Mr Cole's house and I shall value it, because it
is the house where I have spent so many happy hours with you, sweet
Daisy, and where I asked you to be mine. My thoughts often go back
to that morning when I broke through the prosaic shorthand lesson …
Whenever I come across a proposal in a novel, darling, I always think,
'I wish I had done it like that' … However, all's well that ends well …
perhaps you weren't in a very critical mood just then …

16th   Went down to Emily Cole's and stayed a bit in the morning. Mr Millins, Grand
       Chief Templar of England, sent me his photo; Emily Cole gave me hers and
       Alfred's. Wrote to Aunt Wild and Aunt Clare wishing them goodbye.
18th   Went to meet Daisy at the Midland Station by the 7 train. (Went to the Pump
       Room concert in the afternoon.) Had a very happy evening together. She
       brought me so many nice things (darling).
21st   Concert in the evening. My last appearance in Corsham … They received me
       very well and I got on all right with the 'Tremolo', and played 'Le Tambourin'
       for an encore. Daisy was everything that could be desired; she was dressed very
       simply in white and gold and I got her a bunch of daffodils from Mr Mayo's …
       The Chippenham friends were a great help …
22nd   In the evening went to Lodge and they presented me with a splendid dressing-
       case and I had to respond.
23rd   Daisy and I went to Bath by the 1.0 train and I bought her a ring, 'Mizpah' …
       Went to the classical concert at the Pump Room in the afternoon and then had
       tea at Sheppey's. In the evening Alfred and Emily Cole came up and Minnie
       and Lewin came in, and we had a family circle in the drawing-room.
24th   (Friday) … At 6 o'clock I had to go to the Town Hall to receive a presentation
       from the inhabitants. Mr Mayo presided and read an address to me, then he
       presented me with a purse of money (which I afterwards found to be £22 4s 6d)
       … Mr Dunlop, Mr Bromley, Mr James, Mr Foster and Mr Kinneir made
       speeches.
25th   Very busy sending off my boxes.
26th   (Sunday) … In the afternoon Dad, Wilfrid, Ernest, Clara, Emily, Sep Kinneir,
       Daisy and I went to Box by train and walked back over the hills; Katie Moody
       came too. In the evening after service Lewin played several pieces on the organ

and Daisy and I sat in the church and listened; it was rather too much for us and we were both upset a bit. We tried Mendelssohn's part songs afterwards, but I gave way in the middle of it and we had violin music instead.

27th Daisy and I walked down to Collett's Bottom and the fishponds; it was a splendid afternoon. We went to the C.E.T.S. in the evening and heard Ernest's paper on 'Prevention is better than cure'. Fred Goold came from Bristol and stayed here.

Clara, Daisy, Herbert, and Wilfrid after a farewell row on 'the pond'

28th In the morning Ma, Fred Goold, Daisy and I drove in Hancock's pony trap to Jessie Goold's place, Easton Piercy farm; we stayed there 2½ hours and had lunch, and then left Fred there and drove back through Castle Combe, reaching home about 4; we enjoyed it very much. Early in the morning Wilfrid, Clara, Daisy and I went down on the lake and had a row with Mr Bartlett; he photographed us near the boat-house. In the evening Daisy and I called on Mr Barnes and Mr Lanham to say goodbye.

29th Went up in the cricket field in the evening; I never saw the ground in better condition; it was beautifully mown. Said goodbye to some of the characters there. The Chippenham bicycle club were over in the evening and Bertie Wild said goodbye. Joe Ward and Stanley Porter came over from Melksham in the evening and spent several hours with us. We had a little music; Daisy sang to them.

30th In the morning went to say goodbyes; Uncle and Aunt Laurie, Miss West, Mr and Mrs Osborne, Grandma (gave her a sovereign) and others. At 11.30 went to Miss Beam's wedding with Daisy; Lewin played the wedding march. Directly afterwards prepared to leave old Corsham and home; I couldn't help giving way when the time came to say goodbye. Dad drove old Israel and I sat with him; Lewin and Wilfrid behind ... Went to the Temperance Hotel on arriving at Paddington, then to Mrs Coxall's where we had a good tea ... Nearly all the Chippenham band and Mr Brinkworth came to see me off at Chippenham station ...

MAY

1st When the tender went off (from Gravesend) we waved handkerchiefs as long as we could see each other.

NOTES FOR 1891

January 6th Uncle Joseph's advice: he himself had married without either money or experience, and had nine children in thirteen years!

March 22nd Easter Communion: refused on teetotal grounds!

April 26th Mendelssohn: it was the song 'Parting' that was too much for him – 'Though far from you I wander, etc.'

A REMINISCENCE

Poem by Daisy Goold (early 1891?)

I was five and you were six,
In the garden we were playing.
You were chasing butterflies,
I adown the path was straying,
On a summer afternoon,
In the pleasant month of June.

Then together hand in hand
Wandered we among the flowers,
Childish confidence exchanged,
Whiled away the sunny hours.
I, a chubby blue-eyed maid,
You, a laddie, true and staid.

But alas, the fairest day
Has a cloud or tinge of sadness.
So it was – I know not how –
Fate stepped in, and stole our gladness.
And we gently slid apart,
Sorrow in each childish heart.

Then with injured queenly air
Forth I went alone and stately.
You with downcast tearful eyes
Followed slowly and sedately,
As I said with darkened brow,
"Herbert doesn't love me now".

Softly to my side you stole,
Spoke in accents sweet and pleading,
Looked with earnest wistful gaze
In my eyes, forgiveness reading.
Longer I could not refrain,
So we made it up again.

On that golden afternoon
Soft and sweet and warm and hazy,
To a simple childish tune
You sang these words: "I love Daisy".
Shall I e'er forget it? No!
Though 'twas twenty years ago.

Tell me, love, have you forgot?
Shall the years our friendship sever?
Can you say the same today?
Do you love me still as ever?
With a love as true and pure,
Childish then, but now mature?

Ah, my darling, times will change,
June will pass to dull December.
Will you through the fleeting years
Still your childhood's vow remember?
Will you always be my friend,
With a love that cannot end?

Herbert Spackman, home again, early 1900s

APPENDIX I

The fire of 17th January 1849.

There are several long accounts in *Keenes' Bath Journal.* Here are extracts from the most detailed:

FATAL FIRE AT CORSHAM

On Wednesday morning last a fire of a very alarming character occurred at Corsham, which ... has caused an immense sensation in the neighbourhood. The fire broke out early in the morning on the premises then in the occupation of Mr H. Spackman, consisting of a large general shop fronting High St, in connection with the dwelling-house, storeroom etc., the whole of which was consumed, and most distressing it is to relate that Mr Spackman himself fell a victim to the devouring element ... [Details follow as to how the fire was discovered, and spread. The proprietor, his son, and his nephew – Herbert Spackman's father – all tried to save valuable documents, ledgers etc. on the ground floor but in vain. Then, with misguided Victorian decorum, uncle and nephew rushed upstairs 'to get a little of their wearing apparel', but the fire reached the stairs behind them and cut off retreat. The nephew escaped through his window but could not reach his uncle in the next room.]

On the alarm being given, by the beating of a drum etc., people began to assemble, and the town engine, and another belonging to Lord Methuen, were quickly on the spot and at work with great energy. A very powerful engine from Chippenham was promptly in attendance, and rendered most efficient aid ... All was done that could be to preserve some of the outbuildings and the houses on the opposite side of the street ... The heat was so great across the road as to blister the paint inside the window shutters. It being known that large quantities of powder were kept in the attics, great fears were reasonably entertained for the safety of the people surrounding the burning pile. Explosions quickly succeeded each other, and the loudest was heard by several at Tytherton, and Bromham, a distance of 8 miles.

When it was reported ... that Mr Spackman was missing ... the consternation was beyond description ... The worst fears were, unfortunately, but too well founded; for among the ruins ... they found his remains ... with scarcely a feature left by which he could be recognised ...

A more affectionate father than Mr Spackman never lived. His children are inconsolable for their irreparable loss. His private charities are now coming to light, they were constantly flowing. He was in the daily habit of supplying bread and meat from his larder to the indigent poor who came to his shop, and of liberally affording them other means of relief. His place in Corsham will not soon be supplied. The Baptist connection has lost in him its greatest benefactor.

The premises and stock were insured, but no doubt the book debts amount to thousands of pounds, the collection of which, as the Ledgers were consumed, will be next to impossible. All the valuable deeds etc. were entirely destroyed.

257

From the *Bath Journal* of January 27th, 1849:

CORSHAM
Funeral of Mr Spackman.

The funeral of the late Mr Spackman, who died from suffocation during the conflagration of his house ... took place on Tuesday last at two o'clock, and never has Corsham witnessed so solemn and imposing a scene. The old and the young, the rich and the poor, were seen attending his remains to the grave. Every householder in the place, habited in a scarf, out of deep respect and sympathy, joined in the mournful procession. On the way to the chapel it had to pass through the principal streets and by the ruins of his late happy habitation. All the shops were shut and business suspended, and every house mourned as if for a relative ... Never will the recollection of the awful circumstances, which have been recorded, be obliterated in Corsham.

(The gunpowder stored in the attic was for use in the construction of Box Tunnel.)

APPENDIX II

Written by Daisy Goold in the person of her mother! (Clara Goold). 'Mary' was the household drudge at Stratford House.

OUR HOLIDAYS

Now Daisy, Ernest, Amy, All!
The holidays draw nigh,
  And we must recreation find
In *cleaning* low and high.

Mary, what are you dawdling for
When there's so much to do?
  As if you had no aim in life
(And so untidy too.)

Take up your dustpan and your brush
Begin right at the top
  And, till you reach the cellar door,
I beg you will not stop.

Sweep all the ceilings, blinds and walls,
The wainscoting and doors,
  Take up the carpets, scrub the bath,
And scour all the floors.

Then clean all handles, taps and rods
With scant Sapolio,
  And rub the furniture until
It wears a ruddy glow.

Now, Dad, I hope some time today
You'll see to all the chairs.
  The legs and backs are coming off
For want of due repairs.

And label all these bottles too;
I've put them in a row.
  The wonder is, we haven't all
Been poisoned long ago.

Ernest, I hope tonight will see
The blinds in good repair.
    Re-ladder all throughout the house;
The pictures hang with care.

    Rene, these dusters are for you.
Machine them all today,
    Answer the door, take round these notes,
And brush the crumbs away.

    Now let the drawing-room be cleaned.
Bertha, you turn it out,
    And put away such books as you
May chance to find about.

    Those boxes, too, want covering
Outside my bedroom door.
    You'll find some chintz and tintacks too
Upon the attic floor.

    Get in some fruit to make the pies,
Put in the meat at ten –
    Just take these sheets and mangle them
And bring them back again.

    Now, Amy, pray don't stand about;
There's plenty to be done.
    This pile of clothes must all be pressed
And put away by one.

    And when this afternoon you go
To Nora Hill's to tea,
    Just post these letters on your way
And start at half past three.

    Ah, there sits Edith, book in hand!
My dear, just rouse yourself;
    Collect your things to pack and leave
Your book upon the shelf.

Then go and see about your dress;
Miss Black will try it on.
Answer this note, and fetch me then
Your mending to be done.

Daisy, just bring your notebook here;
I'll tell you what to do.
Mark all the sheets with "G" in red,
And pillow-cases too.

The music must be all arranged
And Stanley packed for school.
Make him some cake and butterscotch
And give it time to cool.

Then go to Kelsall's Registry
And see about a maid.
So idle Mary is, I cannot
Keep her, I'm afraid.

Take Edith to the dentist's, call
And pay this bill at Hoe's;
Get in tomorrow's dinner, and
Mend all the children's clothes.

Bertie, Bertie (you naughty boy,
I've had to call you twice)
The knives want cleaning, and the boots
Are far from looking nice.

Now children, if your work is finished
Very well indeed,
Tonight the great treat you shall have
To *sew*, while I shall read

From that delightful book that Kate
Has sent from far away.
Then say good night, each having spent
A profitable day.

But run off to your duties all;
I've scores of notes to write
    And winter things to put away –
I shan't get done tonight.

My head is in a dizzy whirl,
My scorching brain's on fire.
    With such a pack of selfish logs
I scarce can check my ire."

This, gentle reader, feebly shows
How Stratford Workhouse thrives
    With inmates as industrious
As bees within their hives.